for.
Richard
[signature]

NO DAUGHTER OF MINE IS
GOING TO BE A DANCER!

*Dancing for Agnes de Mille and the
Giants of Dance in the 40s*

By

Sharry Traver Underwood

Foreword by
Deborah Jowitt

Dedication

To

Wynn Underwood

Who lovingly sustained me through all the years

Table of Contents

1942 Summer
Harrisburg, PA
   It is my dancing!
   WWII raging. Dance while others die?
   Dance at Syracuse University
   Jungle Rhythms
   The plan: to go to Jacob's Pillow University of the Dance
   My dance training; is there any?

1942 Summer
Jacob's Pillow
   Opening Season of Jacob's Pillow University of the Dance
   First day in class with Joseph Pilates, Steffi Nossen
   Ted Shawn, Bronislava Nijinska, Elizabeth Burchenai.
   Classes with Anna Duncan, Arthur Mahoney, Thalia Mara,
      Dr. Margaret d'Houbler, Dr. Anne Duggan
   A spectacular class with Ruth St. Denis
   Performance dance artists: Ted Shawn, Barton Mumaw, Helen
      Tamiris,
   Asadata Defora, Elizabeth Waters, Miriam Winslow, Marina
      Svetlova.
   Comprehension of Dance as A Living Art
   Ted Shawn proclaims Body, Mind and Spirit inseparable!
   Ted Shawn's appraisal of my dancing.

Test of character
Audition for *Starlight Operettas,* summer theatre in Dallas

Show closes midsummer

List of Illustrations (Between Pages 172-173)

Frontispiece: Shirley Traver Jacob's Pillow Dance Festival, Lee, MA August 1943
   Lindquist Photograph, Copyright © Harvard Theatre Collection, Houghton Library

Photo 1. Shirley Traver 1927, five years old, Paxtang, Pennsylvania
   Underwood Collection

Photo 2. Ted Shawn Jacob's Pillow University of the Dance, Lee, MA August 1942
   Underwood Collection

Photo 3. Ruth St. Denis at Jacob's Pillow University of the Dance, Lee, MA August 1942 (Tommie nickname)
   Underwood Collection

Photo 4. Barton Mumaw as Pierrot at Jacob's Pillow Dance Festival, Lee, MA August 1942
   John Lindquist Photograph, Copyright © Harvard Theatre Collection, Houghton Library

Photo 5. Student dancers August 1943: Jacob's Pillow Dance Festival, Lee, MA Front row: Virginia Bosler, Ruthanne Welch, Jean Tachau, Marian Kirk , Back row: Geni Whitlow Betty Jones ,Shirley Traver
   Lindquist Photograph, Copyright © Harvard Theatre Collection, Houghton Library

Photo 6. Shirley Traver on roof of Administration Building at Texas State College for Women, Denton, TX April 1945
   Photographer Diane

Photo 7. Starlight Operettas Program for 1945 Season, Dallas TX

Photo 8. Shirley Traver as Cancan Girl in *Maytime* Starlight Operettas, Dallas, TX 1946
Photographer Thomas Cone

Photo 9. Shirley Traver as Gypsy in *Maytime* Starlight Operettas, Dallas, Texas 1945
Photographer Thomas Cone

Photo 10. Bloomer Girls in Act I *Bloomer Girl* in performance at Biltmore Theatre, Los Angeles, CA June 1947 Gisella Weidner, Carolyn George, Margit Dekova. Jean Kinsella, Sharry Traver, Susan Stewart
Photographer Jerome Robinson

Photo 11. Sharry Traver in *Bloomer Girl* in performance at Biltmore Theatre, Los Angeles, CA June 1947
Photographer Jerome Robinson

Photo 12.Hubert Dillworth (Bill) singing *Eagle and Me* *Bloomer Girl* in performance at Biltmore Theatre in Los Angeles CA 1947
Photographer Jerome Robinson

Photo 13. Women in *Bloomer Girl Civil War Ballet* Biltmore Theatre Los Angeles, CA. Betty Jones, Gisella Weidner, Carolyn George, Cecil Bergman, Sharry Traver
Photographer Jerome Robinson

Photo 14. *Bloomer Girl Civil War Ballet* Biltmore Theatre, Los Angeles, CA June 1947. Carolyn George, Cecile Bergman, Ruthanne Welch (far Right John Begg)
Photographer Jerome Robinson

Photo 15. Celebrating War End in *Bloomer Girl Civil War Ballet* Los Angeles CA 1947. Biltmore Theatre Sharry Traver, Scott Merrill, Margit Dekova & Dancers
Photographer Jerome Robinson

Photo 16. Coda to Civil War Ballet in *Bloomer Girl* Biltmore Theatre in Los Angeles, CA 1947 Frank Reynolds, Jean Kinsella, Scott Merrill, Margit Dekova, Sharry Traver
Photographer Jerome Robinson

Photo 17. *House Divided* Charles Weidman as Abraham Lincoln, Spencer Teagle as His Voice. Charles Weidman Dance Compan, Mansfield Theatre, New York, NY April 1948
Photograph by Fred Fehl
Courtesy of Gabriel Pinski

Photo 18. *House Divided* Charles Weidman Dance Company Mansfield Theatre, New York, NY April 1978 Emily Frankel, Peter Hamilton, Sharry Traver, Charles Weidman, Betts Lee, Marc Breaux, Nick Vanoff, Felisa Condé Carl Morris
Photograph by Fred Fehl
Courtesy of Gabriel Pinski

Photo 19. *Lynch Town* Charles Weidman Dance Company 1978 National Tour: Sharry Traver, Betts Lee, Emily Frankel, Felisa Condé
Underwood Collection

Photo 20. *The Courtship of Arthur and Al* pose on 1978 tour Beavers: Emily Frankel, Sharry Traver, Felisa Condé, Jack Ferris, Charles Weidman, Carl Morris, Betts Lee
Underwood Collection

Photo 21. *The Owl Who Was God* Charles Weidman Dance Company, Mansfield Theatre, New York, NY April 1978 Sharry Traver, Betty Osgood, Felisa Condé, Carl Morris, Betts Lee, Marc Breaux
> Photograph by Fred Fehl
> Courtesy of Gabriel Pinski

Photo 22. Weidman dancers & accompanist on 1978 National Tour: Betty Osgood, Emily Frankel, Betts Lee, Freda Miller, Accompanist, Sharry Traver, Felisa Condé
> Underwood Collection

Photo 23. *And Daddy Was A Fireman* Charles Weidman Dance Company at Baltimore Arts Museum, Baltimore, MD 1978 tour Betty Osgood Marc Breaux, Sharry Traver, Charles Weidman, Felisa Condé, Nick Vanoff, Emily Frankel. Program
> photographer unknown

Photo 24. Photo Posing outside The Music Box Theatre during *Ballet Ballads*: Sharry Traver, Katherine Litz, Margaret Cuddy, Ellen Albertini June 1948 New York, NY

> Underwood Collection

Photo 25. *Susanna and The Elders* in *Ballet Ballads* The Music Box Theatre, New York, NY June 1948 Foreground: Sharry Traver, Margaret Cuddy , Katherine Lizt (seated), Ellen Albertini
> Photograph by Fred Fehl
> Courtesy of Gabriel Pinski

Photo 26 *Susanna and The Elders* in *Ballet* Ballads The Music Box Theatre New York, NY June 1948 Foreground

Sharry Traver, Margaret Cuddy, Katherine Litz (seated), Ellen Albertini
Underwood Collection

Photo 27. Dancing on stage in *Willie the Weepier* in *Ballet Ballads* at The Music Box Theatre New York, NY, 1948 Dancers surround Paul Godwin as Willie
Underwood Collection

Photo 28. Dancing on stage in *Davy Crockett* at The Music Box Theatre, New York, NY June 1978 Barbara Ashley, Ellen Albertini, Margaret Cuddy, Sharry Traver
Underwood Collection

Photo 29. *Ballet Ballads* rehearsal with Annabelle Lyons, Hanya Holm, Jerome Moross, John Latouche, NewYork, NY May 1948
Underwood Collection

Photo 30. Final pose of *If this Isn't Love* dance in *Finian's Rainbow* 46th Street Theatre New York, NY 1948 Margaret McAllen, Anna Mitten, Sharry Traver, Kathleen Stanford, Erin Harris, Eleanor Gregory, Harry Rogers, James Tarbutton, Gene Wilson, James Flash Reilly, Roger Orthadiene
Photographer William Hawkins

Photo 31. Margaret Cuddy, 1948
Underwood Collection

Photo 32.Virginia Johnson Program for *The Invisible Wife* 92nd Street YMHA/YWHA New York, NY *1949*

Photo 33. Sharry Traver as Mother James Nigren as Son in *The Invisible Wife*

Courtesy of *Dance Magazine,* August 1949
Photographer Otto Fenn

Photo 34. Margaret Cuddy, Bob Patchett, James Nigren *The Invisible Wife* 92nd Street *YMHA/YWHA New York, NY* 1949
Photographer Max Wallman

Photo 35. Sharry Traver as Wife & James Nigren The *Invisible Wife* 92nd Street YMHA/YWHA, New York, NY May 1949
Photographer Max Wallman

Photo 36.*Woman Working* Sharry Underwood Boston MA Fall 1950 *Lindquist Photograph, Copyright ©Harvard Theatre Collection, Houghton Library*

Photo 37.*Woman Waiting* Sharry Underwood Boston, MA Fall 1950
Lindquist Photograph, Copyright © Harvard Theatre Collection, Houghton Library

Photo 38. *Woman Loving,* Sharry Underwood Boston, MA Fall 1950
Lindquist Photograph, Copyright © Harvard Theatre Collection, Houghton Library

Back of book photo Author Sharry Underwood
Baltrami Studio

Permissions

The search to locate various dance photographers of 1940s productions often has been fruitless. Thanks to their assignments or their impulses on the moment, many of their pictures survive to document the dances. Some were professional jobs, such as Fred Fehl's pictures of the Weidman Company or Jerome Robinson's shots of *Bloomer Girl*. These, as most of the pictures, were taken during performance, giving an immediacy posed photographs lack. Now such photographing during the show is forbidden. Some shots are just informal photographs from the author's private collection. Photographer John Lindquist faithfully photographed dancers at Jacob's Pillow Dance Festival year after year. Seven of his photographs are presented here through gracious Permission from The Harvard Theatre Collection at Harvard University, Houghton Library with the generous assistance of Ms. Pamela Madsen. I appreciate Attorney Robert Kosiniki's assistance in helping me reach Avivah Pinski and Gabriel Pinski. I thank Mr. Gabriel Pinski for his permission to include four rare photographs by Fred Fehl of the *Weidman Dance Company* and *Ballet Ballads* in 1948. Susanna Tarjan, daughter of Jerome Moross, co-creator of *Ballet Ballads,* has most generously given permission for use of copy and "any material regarding *Ballet Ballads.*" Wendy Perron, Editor-in-chief of *Dance Magazine* and Hanna Rubin, Executive Managing Editor, have given their permission to quoting particular dance reviews and copy in their magazine under the Fair Use Rule. Specific permission was granted regarding Pilates text; The section on Joe Pilates is reprinted courtesy of Dance Magazine, copyright, 2011. I have a file of failures to prove my efforts at the New York Public Library Dance Collections, on the Internet and searches through ephemera. The production offices of *Bloomer Girl* and *Finian's Rainbow* '48 are extinct. However, each known photographer is given credit. Their work is being kept alive here.

Lost photographers: Jerome Robinson (Bloomer Girl)
        Otto Penn (Invisible Wife)
        Max Wallman (Invisible Wife)
        William Hawkins (Finian's Rainbow)

I would welcome any of the photographers or heirs I could not locate to report for appropriate recognition.

i

Foreword

by Deborah Jowitt

These days–when scantily attired young women compete to air their dancing skills before thousands of television viewers in sexily aggressive choreography, and besequined little girls wiggle their tiny hips in studio recitals–some people may have trouble understanding a father who would say in 1942 to his offspring, "No daughter of mine is going to be a dancer." Shirley Traver's dad felt that "no nice girl" would display her body on stage, and, as a loving parent, he feared the hardships that a performer's life entailed. But Shirley (later Sharry, still later, by virtue of marriage, Sharry Underwood) was not to be deterred. At 20, having taken only some tap classes paid for out of saved-up allowance money and studied modern dance for Physical Education credit at the University of Syracuse, she, like many other dance–drunk women, left home and ran away from the life her family had envisioned for her.

Luckily for a girl who had always considered dancing on a par with the air she breathed, her first in-depth experience of it as a demanding discipline also involved freedom of expressions. In 1942, Ted Shawn had just established a summer school, Jacob's Pillow, in Becket, Massachusetts–America's entry into World War II having deprived him of the young men who made up his all-male dance troupe. Shawn, like his former wife, Ruth St Denis, had high–minded ideas about dance's ability to express spiritual values without sacrificing its ability to entertain. And young Shirley had the delirious experience of performing a gypsy duet with Shawn himself.

In her tale of a dancer's life in 1940s America, Underwood reveals both the rapture she felt in dancing and her refreshingly spunky approach to a career. Over the decade, this young woman–experiencing a wide range of performing styles and training techniques–matured and developed as an artist and a person. Her reminiscences, written in the vivid prose style she cultivated in her mature years as a dance critic in Burlington, Vermont (where for decades she also performed, choreographed, and ran a company), she provides an illuminating view of theater and dance during the war and the immediate postwar years. Back then, few dance companies provided a living wage, and performers moved easily between Broadway and the concert stage. Underwood invites the reader into her classes with Hanya Holm and her performances with another modern dance pioneer, Charles Weidman. She describes rehearsals and backstage maneuvers in Dallas at the Starlight Operetta season of light opera (an almost forgotten form). She survives teaching and choreographing (while completing an MA degree) in the Physical Education Department of Texas State College for Women and relishes performing on Broadway and on the road in *Bloomer Girl*, one of several musicals choreographed by Agnes de Mille that revolutionized the image of the chorus girl by developing individual characters and believable behavior.

These experiences and more mingle with Underwood's zesty saga of surviving disappointments, poverty, waitressing jobs, and disastrous roommates, as well as fending off (or not) would-be suitors and stage-door Johnnies. Resilience, determination, wit, and a rambunctious honesty saw her through it all.

Underwood's greatest asset in chronicling an era is her gift for recreating scenes, dialogue and all, and for describing the action of a plot or the steps and feeling of a particular dance from the viewpoint of an insider. She relives the experience of performance, while adding the insights and sharp perspective she developed as a dance critic. Cast as one of two trees in Katherine Litz's "Susanna and the Elders", a number in the experimental 1948 *Ballet* Ballads, she writes: A fervent tree climber, I soon added tree rhythms to the rising/falling basic motions. Depending on the story's action as the Elders spied on Susanna, I imitated the effects of riffling breezes, with that quarter-second after-beat just stirring the leaves, and heady winds that stirred the trunk itself to the roots and began a counter-swaying. Wild winds sent my "branches" careening, lifting, then clashing in dismay. I used them all, usually in succession to keep from looking drunk."

After her stint in *Bloomer Girl*, Underwood received a telegram from her father. "We knew you could do it." (irony unintentional) And what was "it"? Early on, mulling over her career in dance so far, she realizes that it comes at a price. "A big one, in that choosing a life of action instead of things, there will never be anything left of it to put like a bright pebble in my pocket." She was wrong. Her memories are that pebble, and they gleam for readers of this book.

Deborah Jowitt has been writing about dance for *The Village Voice* since 1967.

She has published two collections, and her essays have appeared in numerous journals and anthologies. Her most recent books are *Time and the Dancing Image (1988) and Jerome Robbins, His Dance (2004)*. She lectures and conducts workshops worldwide, as well as teaching in the Dance Department of New York University's Tisch School of Arts. Her awards include a Guggenheim Fellowship in 2002 and a Dance Magazine Award in 2010.

Acknowledgements

The *raison* d'être of this entire book is to acknowledge the dancers who brought dance in America to a theatrical art form during the decade of the 40s. It takes a whole book just to begin to credit the direct and indirect ways these dancers inspired and provided for my generation with their work.

I am ever grateful to have danced with and for these seminal artists. They changed and sustained my life. Ted Shawn gave me faith in my abilities. Ruth St. Denis revealing her spirituality in dance verified its beauty in my soul. Through her sister Anna, Isadora Duncan taught me to trust my wayward way of dancing. And so it went as one teacher, one choreographer, one dancer after another helped me to find the intelligence in dance; its generosity, its stature as an art.

It is my obligation in turn to share these gifts by performing, teaching, and recording them for the next generations of dancers.

I am indebted to Norton Owen, Curator at Jacob's Pillow Dance Festival, for his contributing vintage film to my Modern Dance History DVD *Fountain.* My debt to Dance Critic Deborah Jowitt began years ago as she told me; "You can't use third person. What you are telling is the truth." Years past until Dance Critic Claudia Gitelman insisted I revive my book. During these years, Deborah Jowitt was Dance Critic for *The Village Voice* and writing significant books on Dance. That she has the charity to write this Forward is a gift forever.

I thank Reader dancer/poet/writer Lynn Swanson, for so generously and wisely seeing me through.

Thanks go to Reader Pat Goudey O'Brien for recommending my book for publication and her book publishing savvy.

Wendy Perron, Editor-in-chief of *Dance Magazine,* has my gratitude for supporting my dance writing in the Magazine, including *Turning Exercise On Its Head.* A section on Joe Pilates is reprinted in Chapter Two, courtesy of *Dance Magazine,* copyright 2011.

I am grateful to these photographers for making a visual record of dance in the 40s: Fred Fehl, Jerome Robinson, Thomas Cone, Otto Fenn and William Hawkins. I thank John Lindquist for his photographs of my dancing in Boston.

To computer consultants: Walter Chesnut for his expertise in design and to Jason Hyerstay for crisis solutions.

To grandson Henry Underwood, eternal gratitude for his timely Academic Wizardry.

To everyone who ever danced with me, thank you for all the beautiful times dancing together.

And an obeisance to my Muse Terpsichore for blessing me with Dance.

INTRODUCTION

"The cup contains; the fountain overflows," wrote William Blake.

Dancers are fountains. It is not enough to *know* something; we have to dance it out body, mind and soul. So it is exciting to know how these flowing spirits from two strong women dancers changed the art of Dance in America. In 1910, the great Russian Ballerina Anna Pavlova brought Ballet to America as the American Isadora Duncan brought her free-spirited dance across America to Europe.

Dance as an art form took decades to evolve in American theaters. It grew primarily from individual dancers' strong dissatisfaction with the *status quo*. Desire for change grew stronger after World War I. Rejecting dance as spectacle or entertainment, a nucleus of dancers determined to dance about aspects of their own lives. The 20s and 30s were years of ferment and experimentation in dance as a voice for humanity. Dancer Agnes de Mille brought the influence of Modern Dance to Broadway. Modern Dance slowly became an art on the concert stage. By the 1940s, American Modern Dance was being introduced into college athletic programs.

During this time, however, only the sensational stars in movies or vaudeville received a patronizing respect. Otherwise it was immoral to be a dancer. Nevertheless, American girls and boys began to run away to be dancers. I was one of them.

Halfway through the 20th century, I danced with the earliest icons of American Dance: Ted Shawn, Ruth St. Denis, Anna Duncan, La Meri, Charles Weidman, Doris

Humphrey, Martha Graham, Hanya Holm, Elizabeth Waters, Alwin Nikolais, Agnes de Mille, Michael Kidd and others. The riches in originality in dance technique and philosophy these artists shared with their dancers and their audiences provided the roots for the development of our own American Theatre Dance.

It has taken half a century but there are now ballroom, swing, jitterbug, break dance, hip hop, belly dancing, East Indian and American Indian dance, African, Irish, square and round dancing, contra dancing, disco, and any form of ethnic dance. And lately there is spontaneous "flash" dancing as one person just starts to dance, people nearby join in and, in minutes, whole streets are full of people joyfully dancing away.

If you have a heartbeat, you have rhythm. You've got rhythm? You can dance. But what if you are forbidden to be a dancer. Then what?

CHAPTER ONE

Harrisburg, PA
August 1942
  No Daughter of Mine Is Going to Be a Dancer

On the train from Harrisburg to New York, I would not let myself think about it. Later, I must. I knew that. Now it was hard not to consider what I had done to my family. I had surprised—no, shocked—my loving parents and surprised myself. I had meant to finally reaffirm what I had told them all my life and get them to accept the facts. But would they? The same denials and arguments. My Dad had his litany of reasons:

No daughter of mine is going to be a dancer.
No nice girl is a dancer.
The stage is a hard, sordid life.
Dancing on the stage is nasty, showing off to noisy crowds.
Dancers are a dime a dozen.
You would be hitting your head against a brick wall to try.
And I love you too much to let you go into that kind of life.

Then Mother, smiling wistfully, had said, "You are twenty. You are too old now, dear."

"Oh! And whose fault is THAT!" I shouted. "I AM GOING TO BE A DANCER AND YOU CAN'T STOP ME!" I had slammed out of the house—slammed the door so hard the knocker gave an extra bang for me. My fury hurled me down the street, over to the path by the Susquehanna

River where I ran and ran and ran until I dropped onto the green grasses.

I sat up suddenly.

Suddenly I was free.

FREE! Such an airy feeling! It stayed with me as I rose and tested it, spinning around slowly, arms to the sky. Ah! Weightless but not weak, no, not at all. A smile, and when I thought of what I had done, I laughed out loud. Wow! They were stunned! Well, it had taken twenty years to do it. It had to be done. Now my parents could no more keep me from dancing than keep bubbles from rising in air.

But I had only five dollars toward my escape. Two weeks went by without finding a job, but I kept practicing twirling and jumping in the our recreation room. Finally, I got a job typing invoices for the Pennsylvania State Police in a brick building beside a brewery, wafting its beery smells our way. But every day the dollars piled up. By July 30, I had earned enough to go. I dressed for traveling, wearing my navy polka-dot suit with its matching beanie, white gloves and spectator pumps. ---

"Pennsylvania Station, comin' up! Pennsylvania Station, everybody!"

Pennsylvania Station was awe-inspiring. It was almost overwhelming with so many soldiers and sailors rushing in all directions. A college girl was expected to change trains without panic and, with only one question, I did it. Now on the train north to Lee, Massachusetts, I could no longer procrastinate.

Thanks to my darling Aunt Pummie who knew a Mr. Bob Bergh who knew Mr. Ted Shawn, I had been accepted for three weeks' study at the Jacob's Pillow University of the

Dance in its first season this year, 1942. What would I tell Mr. Shawn when he asked about my dance training?

Was there any?

Born in 1922, Elsie and Charles Traver named me Shirley, with a middle name "Marie" for Elsie's sister (aka, Pummie). I had known I was a dancer as soon as I knew anything. I came by it naturally: my father had been a superlative athlete, my mother was musical. So I knew I was not just someone who dances, but A Dancer! And as it turned out, I was also a lefty.

As a child, no one seemed to mind my dancing unless I got in the way or I could not stand still when spoken to. Then I was sent outside where it was deliciously delirious to spin fast with my eyes shut until I tumbled over. Or to move so s-l-o-w-l-y and q-u-i-e-t-l-y not even the fairies in the red tulip cups could hear me. Best was on the playground, sailing around on one foot with my dress afloat, singing, *"I feel...I feel...I feel like a morning star!"*

I told anyone and everyone I was a dancer and no one would believe me. When I began to insist I was a dancer, they insisted that I should not be.

Then, in 1927, my parents were in a devastating auto accident. Mother was thrown through the windshield, critically injured. Ultimately she survived but, her vocal chords cut, she could not speak aloud for seven years. At that time, my sister Jane was nine, I was five, and Phyllis, two years old. We were taught never to yell in the house and not to argue. Indoors was disciplined, but it was also intimate, as adults never raised their voices to us. If disobedient, I was told to sit still on a chair to "Think about it. You must learn to be of good person."

Our mother did not become an invalid; gradually she could go about with my father or with friends. Good days, Mother would play the piano while Daddy strummed his ukulele and sang *On the Road to Man-da-lay* for us. Mother would whistle. Trying to whisper, she would hold us to her. I would look deep into her eyes, trying to understand.

Our mother's mother, Nana, came with her Bible to live with us, helping in all kindly ways: Despite the Depression*, we* also needed Anna, our scolding, enfolding black cook, part-time. With my Daddy's daily bear hug, it was easy to believe I was loved. And I loved them all back. Being loved and loving was a strength that opened my heart and freed me from fear. Coming early, love was set as a truth of life for me.

There was just this one contrariness. Danc*ing* seemed to be all right. My parents soon went out social dancing about Harrisburg. Danc*ing* in a school May Day program was allowed. *Being* a danc*er* was not all right. Dance lessons were strictly forbidden.

But how could I not be what I already was? The beauty of dancing was that it was made of me and therefore available anytime. Furthermore, no one could take it from me. So I pounded cleats onto the toes of my school shoes for tap shoes. I sold the most Girl Scout Cookies, but the prize money went to my troop, not to me. When I pleaded for lessons again, my father began to fine me a nickel from my fifteen-cents allowance every time I mentioned *dance*. That was serious. I waited until my allowance was a quarter, than ran to the Paxtang Municipal Building where my friends took tap lessons every Saturday. My school shoes made little sound, but the teacher nodded to me as I tried the steps. My father was not pleased, but he did not go back on his word that our allowances were ours to spend. Then the Great Susquehanna Flood of 1934 washed out Harrisburg and the tap classes. The Paxtang Municipal Building became a Refugee Center.

That same spring in 1934, I was asked to be Gypsy Ann in our grammar school presentation of *The Magic Beanstalk*. My dance went well, but then something awful happened: I was to sing my fortune telling, but my alto voice could only squeak at the high notes. The only way to keep my dance was to pretend to sing while Charlie, the student who played Jack, sang for me offstage. The night of the performance, Jack was on stage left, but his beans were at stage right. So with the black jellybeans in my hand, I danced, twirling and stamping to the music in my red skirt and black, oilcloth boots. As I took my bow, I felt a glow inside I had never known before. It was as though I had given something from inside myself.

That very summer of 1934 was a watershed year in the exciting development of American Modern Dance. Dancers Martha Graham, Doris Humphrey, Charles Weidman and Hanya Holm met together at Bennington College in Vermont. They worked with open minds on a new *modern* dance vocabulary that spoke of their opinions and attitudes on what American dance could be. For example, they included the very floor as dance space not merely to dance over or stand upon, but as another place to locate dance. Teaching, choreographing and performing in new styles to modern music, these four dancers would become known as the Four Pioneers of American Modern Dance. What they did that summer would change my life.

The following year, March 16, 1935, the great Soviet ballet director, Colonel W. De Basil brought his *Ballet Russe de Monte Carlo* to the Zembo Temple stage in Harrisburg. My mother took me to see it as a consolation for the continuing Edict of No Dance Lessons. *Les Sylphides* opened the program, my first *ballet blanc*. I caught my breath as these ballerinas swept me into a mystical beauty never before known. The entire program opened up a new world of dance. Oh, to dance like that! Both *Union Pacific* and *La Beau Danube* showed stories could be told through dancing in the most exhilarating fashion. And that men did all these dances too! And here on stage, live, dancing was more dangerous and more intimate than seeing dancing in the movies.

But what did I know? Nothing.

After glorious Fred Astaire and Ginger Rogers, Sonja Henie came onto the silver screen, dazzling us with her pretty, perky, twirling skating. By then my sister Phyllis was proving to be an excellent athlete and was attracted to figure skating. I saw it as a cover for a lot of ballet moves. Insisting it was "a sport, Daddy," we gleefully got permission to take figure skating classes at Hershey's new ice palace. I was a high school junior when the *Mirabel Vinson Ice Skating Show* came to the Zembo Temple. Waiting around after the show, I got a date to audition to join the company. Next day I hid my skates in my jacket, cut school and ran over to audition, ready to run away from home. All the doors were locked. The show had already left town.

My older sister, Jane, was smarter than I. She hid her passions. Jane went to Syracuse University, majoring in Liberal Arts. It soon appeared I was not the only one thrilled with the theatre. Once there, Jane daringly went ahead and changed her major to Theatre Arts. She came home on holidays, excited about the Civic Theatre the University had in town, and more. The theatre students put on their own musicals! Dancing? Of course! When it was time to choose my college, Syracuse University was the only one I would consider. No to Rutgers, my father's college. No to Goucher, my mother's college. No to Holyoke, Vassar or Wellesley. Finally, in 1940, I was allowed to go to Syracuse and major in Theatre, as long as I took classes in Typing and Shorthand.

By 1940, the Four American Modern Dance Pioneers had produced many new works at Bennington. In 1935, Doris Humphrey and Charles Weidman evolved their *New Dance,* a major work "representing the individual in relation to his fellow in an ideal state." In 1937, Hanya Holm made her statement about social decay in *Trend.* In 1938, Charles Weidman performed his *Opus 1.* In 1940, Martha Graham premiered *El Penitente* there. By 1940, the results of their teaching workshops were spreading across America. Most summer students had been Physical Education teachers looking for new material for their classes. These teachers brought Modern Dance to campuses.

When we freshmen registered at Syracuse University in 1940, we had to answer a lot of questions. One: What do you want to do most in the world? I wrote: "Make people happy." (I would do this by dancing for them.) Freshmen also had to take a Physical Education credit. Among the sports for women coeds was Modern Dance. I signed on for that. Our teacher, Barbara Nash, was a product of the intense summers of modern dance held at Bennington College. Miss Nash was lovely and slim. She moved silently, in a state of grace. We wore little body suits, leotards, and no shoes. Class started with stretches, standing, then sitting on the floor, bending over with knees bent, then legs straight and then with legs wide apart. We were uncomfortable seeing Miss Nash stretch with only a bit of fabric between her legs. She serenely demonstrated that we were learning more about our bodies. Most of the instruction was in ordinary ways of moving: walking forward and backward, hopping, running, turning as she beat a drum. She also taught us how to fall down: back, side, even forward. Leaping came last and I was the best. And why not! I had been leaping over everything for years. But class was not dancy with steps, and there was no music.

Miss Nash tried to form a performing group to create our own choreography. I was included and tried to experiment but each attempt proved I needed stronger dance technique.

Now I was on my way to get it.

At first my train made many city stops; service men getting on and off. I thought about my Syracuse boy friends that left to join the armed services right after Pearl Harbor. About my other reason for this trip: deciding what to do with the rest of my life. It had come to that as I had stood in the Maxwell Citizenship Building staring at my country's flag, the chimes in Crouse Tower still ringing out the alarm of the Pearl Harbor attack.

What good was a dancer in a war?

No good at all.

How dare I dance as others died!

Why was it that dancing, the most innocent, beautiful thing I knew, always got me in trouble? First with my parents. Then my church. And now my country. I loved my country, owed it my civic duty as any other citizen. But I was at heart and mind a pacifist. Ever since I had seen the life-size bloody horror of war in the painting of the Battle of Gettysburg in our Pennsylvania Capitol building, I hated war. No good at hitting back, I'd get sad instead of being mad. How selfish now to still want to be a dancer!

I was going to Jacob's Pillow to see whether I had any talent and then decide what I must do. Would I have to audition before they let me stay?

Would Jungle Rhythms be enough?

As our train began wandering through the Massachusetts countryside, I closed my eyes and was back on stage at Syracuse University's Civic Theatre. I had gone down to the theatre the first time wearing my pink sharkskin shorts and cotton top, just like Ruby Keeler in the movies. I made it through the audition for the student musical *Tambocade,* vowing to learn everyone's part. When our Rumba Star thought she was too good to bother with rehearsals, I got the lead.

In my turquoise and orange ruffled skirt and midriff, I waited offstage for my partner John Moe to lead me center stage in the dark. As we turned back to back, he squeezed my hand for luck. Then the bongo drums set the pulse; the subtle melody of *Siboney* began our Rumba, small and close. As the dance grew and expanded across the Civic Theatre stage, other dancers joined in. Shoulders and hips alternating, knees circling, legs thrust through the slit skirts. At the given moment, all exit but John and me. Blackout! Silence. Sudden spot on John and me in close pose. Spot on bare-chested Native Drummer, doubling the beat, thrusting us into a fast, wild, Native Rumba with larger undulations and sensuous twists. The excitement grows! We throw ourselves into leaping turns as the chorus joins us in a spinning shouting crescendo!

Heeding audience reaction, Sawyer Falk, production supervisor, has wisely shifted the Jungle Rhythms sequence to directly before

the finale. The dancing of Shirley Traver and
John Moe, and the weird lighting effects in
this scene, made it the hit of the show, judging
from audience applause.

Syracuse Banner, December 16, 1942

I had been surprised and thrilled to find people
praising my dancing. Oh, I always knew it felt good to me,
but now it was officially approved. It was like being allowed
to breathe.

"Lee next! Lee, Massachusetts, comin' up! Lee,
Massachusetts! Lee, comin' up!"

CHAPTER TWO

Summer 1942
  Jacob's Pillow University of the Dance

Many other people got off the train. While we were all gathering luggage, a large, blonde, energetic woman came rushing up. She flashed brilliant smiles, calling greetings and embracing several people. Seeing me, she called out, "Hello, darling! How was the trip? Come along!"

"Oh, I'm not... I'm to go to Jacob's Pillow!"

"So are we all, darling. Come, come! I'll take you!"

Squashed in the old station wagon with the others, I was impressed that Mr. Shawn had sent someone for me. A few minutes listening to my companions impressed me even more. They were journalists and photographers from *Life Magazine* up to do a story on Jacob's Pillow. The car turned off the mountain road onto a dirt way leading through a wood, trundled along and turned into an open yard. A large, white clapboard house stood on the right with a stone cottage attached to it. Across the way was a large barn, its two wings at right angles. The *Life* crew was swept into the house, but the blonde woman did not forget me.

"Just go find Esther, darling, if you haven't had any supper," she called over her shoulder. Looking about in the fading light, I saw no one but heard sounds from the cottage. The door was locked, but I pounded on it anyway and in time, a brusque, stout woman pulled it open a crack.

"Supper's over," she said and began to close the door again.

"I haven't had any. I'm new," I complained.

With a world-weary sigh, Esther let me in and provided a bowl of soup, a slice of bread and a glass of milk. Although I was very hungry after so long a day, she made it clear that would have to do.

Outside again, I looked about. It was odd. I was here at Jacob's Pillow but apparently invisible to the few people who went hurrying in and out of the buildings. Wandering, I found the larger barn was a theatre. Musical sounds emerged but no one was at the box office. I explored the smaller barn, discovering it was a studio. A shadowy image of myself in a wall of mirrors was the clue. Opening my arms, I took a little turn and hugged myself with glee. Another door opened in the far corner of the studio and a young man ran through cursing loudly. Very quickly he was back running, carrying a costume. The door banged open but was shut very quietly. I was just realizing that I must be missing a dance performance, when lights suddenly blazed in the garden and people came pouring out of the theatre, talking excitedly. When they returned after intermission, I went with them, slipping into an empty seat.

The theatre looked like a new barn turned into a steep auditorium with a stage. A fresh, new-wood scent lingered in the air. On stage, a large, blond girl was bounding about, smiling happily as she twirled to folk music. Next, a slim wisp of a girl wearing a blue draped costume with a hood moved solemnly, almost religiously, in a modern dance. The audience rejoiced over both these dancers. There was a curtain call and the show was over.

Trying to pay for my ticket at the box office, I was promptly turned over to Mrs. Butterfield, the housemother. Middle-aged with dark, wavy hair and a distracted smile, Mrs. Butterfield explained everything she was doing or going to do aloud. Then she led me to her car and drove me off into the night away from The Pillow. When we stopped, she flashed a light on a wooden building off in a field and said, "Take any empty bunk and ask the girls anything else tomorrow. See you in the morning!"

In minutes I was scrunched down under a blanket, trying to read tonight's program by flashlight. The blonde must have been Helen Tamiris and the other, Miriam Winslow. Circling the cabin with a flashlight found a hanger with black tights; there under a bed, two worn, pink ballet slippers, a flower pot of ribbons on an orange crate, a black ball of yarn near two knitting needles with a few rows on them. Dancers. With the light out, it was as though my narrow bed was floating in the dark somewhere in the Berkshires under a starry sky. Smiling, I snuggled down and slept.

The alarm went off at 6:30 a.m. Breakfast at 7:00, and it was a mile back down the hill to The Pillow. The girls were friendly but preoccupied, for today would be the great *Life Magazine* picture taking. No part of that. I hung around to learn what I could. On the walls of the studio were pictures of Ted Shawn and other male dancers. This must be the man who had headed the dance company of all men that Jane told me about. I studied the pictures of strong men looking almost like statues. These men were dancers!

Shawn had disbanded his group, *The Men Dancers*, in 1940 before World War II broke out. Now all the men were in the war. Shawn thought he would have to give up dance at Jacob's Pillow. However, with the encouragement of fellow artists and neighbors, Shawn and his Board came up with the ideas of a dance school. The University of the Dance's Mission was:

to provide students with the finest possible dance education,

to provide many dancers with the opportunity to reach the public and

earn money for scholarships for talented pupils unable to pay full tuition,

and to offer the public both entertainment and education of the highest order in the art of the dance.

How Beautiful Upon the Mountain, Ted Shawn, 1942 (Published privately)

Conceived in 1941 and brought forth the following June, 1942, Jacob's Pillow was one more war baby, struggling for life in this first dreadful, dark year of WWII. It would be a one-parent family were it not for all the artistic foster parents who gave generously of themselves for its survival. Jacob's Pillow University of the Dance was the school; Jacob's Pillow Dance Festival was the performing branch. Defying its very isolation, plans had gone ahead to build the first theatre in America devoted to the Dance. It was designed by Joseph Franz in harmony with the barn studio next door and named the Jacob's Pillow Dance Theatre (later changed to the Ted Shawn Dance Theatre). Its very first season opened with great excitement.

Shawn had chosen The American Dance as the theme for this first summer, gathering native American dancers and exotic dancers from countries that came here to dance and teach. To christen the stage for its first performance, Shawn asked his neighbors in Otis and Becket, Massachusetts, to perform their traditional square dance.

New York Times Dance Critic John Martin wrote:

> If these ageless dances are simple and
> unsensational, they are formally of great
> perfection, and when they are done as simply
> as they were on this occasion, they have the
> power to bring tears perilously close to the
> eyes of the spectator who is in love with his
> country and its culture.

The New York Times, 1942

Monday morning I was up like a shot. With a gulp, I pulled on my black mercerized-cotton leotard and buttoned it at the shoulder while wiggling into my sandals. Grabbing a sweater, I bolted back down the hill with the other students. Oatmeal, toast, coffee or cocoa for breakfast. Then I headed for the studio. Peering cautiously into the room at first, I saw a splash of sunlight on the floor and went to it for warmth.

"Gut Morgan!" said a voice with a strong accent. I wheeled around having seen no one, then spotted a man in white shorts and shirt standing on his head in the corner.

"Oh! Good morning!" I twisted upside-down to smile at him.

This amused the man. Laughing, he hopped down from his headstand with a little bounce and strolled over to me. Strength worthy of note, solid strength quieted but a hair from expulsion, dwelled in this short, rugged, but nimble man.

"No, no! You stay. Always start da day fifteen minutes on da head. I am Joseph Pilates. You new girl." He gripped my hand with a quick, numbing grasp. "Turn 'round—turn 'round!" he ordered, firmly pushing on my shoulder. I hesitated. (Who was Joseph Pilates?)

"Auk!" His hands clapped smartly together. "Za back iss no gut!" Pilates gave a hearty laugh and with a couple of hard claps on my arm, promised, "Ve fix you! Ve fix you!"

Others were entering the studio with towels or small rugs. Those without quickly seized the mats along the wall, pulled them into the center of the studio and sat on them with a proprietary air. I found a bare space on the floor and prayed those aids did not imply acrobatics. Exactly at 8:00 a.m., with the now familiar smack of his hands, Pilates set us off on an hour of arduous body alignment that had my adrenals pumping steadily. As he shouted out his commands, everyone instantly flung into energetic contortions. Within minutes, we were all sweating, breathing heavily while stretching to a new degree as he shouted, "Hold it!"

In no time I dearly coveted the mats or even a scrap of worn toweling. Every exercise seemed to grind this joint or that into the floor as we shifted from "onza stomick" to "onza back." It was a relief to have a few exercises standing up. One order sounded as through he had just told us "to hug a tree". I bit my lip not to laugh only to understand that was indeed what he ordered. With arms wrapped around an imaginary tree, we were to "squveeeze!" Hard. I looked at the others who had feet astride, knees bent and arms encircling before them, trembling with tension. Veins stood out on foreheads. Seeing my bewilderment, Pilates strode over to me. Clapping a heavy hand over my left breast and jiggling it up and down, he roared, "You vant schloppy pectorals? You squveeze!" He pulled both arms into a circle to get me started and went on to another student while I thought I would die of mortification.

Nobody laughed or paid the slightest attention. As class went on, I was often a beat behind the other dancers who knew Pilates's exercises. Slowly I began to realize that here, it was allowed to make mistakes. Corrections might be quick and clear, but there was no malice or shame in them. The concentration was on learning. And I suddenly felt free to learn, to think my body through the exercise itself.

We make strange faces to stretch face muscles, then tried to balance on our hips. Round-the-Clock was the last exercise. From a complete body flexion to a complete body extension without head, feet or arms touching the floor, the student performs one set at every point on the twelve-numbered clock, and then reverses.

"Flex, two, three. Release, two, three! Knees to forehead! Twenty-four dimes! Tvelve, you new girl!" Finally, after a flat-out collapse on the floor, we rested.

How had I lived this long without knowingly discovering these positions?

Pilates stopped me one more time on the way out of the studio. Placing both hands on my hipbones, he tipped my pelvis under so his thumbs pressed into my flesh in a most ticklish way. Distress kept me from yelping. "Ziss vay. Only ziss vay, you," he frowned, then smiled.

How had I dared to come!

In minutes the students were back, this time taking places at the *barre* along three sides of the studio. Not wanting to take a former student's place, I lingered and ended up in center. Chitchat ceased.

Wearing a white terry bathrobe, a tall, tanned, handsome man with a touch of white at his temples swept into the studio. Ted Shawn.

He stood easily at the piano, one foot at the arch of the other, eyes searching the room, commanding attention. "Good morning, children!" he smiled. As we responded, a pretty, white-haired woman carrying music books came in and seated herself at the piano: Mary Campbell, Shawn's accompanist. Again I had an awkward moment: go introduce myself at once (disruptive) or just take the class (presumptive)? The music began with two strong chords and the only thing to do was follow everyone as they stretched upward, rising on toes, then bending down from the hips halfway to swing the body right-left-parallel again, then drop relaxed, knees bent. Shadowing again, I managed not to be corrected. After more exercises, Mr. Shawn announced today would be his Line Study, beginning with walking.

As it was my turn to walk on the diagonal, Shawn stopped me. "Oh, are you the friend of Bob Bergh? Glad to have you! Now let's see if you can walk." Before I got very far, Shawn stopped me again. "Oh, dear. What's wrong, children?"

"She didn't place one foot directly in front of the other," they chorused. Dear God, I couldn't even *walk* here.

Shawn took me by the hand and started me over again. I felt like a tightrope walker, but as he called out "Bigger steps!" my walk smoothed out and I could feel the difference. Before class ended, we were all making plane geometric designs—floor patterns, Mr. Shawn called them. The remarkable discovery was that I was making floor patterns all the time I went anywhere. Not visible patterns like you make on snow or sand, but foot patterns just the same. And so was everyone! Fern Helscher, Shawn's Girl Friday, running to the telephone. Mrs. Butterfield buzzing along her circuitous ways. Mother at home. Eleanor Roosevelt in Washington. The men at war! What a gigantic worldwide Gordian knot. Lucky these foot patterns were all invisible!

"Hey! Steffi's class is starting!" a girl called to me. Steffi Nossen proved to be the energetic blond who picked me up at the train. Steffi was Scandinavian. An associate director of The Pillow, she was teaching here all summer. Winters she ran a studio in Westchester, New York. She was very popular here, teaching Modern Dance. Many of her exercises were similar to Miss Nash's, but here, classes were an hour and a half long. What a difference in temperament! Steffi was a stouthearted rabble-rouser, shouting corrections, darting among us to enforce them, dashing up front to lead combinations. She carried my college classes off the floor with jumps into cannonballs, one-legged and full-air turns. We even jumped before our falls. "Bend those knees when you land!"

The word *preparation* took on a vital meaning as I learned that a small move, often in the opposite direction, was ignition for larger co-ordinations. When Steffi could not stand us working in place, she divided the class in two and sent us to opposite corners. This meant high prancing, small leaps, then big-bigger-biggest leaps. Inspired by her nonstop cheering, I shoved off into the air light and fast as a shuttlecock.

"Great elevation!" she shouted. She wore us out, then laid us out on the floor to close our eyes and roll relaxed as rag dolls. "Think of yourselves as old socks under your bed," she suggested. Then she lined us up against the studio walls, feet up. Resting, I realized I had been in motion four hours straight.

Time for lunch—which eluded me because I did not know the ropes. Sit beside others in a sweat-soaked leotard? Not my mother's daughter! I ran to the locker room to wash and change before falling in at the end of the line at the cottage. That cost me my soup and half a brownie. One of the students, Betty Jones, asked, "You going back up to Madame's class?"

"Ballet? Yes."

"Well, you better put your hair up. Madame doesn't allow anyone in her class who doesn't."

Alarmed, I asked, "Go back where?"

Enjoying my consternation, Betty explained that Madame's class was in another barn studio back up the hill near our dorm Hurrying briskly along the mile back, I passed a slim figure, recognizing Miriam Winslow from her performance. Was I taking class with professionals? Lordie! At my dorm I dashed to the latrine and back to frantically braid my hair in two pigtails, pinning them together on the top of my head. The ends stuck up like two insect antennae, taking more precious time to subdue. Hysteria paid off as I was among the first three in class.

"Can you please tell me Madame's full name? I'm new and have not met her yet," I explained.

"Madame Bronislava Nijinska," one answered, adding, "She's Nijinsky's sister." I had heard of him, the great Russian ballet dancer whose jumps were almost like flying.

Class filled promptly, students taking places along the *barre*. In moments, a young man with a well-developed body came bouncing in wearing a navy-and-white striped jersey, tights, white wool socks up to his calf and white ballet slippers: Nikita Talin. He held a kerchief and, tying a knot in each corner, placed it on his head. Then he began posing before the large mirror. Next came a tall, thin man in a black business suit who promptly seated himself at the piano: Mr. Singaevsky. He lit a cigarette, holding it in the center of his mouth, rubbed his hands together and began to play chords.

As the next person arrived, all in class were instantly at the *barre in* first position. Madame Bronislava Nijinska was here. She was short, a little puddin' of a woman with a round face and short grey, ear-length hair, parted in the middle. Her slacks were black and she wore a dark grey, snug-buttoned jacket over her white cotton shirt. Moving slowly, quietly, in her black ballet slippers, Madame went over to the piano, disregarding the class, and also lit a cigarette. Holding it in the corner of her mouth, she returned to center before the mirror to face the class. With a slight nod to the pianist, she clapped her hands patty-cake style to set the tempo and began counting aloud between her teeth: "Wan—y—doo—y—tree—" The music began, the students began, and I did my best to second guess what the *barre* would be. Madame Nijinska gave little vocal direction; she spoke little English.

It was a brisk class with Madame demonstrating the next step with her hands. Now and then she would move a foot from front to back and vice versa, but seldom did she move to the side or mark a floor pattern with her feet. Periodically she would stamp a small foot, then cross and re-cross her hands to indicate disapproval or misunderstanding by the class. She would then approach the pianist and a rush of Russian would pour forth. Then Mr. Singaevsky would try to explain, using his basic English. "Two dimes turn" or "Up, up ze toes," responding to Madame's hand gestures that a jump was not called for, but half toe.

If it was at all as frustrating to Madame as to the students, she gave no clue beyond chain smoking. Her face was impassive on long adagio phrases, twice calling on Nikita to demonstrate. Then she would nod slightly and class would continue. Class was divided for *pirouettes,* one foot turns, forward and backward on each foot. As rows were rotated, I was brought front before her and the mirror with others. Now Madame indicated she wanted *fouetté en tournant* (a turn on one foot with the other a whipping leg, new to me). When it was our turn, the girl next to me traveled and crowded me off to the side. Madam nodded to me to come back in and I tried the turn on the repeat. Traveling again, my neighbor's whipping leg caught me right in the belly and knocked me flat. Dazed by the jolt, I heard her say, "Get out of the way! My God, you're stupid! Oh, my foot!"

It happened fast but noisily. I was mortified a second time this day. But again nobody else paid attention; they were lining up at the corners for *grand jeté (*a split leap from one foot to the other) across the floor. At my turn, my knees were still trembling, but twice before leaps had saved my self-respect. I took a breath, galvanized my energy in the preparatory two steps and soared into the air to land neatly on one foot and repeat it. Madame showed her approval with the slightest nod of her head and a blink of her eyes. To me it was permission to continue to live. Class ended with a deep curtsey, a *reverence,* as respect to Madame Nijinska. Then everyone clapped enthusiastically. Madame gave her slight nod with a bare hint of curve in her lips.

No time to rest. Back down the hill for the next class, American Folk Dance. Goodness! Didn't we all already know that? Tall, middle-aged, Elizabeth Burchenal was introduced by Papa Shawn as the President of the *American Folk Dance Society.* She smiled generously as she told us that folk dance was primarily for fun. Dance was first a social institution and, secondly, a performance art. We were to remember that the primary impulse for dancing was the dance itself by the ones dancing. After that, folk dance might be considered for spectators. We did realize, did we not, that professional dancing was a very, very small part of dance on a worldwide basis.

Elizabeth Burchenal started us off with *Buffalo Girls, Oh! Susanna!, Life on the Ocean Wave,* and in no time reluctant students were having a great time singing and laughing as we danced. Papa Shawn came in to watch and praise Elizabeth for her book *International Folk Dance,* defining it "as that dance that provides the roots for all concert and theatre dance."

In this very first day at Jacob's Pillow, my scope of dance had exploded geometrically from personal joy to the deep implications of each new dance form. And the day was not over yet. Esther's spaghetti that night was terrific but filled me sooner than I thought. The beautiful white milk— good, cold friend since childhood—sustained my weary body.

After supper, hanging out in the old barn entrance, getting to know a few people, we learned that Madame was rehearsing in the studio. Quietly we crept into the small observer's bench above the studio mirror. There we watched Madame Nijinska place Nikita in position, and then demonstrate the *porte de bras* (carriage of the arms) for a very pretty ballerina, Marina Svetlova. When Madame decided she did not like her idea, she would let loose a stream of Russian, waving her arms vigorously. Then Papa Shawn shoo-ed us out, so we went over to the theatre where Asadata Defora was rehearsing with his Sierra Leone drummers.

When Asadata gave us a master class in Primitive Rhythms, another earthy territory of dance and life rhythms was revealed. (For a girl taught to keep her knees together, it took a minute to squat and let go in the beat.) There were other master classes given by the current guest artist: Elizabeth Waters. Alwin Nikolais performed with her dance company, *Dancers On Route*. Waters taught us about investing our personal energies in dancing Modern Dance, the one thing I already knew. Her artistic independence was an inspiration to us. She was glad to talk dance to us, chatting with a quirky sense of humor.

"Barton's coming! Barton's coming! And so is Jess!"

Barton Mumaw had been Papa Shawn's lead dancer and Jess Meeker had been the accompanist and often composer for the dances. Barton was in the war, stationed at Keesler Field in Biloxi, Mississippi, where he was in Special Services, dancing to entertain the troops. Now he was on leave, coming to The Pillow to give performances. Papa Shawn beamed like the sun. Jess had managed to get leave at the same time, so there was great excitement.

Barton came to Shawn's class, demonstrating and teaching us selections from his repertory. Shawn had been teaching us *The French Sailor,* urging us to land "like ink in a blotter". With a grin, Barton showed us it was possible. He danced with such easy strength that physical effort was invisible. Barton's solo program at the Jacob's Pillow Dance Theatre, Friday, August 8, 1942, astonished me with what an American young man could—and would—dance. I had never seen anything like it. There was Barton's bounding joy as the

Banner Bearer in *Olympiad,* then his primitive, fearsome skill as the *Mongolian Archer.* Next, with great poise, he danced *Hellas Triumphant* in that short, flouncy, white skirt and shoes with big, black pompoms, the traditional attire of the Evzone, the Greek Royal Guard.

No man I knew would be caught dead in such an outfit, but here at Jacob's Pillow, sincerity seemed to dignify any strange or exotic arrangement of cloth, ties or feathers about the human body. *Hellas Triumphant* gradually captivated me with its short story of the Greek soldier, but two others of Barton's dances affected me more deeply. Barton's own choreography in *War and the Artist* justified my hatred of war. It was an agonizingly personal dance, illuminating the conflict of conscience and duty, the surrender to killing, the following self-loathing and sorrow. I wept in the dark, tears streaming, for him, for my boy friends in the war. Oh, how did horrible Hitler come to be? How turn peace-loving men into killers! What if even the artist lost his way? Frightening!

Barton closed his program with a romance in a minor key, his beautiful solo, *Pierrot in the Dead City.* Here was the aching pain of the heart. It touched me, illuminating the private, intimate longings, regrets and suspended dreams I shared with no one. On my own and in over my abilities, this was a serious risky time for me. Barton's lost Pierrot in his lonely wistful way danced it all out for me. The dance must have touched the entire audience for there was a long silence before applause. After his dancing, Barton came out into the audience to watch Shawn and Steffi keep their promise to dance a Viennese waltz for him. Here was the performing hero at ease, unpretentiously enjoying their dancing. I was still weeping.

The following week was devoted to dances of the First Generation of American Dancers: Anna Duncan, Ruth St. Denis and Ted Shawn. Papa Shawn started us off with dance history, including many references to important books: Isadora Duncan's *My Life,* Shawn's own *Dance We Must,* Sir James Frazer's *The Golden Bough,* and Havelock Ellis' *The Dance of Life.* Shawn quoted from Ellis: "Dance is life itself. Dance is the Mother of the arts." He went on about The Philosophy of Dance, presenting a consideration of dance as intellect and a force native to mankind since the Beginning. Dance was a serious concern of philosophy and anthropology involving mind, body and spirit.

Like most of my peers, I had been raised to have my mind educated at school, my body playing outside and my soul in Sunday school. This separation was emphasized. That there was tension between all three was drummed into us as a fearful fact of life that was reinforced the older we grew. Body health was good, of course. We were also taught that the body was "weak," giving into emotions and desires. Emotions were signs of loss of control. A pure spirit worthy of Heaven was the goal.

Now Shawn was saying the body, mind and spirit coexisted inseparably! I listened with wonder and relief for I had never been able to successfully divide these personal dimensions. It made great sense to me. Guilt fled. Freedom rang.

All this information was prelude to Shawn's introducing Anna Duncan, a seemingly frail older woman wearing a gown and a turban. Anna instructed us on Isadora Duncan's Principles, illustrating them with stories of her performances and schools. Having been freed already by Isadora's dancing barefoot, this idea was no longer defiant.

The simple movements Anna showed us seemed childish, almost too simple. Gradually we learned the sweep of energy they required. Skipping with leg swings...walking long distances on half toe...the carriage of the arms, hands open, bent back at the wrist "to offer a gift"...the head on a long neck, and where we were to look. Not face: *look!* Besides bringing Isadora's style and intimations of her passionate dancing, Anna impressed us with her dedication to keep Isadora's ideas alive. With her humble demeanor and quiet voice, Anna showed another kind of dancer personality.

Education in the ways dancers defined themselves was advanced with the arrival of Ruth St. Denis, a.k.a. Miss Ruth. Hers was an aura of spirituality. First seen from afar, Miss Ruth was a willowy creature in a long white gown, drifting across the pathway to The Main House. Even viewed from the back, Miss Ruth conveyed another demeanor. I fully expected her to float into the house, and found it contrarily ordinary when she had to open the door by hand as the rest of us did. The following morning, we received a lecture and class from Miss Ruth.

As Papa Shawn had promised pearls of wisdom, I had brought along a notebook. Shawn introduced her with lavish praise, telling us of her famous roles: *The Incense, The Cobras,* and her Indian Nautch Dances, her productions of *Radha* and *Egypta.* It was now eleven years since they had danced together, but revivals were in the works. Miss Ruth was currently devoting her energies to Spiritual Dance in California but happy to be here for the very first season at Jacob's Pillow Dance Theatre. The two partners exchanged looks that only could be called loving. Wasn't dance wonderful? Here were two divorced people supporting each other, celebrating each other's talent instead of bickering.

Miss Ruth smiled grandly, settling herself on the patio bench as we gathered around her feet. Quickly I jotted down a description: clear sapphire blue eyes...nice smile...pure white hair in a cloud about her head...covered with a black hair net...long curling eyelashes...heavy mascara...wine-colored lipstick...matching nail polish...chalky peach skin...surprisingly few wrinkles for her age, 65! She wore a long, white jersey gown, soiled around the edges...purple, rough cloth coat, worn open over dress...silver belt engraved with Indian designs...no other jewelry...freckled hands and neck...white socks and brown sandals...horn-rimmed glasses, one side-support gone...papers in hand, some typed, some handwritten, clasped together with a safety pin.

St. Denis welcomed this opportunity to talk to us, preach to us. Her lecture was a combination of performance and declamation of her Credo of Dance. She used many facial expressions, gestures and bodily movements for emphasis. Her eyebrows were fascinating and involved in changes of feeling. At times her eyes were merry with amusement, her verbal expressions jarringly worldly. Then her lovely, clear eyes would gaze far beyond us into a mystical somewhere as she spoke of Truth, Beauty and Love. Her voice was low, her diction exacting the value of her consonants.

Miss Ruth described her Society of Spiritual Arts, which she had founded in 1927. Her dancers, she said, were instruments of religious worship. At their services, she would speak what was on her mind, then they would rise and dance. The Three Stages of Prayer were supplication, gratitude and sharing, or prayers for others. Her method was to create through thought or emotion and then "rhythmatize" in action.

Readings from the scripture were also inspirational for her Rhythm Choir Knights.

"Start out to make Beauty, or even History. Not money," Miss Ruth told us. "Money is the byproduct of a job well done. It is of the greatest importance to heal and bless, rather than astonish with dance. The way to develop a spiritual attitude is first to understand the self as a spiritual being. This is the beginning of spiritual dance."

Her blue eyes were penetrating as she caught the eye of this student or that, demanding rigorous self-examination. Were any of us worthy or sufficiently pure in heart? My concepts of dance took a monumental leap. I had farther to go than I ever dreamed. Next Miss Ruth added homework! We must all read *Man the Unknown* by Dr. Alexis Carrel, which stated man was the measure of all. We must study early civilizations; their arts influenced her in her work. To her, Greek sculpture demonstrated the finest, most balanced art of the body. Egyptian architecture and sculpture demonstrated the importance of symbolism. Hindu arts brought her the joy of the diametric. Diametric? There had been scoffing by students who would have preferred a technique class to listening to a "65-year-old dancer who probably could hardly move." What would she know of contemporary dance? No one expected an intellectual mind to accompany her spiritual presence. She kept us off balance. Then she raised her arms, calling us into the studio where we were to dance out Good and Evil!

Centering herself in the studio with us in a ragged circle about her, Miss Ruth first gave a dramatic gesture to her thin, intense accompanist. Then she bent low to the floor before turning in ever-rising circles, her white gown flowing, following every motion. She began to chant, "I am the center of All Good. Come unto me and let me feed you that you may spread joy in the world. Yes! Touching and not touching, this strength you must share. Oh, you evil ones that dare not expose your hearts but mock the good about you! Cast down your trembling. Let good open the heart. Evil makes the heart shrivel, binding the strength inward. Spin off evil thoughts—faster—faster! Free the self! Lose the self! Open the heart to Good!"

Unwilling or not, phrases such as these drew us into Miss Ruth's vortex of motion. Her exhortations matched the rolling, tumbling dynamics of the music: first light and swirling, the accompanist fingers rippling from bass to treble; then low thunderings and tremolos as Evil threatened us all! No one escaped her calling. Those who joined tentatively were soon crouching and contracting with violent twists, then rising into statuary poses. We jumped, leaped, rolled on the floor then joining in two and three as Miss Ruth gathered and released us as the frenzy grew. First shy as Miss Ruth cried out for "Openness!" I now felt my chest would surely split and my beating heart burst from within to sail far out to the ocean. St Denis demanded, "Close! Feel the Evil you must resist!" Everything knotted inside me. In! Out! The orgy climaxed and was suddenly over. St Denis stood center, arms raised but relaxed, face lifted in serenity, eyes closed: the rest of us in states of prostration on the floor about her. Good apparently had won.

Dazed, exhausted and not a little bewildered, we gathered ourselves to our feet and managed a ragged applause. St. Denis bowed her head and nobly withdrew.

It was a singular experience, a profound lesson in personal magnetism. As others, I had been literally within her power, possessed. The hypnotism left me with a pervasive uneasiness that I determined to avoid in the future. At the same time, I recognized that this orgy was benign, and I was grateful to now know the experience. Yes, we were manipulated by St Denis, but divinely. Once I was my own person again, I could only admire and respect this astonishing woman. By the time she performed for us all in the theatre, I simply loved her.

In performance, Miss Ruth was just as hypnotizing. None of us had seen her perform; all were curious to see how her presence would project in her dancing. Some students were outspoken, saying that no one else her age would be allowed so much stage time; that it was nostalgic and pathetic, that she and Shawn too should retire. After her performance, such remarks were scarce. Granted the range of technique was limited to walking, bending, turning and mannered steps derived from Far East origins, but it fit the ceremonial style of her dances. Her integrity in being the priestess, combining the sensual with the spiritual, radiated through every movement. The theatrical lighting created an interior space: a mosque, a cave, an altar on the stage, but it was St. Denis who provided the aura: in a word, incandescent!

Wearing green jewel "cobra eyes" rings on her fingers, Miss Ruth created one of those "Is it a man or butterfly?" conundrums. The "boneless" cobra arms seemed to possess the woman, then the woman seemed to tempt danger in intimacy with the cobras. The dark side of sexuality was invoked and revealed by this 65-year-old dancer. Papa Shawn had told us of Miss Ruth's extraordinary suppleness and strength that allowed her to ripple her arms for long periods. He taught us how to initiate these successive moves, but we all failed to sustain them correctly or for long.

St. Denis's duets with Shawn were more worldly. She became demure and flirtatious in their revival of a favorite, *Josephine and Hyppolyte.* Miss Ruth wore a dark wig and a small tiara to accent her long Empire gown. Shawn looked dashing in his Hassar uniform. They gave us a lesson in style and professionalism that had nothing to do with technical pyrotechnics. If my parents could see this, they would understand that this was true elegance, not the cheap dance they feared. We watched as John Lindquist photographed them in costume outside after the program. Handsome and beautiful, intelligent and witty, talented and sensitive, these two human beings now represented the best a person could be. Consciously or subconsciously, gradually, they became surrogate parents for me.

Curtain time for the Jacob's Pillow Dance Theatre was set at 5:00 p.m. to allow patrons to see the performances and still get back home before the Blackout. If we students were not assisting an artist or preparing cucumber sandwiches for the intermission in the Tea Garden, we were allowed to watch all these artists work. Nijinska presented her new ballet, *Etude,* to music of Johann Sebastian Bach, and *E-Minor Concerto* to music by Frederic Chopin. Nina Youskevitch had come up to join the principals in the ballet, Nikita and Marina (who practiced in tennis shoes). It was a rare opportunity to see Nijinska's choreography but since I was a novice, much passed me by. Shawn also performed on this program. And so did I!

Shawn did not omit Dance in Education from his University of the Dance. He invited two pioneers in college dance to teach. One was Professor Margaret D'Houbler from the University of Wisconsin, where she had founded a Dance Major. Exciting news. Dr. D'Houbler had written a book,

Rhythmic Form and Analysis, which we all had to buy and study as we took her classes. Action became cerebral as we learned to clap primary, secondary and resultant rhythms; offbeat, on-beat and counter-rhythms. Didn't dancers learn the rhythms of each dance anyway? Shawn insisted and to press his point, gathered us all together, reading Stephen Vincent Benet's narrative poem, *The Mountain Whippoorwill.* The poem is about a young fiddler who goes to a fiddle contest with old-time fiddlers, competing with The Devil and winning. We were going to explore the various rhythms in the poem with Shawn in dance. Would we be asked to make up the dance steps? Choreography was a new, big word. We were learning this from the second dance educator, Dr. Anne Schley Duggan, from Texas State College for Women in Denton, Texas.

Unlike Dr. D'Houbler, who wore street clothes, Dr. Duggan wore custom made outfits: crop top, bare midriff, long skirt and always flowers pinned above the center of her forehead. She taught *Fundamentals of Movement, Rhythm and Design,* basic tools for choreography. Dr. Duggan seldom danced; rather she stood beating a drum, calling out instructions as her Junoesque redheaded assistant, Jeanette Schlottman, happily demonstrated all. Fundamental movements were put to use in 4/4 time and 3/4 time, then combined to achieve resultant rhythm (1-4-5-7-9-10), which was then to be translated into a dance movement. We were not to use dance vocabulary previously familiar. This exercise added new mental processes to dance for many of us. One thing brought home to me was how obedient dancers were. All day we followed instructions, corrections, rules of dance forms and teachers' examples. Dance was handed down vocally from teacher to student and dancer to dancer.

When told to move any way we wished, some of us learned that at times complete freedom is no freedom.

Now Shawn asked for suggestions for *Mountain Whippoorwill*. As we all hesitated, he took over with no end of ideas, explaining his choreographic decisions as he went. Many of us did little more than cross and re-cross the stage with a dancy step but it was a thrill to dance on the stage of the Jacob's Pillow Dance Theatre. As it was still light, the back doors of the stage were opened, providing a mountain greenery backdrop to our set.

When the classes ended in August, my crucial decision about becoming a professional dancer was already made. With new insights into the stature of dance as art, with Bart's program still imaging in my mind to show the way, my choice to pursue dance in the face of war was strong and sure. Everything I had learned these three weeks confirmed what I felt was true: I would strive to be an excellent dancer to dance for everyone.

Then the Big Question: Was there any hope that I *could* be a professional dancer?

Shawn's see-all-do-all manager, Fern Helscher set up an appointment with Papa Shawn for me. Trembling, I went into the Main House. Before I could ask Papa Shawn to sign his picture, he said, "In my mind, you have the talent, the beauty of face and body, and the love of the art to be a fine artist of the dance."

He took my breath away. I told him how wonderful it had been here for me, how he inspired me with great ambitions. "And you'll realize them. I wish I could be as sure of everyone as I am of you."

My experience with Ted Shawn did not reveal him as a man who coddled his pupils or was lavish with empty praise. It was important for me to believe him and I did. He talked to me about the life of a dancer, my parental problems, dance opportunities during the War—everything. It was best that I go back to Syracuse for my junior year as a theatre major and milk every opportunity to dance. He knew a fine ballet teacher to study with in Syracuse, Norma Allerwelt. Next summer he hoped to have about twenty students and five choreographers at The Pillow, including me! I should write to him in January to tell him if I was interested. I instantly assured him I was and thanked him profusely.

August 28, 1942, I now had the right to stand among dancers.

38

CHAPTER THREE

Fall 1942 - Summer 1943
  Syracuse University Theatre & Scholarship Student at Jacob's Pillow

Going back to Syracuse for my Junior year, I took a salesgirl job to afford my new ballet classes with Norma Allerwelt. Her classes were similar to Madame Nijinska's, with an extra emphasis on building stamina. We did everything eight times, from *demi pliés* (knee bends), *grand pliés* (deep knee bends), *relevés* (rising to the toes), *pirouettes* to *attitude turns* (one leg bent back in the air), and *jetés (leaps).* Each class ended with sixteen *grand battements* (high leg extension to side).

I also followed Shawn's advice, insinuating dance solos into many campus events. My repertory was all from The Pillow but new here. The Spanish flamenco dance, *Viva Faraon,* with the heel beats was a favorite. For the Junior Class Ball, I got a fellow thespian from our student musical to dance *Gypsy Rondo-Bout Town* with me also. With Miss Nash's Dance Group, too, I was doing more dancing than acting. It was disappointing when director Sawyer Falk chose an actor to be the ballet girl in William Saroyan's *Jim Dandy,* so her character did not dance. In our student musical, he cut out a duet I choreographed, explaining that though he liked this dance, it made the show too long. At my dismay, Falk said, "You know our theatre motto is *Personal Integrity Through Artistic Integrity.* Do you know what that means?"

Hesitating, "Something about truth," I guessed.

"Close. It means by being true to the principles of your art, you will grow to have integrity in yourself. Think about it."

Later in the year Falk came to me, saying he was going to show the French film, *Ballerina* at the Civic: Did my ballet class have a dance for the program? Yes! As the film was run for the audience out front, we warmed up behind the screen. It was charming to see the shadowy dancers in reverse. Watching their images, I moved to fit in with them, to feel that I was also dancing at the Paris Opera. Then we danced our Chopin *Etudes.* How alive it was to dance live!

There was great excitement in the spring at The Civic as Falk convinced playwrights Florence Ryerson and Clarence Clement that our theatre was the one to try out their new play, *Harriet.* Actress Eugenia Rawls came from New York to take the role of Harriet Beecher Stowe. All the parts were played by University students, except for one community actor and Miss Rawls (who wore slacks to rehearsal!) It was my job to design and run the lighting. We dedicated the play to Eleanor Roosevelt, who had recently come to the campus, speaking about the War. Then the news was that Helen Hayes herself would come to our opening night! The play went well, no crisis with my lighting. Everyone on stage and off joined in the dramatic finale singing the impassioned *Battle Hymn of the Republic.* It was thrilling! Miss Hayes came backstage, graciously complimenting us as we all stood there to receive her. That fall, she opened *Harriet* for a long run on Broadway.

Our next production was Maxwell Anderson's *The Eve of St. Mark,* another war play. Neither our drama nor our campus was isolated from the war. Syracuse was one more college used for training officers, billeting service men in dorms and fraternity houses. There were bond sales, stamp dances (bond stamps for admission), Bundles for Britain and blood drawings, and asking our musical to perform at Army bases. By spring—oh, joy! A letter came from Papa Shawn inviting me to be a scholarship student at The Pillow the coming summer.

Returning to The Pillow was more exciting than going home for Christmas. We came a week early in June to get things ready for the 1943 season, meeting in the stone cottage for our first meal together. Chatter was lively. All hushed as Papa Shawn rose, raising his arms over us in a blessing. With a warm smile, he welcomed us all and announced the events for the coming summer. Joe Pilates was already here. Natasha Krassovska and Grant Mouradoff of the *Ballet Russe de Monte Carlo* would be teaching Classic Ballet. Thalia Mara and Arthur Mahoney, Spanish and 18th Century Court Dance; La Meri, Dr. Duggan and Marina Svetlova were coming later. Fern Helscher was still manager.

"I also want you to know I plan to give you scholarship students some opportunity to perform this summer," Shawn said to instant applause.

As Shawn spoke again his voice was lower, serious, at times held a sardonic humor. There almost wasn't going to be a summer program here at Jacob's Pillow because of the war. The trustees had experienced very hard financial times. Tanglewood was not going to open, nor was the Drama School of the Berkshire Playhouse for the first time in seventeen years. Even the American Dance Festival at Bennington College was suspended. Shawn had taken full responsibility for this summer here with the understanding that the trustees would not be responsible for any deficit. As scholarship students, receiving this opportunity to study without paying, we must be just as responsible and diligent throughout the summer for the work to go forward. "If no one comes, we'll dance for each other!" Shawn declared to rousing cheers.

Next he asked for volunteers for specific assignments. Betty Jones and Ruthanne Welch quickly took KP, a wise move I did not value until I noticed later they were never hungry. My job was to run the Theatre Office, typing press releases, printing the programs, reserving tickets, answering the phone, et al. Papa Shawn himself taught me how to use the cranky mimeograph machine for the programs, saying with wry wisdom, "Anytime you can't learn the composer for a ballet, use Tchaikovsky. You'll be right ninety per cent of the time."

Shawn was demanding, but he kept our rights to class inviolate. Class is a dancer's Daily Bread—sustenance, growth, vigor and repair. At once personal and communal, there were the constant perceptions to receive, to know, to give, seeking ever-elusive perfection. Pilates started us off each morning, challenging every body part. With only twenty- six of us students (22 girls, 4 boys), we got individual attention in theory, practice and at least studio performance. Natalie Krassovska (Natasha) or Grant Mouradoff taught ballet with little better English than Madame Nijinska. Natasha had worked with Madame and also George Balanchine. She danced leading roles in the major ballets. With beautiful, dark eyes deep-set in her oval face, she had a Slavic elegance. She, like Marina, smiled generously and often, sometimes because she understood little English. Where Marina seemed to be airily daydreaming, Natasha seemed deep and soulful. Give them each a mazurka, Marina would skim the stage; Natasha set it on fire.

Perhaps the most vital fact Shawn drilled into us was that dance was eclectic. One form or style did not deny the other. If there were modifications to a dance, then it was not a violation but a new version. If you wanted the strictures of the original dance, you could go to that again. He had respect for the variety of dance forms, styles, traditions, sources and the dancers themselves. Curiously, the only dance style he dismissed was tap dancing. He also disdained acts of certain ex-Denishawn dancers who had "failed him" (Martha Graham, Doris Humphrey and Charles Weidman). Changes could have been made within without destroying Denishawn.

Shawn's classes were also a venue to teach us repertory. One of the most useful was a series of dance vignettes, *Sixteen Dances in Sixteen Rhythms:* march, gavotte, schottische, minuet, tango, bolero, tarantella, polka, galop, waltz, barcarolle, jota, two-step, polonaise, mazurka, varsovienne. These rhythms were choreographed as short dance vignettes, one leading into the next. Shawn gave us a quick run-down on each dance's historical background, spirit, style and costume. After teaching us much of his repertory, Shawn sold mimeographed copies of these dance notes for a quarter to a dollar: I bought them all.

Mary Campbell made sure we got our time signatures and rhythms right. She was a treasure. Mary played accompanist for Shawn's performances and for the professional performers at the Theatre. She played with equal zest for our classes, never impatient, patronizing or judgmental. Mary was a beautiful woman in her late fifties with coifed white hair. Often her piano was visible on stage during Shawn's dances, making her a partner in performance. For these occasions, Mary wore a dark cloak over a long gown.

We had all been measured for toe shoes the first week. I could hardly wait for mine. Natasha spent a whole class going from girl to girl to check each fit. — then tie— then first *plié* then first *relevé*. The first time we used the *barre* to push up *en pointe*. From then on fifteen minutes practice at the end of ballet class.

It was a joyful agony, a thrill to balance up there. It was a thrill to find blood on the lamb's wool stuffing my slippers; that was a rite of passage dancing on point. As pain and blood did not stop, I confessed to Natasha. She asked me to remove my slippers and ballet tights to examine my bare feet more closely. First she looked intently, then sadly. My second toe was longer than my big toe, forcing my second toe to fold under or jam the metatarsal. I had Greek feet. This anatomical problem could only be solved with expensive custom-made toe shoes. Consideration of this financial enormity aroused a vivid image of a dark windy force sweeping down and whisking my beautiful white romantic tutu from my arms forever.

I let out a weepy, "Oh!" All the girls were silent. I managed a shrug. Trying again and healing alternated, but my ballet dreams began to fade. Often I joined the boys practicing elevations with Grant. Natasha took time to perfect my *grand jeté en tourant*, a high leap, turning midair).

Arthur Mahoney taught us that ballet did not exist in a vacuum but had developed from peasant dances in France and Spain. Manner and technique were influenced by the *Commedia dell'arte'* in bows and curtsies. The basic five positions originated there. Dancing lessons were required by all, but only the most skillful performers danced in royal entertainments. In the French court of Louis XIV, it was the very king himself who outshone the other courtiers in dancing. Wearing a glittering gold costume, Louis XIV performed the role of the Sun King in *Ballet Royal de la Nuite* as early as 1633. Arthur performed his version of the Sun King and other court dances with Thalia Mara in the Theatre.

Husband and wife, Arthur and Thalia also performed. Taking the rhythms of the guitarist and in traditional flamenco costumes, Thalia and Arthur performed a fiery, flirtatious flamenco. They taught us three styles of Spanish dances: peasant or country dance, the jota; court dancing, the pavane; gypsy dancing, the flamenco. While we were stamping out *bulerias* or *farrucca* rhythms and clapping the hollow-handed Spanish way, La Meri arrived..

La Meri, a Texas girl, had had the brass to go to India without knowing the language and convince a learned teacher of classic Indian dance that she had the spirit and determination to learn it. She stayed until she did. On she went to Argentina and other countries to master more ethnic dance. In the Jacob's Pillow Dance Theatre, La Meri performed Argentine gaucho, Javanese and Spanish dances, as well as Indian. In class, La Meri wore an East Indian print sari and a red cast mark centered on her forehead. Greeting us formally, palms held together as in prayer, she touched her forehead, her breast and her waist. Quiet was required in La Meri's class. How else could we hear her ankle bells!

She introduced us to Indian culture, showing us how to tie a woman's sari and a man's dhoti without fasteners. She demonstrated the most intriguing hand gestures, foot steps and facial expressions. The *mudras* (hand gestures) were truly exotic and appealing, demanding fine finger co-ordinations and flexible back-bending hands. Walking steps included a scooping toe-in/toe-out step, the big toe held up.

There were different ways to stamp the feet or just the heels. Somehow we had to make all these isolated movements flow in motion, often while singing. We all looked like broken puppets at the start, except Aldo Cadena and Rebecca Harris. Both later joined La Meri's dance company.

For fun, she taught us a genuine hula, chiding us girls for our "ridiculous modesty" that had no place in a hula. There were tricky steps and a very different way with the arms. The dances told history and native Hawaiian stories, as the Indians did in their dances. Our rippling arm work with Shawn helped us see when arm movements were decorative or meaningful. In Indian and Hawaiian dance, the arm movement initiated from within the body out: positive. Miss Ruth's arms in *Cobra* initiated in her hands, undulating inward: negative.

Midseason, I joined with the other scholarship students reminding Papa Shawn he promised to let us perform. So far only Virginia Bosler and Betty Jones with Aldo Cadena had danced a short 18th Century dance for Arthur. Nobody was surprised that they were chosen. Both Betty and Virginia (Winkie) were among the top ballet students here: consistent, clean, accurate and timely. Betty was cheerfully pragmatic. Virginia had a natural ease, readily fulfilling movement.

Then Shawn taught us *Amethyst,* a lyric dance infused with Art Nouveau nostalgia. So much of the repertory had been masculine; we were thrilled with this feminine dance, its subtle moods. Each of us hoped to perform it, including Natasha. She often came to Shawn's class, delighted to be dancing barefoot. Shawn gave the performance of *Amethyst* to Natasha, who was ecstatic. There was a lot of feeling about it. It was our turn to perform. Natasha had many performances. She was too balletic, too stiff, too old. But we knew Shawn had every right to give the dance to her. He had to use star power to get people to spend their precious gas rations to come to Jacob's Pillow performances during the war.

Shawn himself danced frequently, reviving all manner of dances from his vast repertoire. Each performance began with a silence. Then Shawn would enter through the curtain wearing his white terry cloth robe, and welcome the guests, telling them about the artists they were to see until he heard a knock—knock backstage, his cue that all was ready. Somewhere in the program, Shawn would dance *Oh Brother Sun, Oh ,Sister Moon* in a monk's garb; another time appear nearly naked chained to a rock as *Prometheus;* dance a comic folk dance keeping his hands in his pockets; or sweating and bare-chested, interpret the Negro spiritual *Nobody Knows the Trouble I've Seen.*

There was new excitement one morning when Mary came to Shawn's class laden with music books. We were to listen to musical selections to choose for choreography we would create. Finally Tchaikovsky's *Romance #5* was agreed upon. Papa Shawn and Mary guided our understanding of musical form aiding choreographic structure. The music allowed a scenario about a woman in wartime. She parts from her lover as the trumpets of war are sounded, her reminiscence, the repeat of the trumpets, then her resolution to carry on.

We called it *Romance.* It would have been melodramatic were it not for the strength of the music and the fact that this story was a daily truth of lives now. Again we believed one of us girls should dance the role. Alicia Langford's husband was overseas fighting the war. It seemed just that she perform *Romance*. But once more, Papa Shawn gave this chance to Natasha, who had not even been in the class.

Hope renewed when Papa Shawn decided to revive his *Cretan Suite,* which included *Gnossienne, Dance of the Bull God* and *Ariadne.* He also added a Denishawn piece, *Choeur Dansé,* calling it *Choric Danes.* Straight from a Greek frieze, three maidens frolic to a 9/8 time signature in music by N. Stcherbatcheff. Because of my job, I had more daily contact with Papa Shawn and Fern, with an inside track on rumors and possibilities. Fern leaked the word to me that Papa Shawn planned to use me in *Choeur Dansé.* My heart thrilled. My mother was visiting my sister Jane in Boston, close enough to persuade her to come see The Pillow. I would then surprise her dancing on the program. She came, but disaster! She saw Papa Shawn bare-chested as the Bull God chasing Geni Whitlow as Ariadne, and Betty, Ruthanne and Jean Tachau in *Choeur Dansé.* Either Fern was wrong or Papa Shawn did not think I was good enough for this dance. Either way, it was discouraging.

The next day, sad and sullen, I was sitting slumped against the fence outside the Tea Garden when Shawn passed by.

"It can't be that bad, can it?" he asked.

"Yes, it is!" And I told him why.

"Well, how would you like to be my partner? We're planning a big student show with Natasha doing a waltz and Joe, a demonstration. Were you here last summer when I taught *Gypsy Rondo-Bout Town?*"

"Yes! I found a partner and we danced it at the Junior Prom!"

"Good! We'll do it. Now here's the program for this week."

Days went by. He had forgotten. But, no, Papa Shawn finally called a rehearsal. I went early to the theatre to be sure of a good warm-up. When he arrived, he gave the piano a slap, grinned at me and said, "Now to work. Mary?" I zipped offstage left. Mary began to play, and off I went: four running steps, *pas de chat, degagé coupé tendu.*

"Stop! What was that?" Shawn stared at me.

"The first step."

"Oh, ho-no! Not like that! Come over here, darling!"

The first *darling* was gentle, reassuring, but as time went on, *darling* became a euphemism for aggrieved patience, aggravated impatience and despair. "That's all I can stand today. Next time be perfect. Then we'll do it again."

I had practiced incessantly, anxiously for fear he would cancel the dance. As the days went by, I practiced with Natasha in the *Waltz,* with Joe in his *Demonstration,* but not Papa Shawn. I, like others, was unaware how distracted he was about Barton's changing situation in the Army, but there were other severe problems, as well. Papa Shawn called the entire school together in the stone cottage after dinner. When we were gathered, he entered from the Main House. Unsmiling, he took a moment to gaze at us all.

"Do you believe Jacob's Pillow is worth saving?"

Stunned into silence, it was seconds before we all chorused, "Yes! Yes!"

It would take all of us, everybody. The Pillow finances were in crisis. Trustees were looking for ways he could finish out the summer. We had been surviving day-by-day. Now there was not enough money for food. Not even for the next couple of days. He waited as shock waves went through us. He had a plan. God helps him who helps himself. We would have a Save The Pillow Blueberry Picking Contest. God covered the Berkshires with His own blue sapphires, free for the picking. The berries would then be sold for food. There would also be prizes from his private collection for the berry pickers: two Japanese brush paintings; one tambourine; a copy of *How Beautiful Upon the Mountain,* his latest book; and a copy of the poem *The Dithyramb of the Rose,* by the Greek Poet Laureate Angelos Sikelianos

I joined Dottie Spence, a writer for *Dance Magazine,* to pick these blue jewels from the low twiggy bushes. Living in New York City, what could she tell me about dance there? The big story of course was Agnes de Mille's choreography, with the spectacular ballet in the hit *Oklahoma!* You did not really have to sleep with the director to get a job, did you? Did she know many men ballet dancers? Were they *fairies* as was rumored? (At that time, I was not alone in my total ignorance about homosexuality. I had a cowardly attitude; not sure I wanted to know.) We checked in at noon for a peanut butter sandwich and a glass of milk, then back out to the mountains to pick anew. At supper, any doubters were convinced Papa Shawn was not exaggerating when we were served "One of nature's delicacies"—steamed milkweed. There were few takers of the soggy mess. It tasted like wet velvet to me. All the blueberries went off to market.

With a few words for malingerers, Shawn thanked us and awarded his prizes to those who picked the most berries. Dottie came in fourth, choosing the second Japanese painting; leaving the *Dithyramb* for the fifth place winner, me! (OK, I spilled one pail and fell behind.) Shawn closed the evening leading us in singing *Jacob's Ladder:*

We are climbing Jacob's Ladder (outspread arms, rising higher on repeats)
We are climbing Jacob's Ladder
We are climbing Jacob's Ladder
Soldiers (arms crossed at breast)
of the (arms up into a Y)
Cross (arms wide, gaze upwards)

Later in our #9 loft, I read my *Dithyramb,* a long poem with dancing. The rose-covered paper booklet was illustrated with silver tracings of an ever-expanding rose, the Perfect Rose, the hundred-petal rose, the Rose of Love. A quote from Dostoevsky on the flyleaf: *Beauty will save the world.* The story traced Orpheus gathering to him all of the orphans of the world, dancing together, more sorrowing than rejoicing. The lyric was bittersweet with longing, not the Dionysian orgies. It was simple to fall into it for I, too, felt orphaned by my family and my peers for needing to dance. And for my left-handed soul that so often made people exchange looks over my head.

"He who cleaves the shadowy seas of separation
Having ever love in his heart like an Eternal Star
will meet not only with those he had lost,
but also with others
And, like a Sacred Bridge, he will join
Lands with lands, peoples with peoples, enemies with friends,
With life, death, the centuries with the centuries."

The Dithyramb of the Rose by Angelos Sikelianos

I stood up under the eaves and my arms floated up as I looked about expectantly. I wanted to run. To be still. To hold in my arms everyone I had ever loved all at once. Down the stairs I ran, charging up to the Theatre, into the dark calling, "Aldo! Aldo!" I ran down the aisle, up on stage, flinging my arms about him, shouting, "I love you, Aldo! I love everybody!'

Then I slid down on the stage in a heap. "Thanks Aldo. I had to hug somebody."

"Crazy. Could be worse," Aldo observed. "What is... this?"

"I was reading the *Dithyramb*. So beautiful. No one needs to be lonely, not really. If we 'keep love in our hearts like an eternal star!' "

"That's all."

"That's all! I can see how Papa Shawn would think he was an Orpheus, leading all us orphaned dancers. Don't you see that?"

Aldo slowly nodded, then his eyes twinkled. "Except when you rehearse with him!" Aldo was percussionist for Shawn and we shared the same kind of terror.

"Well, there's no rehearsal tonight. I'm still hungry, aren't you? We could walk to Peanuts." (A roadhouse about a mile away, where we often went after hours to dance and have blueberry pie.)

We asked Dottie to come along. "I'm hungry all right, but nobody is going to get me to walk that far after climbing mountains all day. I'd rather starve."

My eyes focused on a distant image. "How about an egg?"

"Egg." Aldo's eyes closed. "I remember the egg."

"Or a cheese omelet. The egg I might walk for," Dottie started to rise, and then sat back. "But not all the way to Peanuts and back."

After a quiet moment, Aldo shouted, "Joe!"

We headed at once to Joe Pilates's private cabin. Joe had the egg. Happily, he scrambled the most eloquently delicious eggs in the Western World and served them with a brisk nod of his head.

"Oh, nothing is better than food when you're hungry!" I moaned.

"More? Any of you, more?" Joe laughed. "Better da milkveed, yah?"

Papa Shawn called a rehearsal for us at last. He seemed preoccupied, then intent in getting through the whole dance. Without comment, we took it from the top twice more. "Time is running out. Just be perfect this time tomorrow, Shirley."

"I'll try," I smiled.

"Don't try! Do it!"

I nodded, blinking. Papa Shawn put his hands on my shoulders and bent down to force me to look into his eyes. "We want to wow 'em, don't we, darling?" I nodded, managing a thin smile. "OK. Four-thirty tomorrow." Shawn picked up his towel and left.

Weary and worried, hot and sweaty, I stood staring through the stage floor. Mary left the piano, and coming over to me, said kindly, "You must learn to listen, Shirley. If Mr. Shawn says 'Be perfect,' he must think you *can* be."

I had one more crisis with Papa Shawn, with my costume. Wrinkled from a hasty mailing, the dress looked so bad he would not even let me try it on. "You used this trashy thing? With gold polka dots? And look at the length of it!

Why, my dear girl, would you have a short skirt going out on the town!"

"I thought you said costumes must not hide the movement," I said.

Shawn gave Fern a baleful look and sighed, "Take it away. Find something else."

Costumes were rare at The Pillow, and mostly men's. Performers brought their own costumes. We girls were making Greek chitons of thin white cotton, gathered at the waist with the new elastic thread, for our waltz for Natasha. I remembered one of Jane's formals for summer, a green flowered chintz with a wide full skirt, three quarter sleeves, and a square neckline with lace. It arrived just in time.

Shawn looked it over. "Better. Put it on."

Fern led me into his office in the Main House where I slipped into the dress. But something was wrong. Boy, had I lost weight! Shawn looked me over.

"Hmmmm. Turn around. Well, the dress is all right. It's just...you look a little...tired," he finished lamely. My heart fell. Now what?

"It's just too big," Fern said crisply. "We can fix that." As soon Shawn left she told me to stuff my bra with Kleenex. Later, sufficiently stuffed, I posed in the studio mirror. It was better when I inhaled, but I looked haggard. Needed a shampoo. Hands on hips, I glowered at my image. Who was dancing with Ted Shawn? Voluptuous bouncing babes? No! Skinny-minny Shirley Traver. Tomorrow!

Our last *Gypsy* rehearsal had gone well. Then Papa Shawn told me to go out front and he would dance his solo *Waltz in Springtime* for me! First I felt like royalty. Then like a fellow dancer. He danced full out, ending with a bow and a smile as I clapped the loud Spanish way. It was a gesture to treasure, for Shawn never let anyone watch his rehearsals.

Saturday, August 14, 1943, everyone at The Pillow involved in the Program was exhilarated. Would friends find the gas to come? Of course my parents would not, but there was a hope that my dear Aunt Pummie and Uncle Herb would come over from Providence for the five o'clock performance. I dived into the theatre to find Natasha more excited about our *Waltz of the Flowers* than her own *Fee Dragee*. She supervised our Romantic Ballet hairstyles and adorned us all with cloth flowers. It would be the first performance *en pointe* for most of us. The ballet was early on the program, then off with the pink toe shoes and into my costume while Natasha, and then Shawn, danced their solos.

At the sound of his applause, I darted into the wings stage left, heart in mouth. After a long pause, Mary began to play. In I ran and had the best time dancing in my life. The steps were right there, the music bright, and Papa Shawn and I hit it off to make it all fun. I was so happy to be dancing, performing on this special stage with this special man. My green flowered skirt sailed wide in the swing time section, swirled gracefully in the ballroom, bounced in the polka and flounced in the cakewalk. The fitted torso enhanced the Spanish steps and the low, lacey neckline, the Minuet. Performing was freedom. Then the dancing was mine, his, ours. As Shawn whirled me out for our bow, he whispered "God bless you, darling!" We came back for several bows. Then he kissed me, saying, "Well, go on over, honey and we'll do it again!" I thought he just meant bow again—he meant an encore! So we danced it all again.

Backstage, Shawn took me by the shoulders and said, "Now it's worth all the discipline, isn't it?" There was a hurt look in his brown eyes. He went on to his dressing room before I could tell him how grateful I was. Next Aldo performed his Mexican Dance and was also given an encore. Joe's *Demonstration of Contrology Exercise* went as planned, and he was dragged protesting onstage for a bow. We had no company bow, so I tried to catch Papa Shawn before he disappeared into the Main House.

He was outside, talking to Jan Veen from the Boston Conservatory Dance Department. When Mr. Veen left, I had a chance to tell Papa Shawn how grateful I was for the chance he had given me. I kissed his cheek. He kissed me back and, arms about each other's waists, we walked toward the Main House. I asked him if he was tired. He answered "yes" but that it was more than that. He hated having to be the person who always had to say "no" here. If he could just dance and be glamorous everyone would like him, but he couldn't. He had to run the school. None of us knew how many problems there were and he had been hurt very much these last three weeks. He had put everything into this school. He didn't know where he was going to live this winter. There was no love here.

All he said was distressing. I caught his hand, saying there was love in my heart and in many others for him. Shawn picked a small blue flower, stood quietly. After a moment, he smiled wistfully, kissed me on the cheek and said, "We'll talk about it sometime." He went on into the Main House.

I ran to the Tea Garden to catch up with Aunt Pummie, Uncle Herb and Phyllis, who had arrived just in time to catch our ballet. They were polite about that but praised *Gypsy,* saying my dancing was a surprise and a delight. How proud they were at the demand for the encore.

At last some of my family had seen me dance. "I am going to be sure to write your parents in great detail about your success," Aunt Pummie promised. And she did.

Dear Charles and Elsie,
We saw Ted Shawn dance with Ted Shawn and the people applauded.

He took bows. Then Ted Shawn danced with Shirley Traver. They took three bows and as many in between—to each other but the people wouldn't stop applauding and finally added stamping their clamor – so Ted Shawn and Shirley Traver repeated the entire dance only to be called forth for more bows. We, her family, became embarrassed and left the demonstration to others.

I hope you will be pleased, because of course the People really know what they like!!

When the company appeared at the end. Mouradoff had Shirley by the hand and kept shaking it and giving her several bows.
Affectionately,
Pummie

Later that night we had a big bonfire at Joe's cottage. A couple of us came up to get some food from Esther. I went on into the Main House to ask Papa Shawn to join us all. He was working in his office, looking tired, sad and lonely. He said, no, he had work to do. Then he put his arm around me and laid his head on my shoulder. Tears came to my eyes so I gave him a hug, touched that this man who had given me so much now needed me. He smiled and said he was writing to

Barton about our dance. I heard the kids calling me but knew when I left he was a bit happier.

None of us students had any idea Papa Shawn paid any attention to the disappointments we felt over *Amethyst* and *Romance*. It smoldered among us, but none dared question his authority to assign dances. Natasha seemed oblivious to any resentment. I too was disappointed, but felt Shawn believed none of us good enough for performance. Now at the bonfire, I told the others how Shawn felt about everything. We all had now performed in the theatre; he had kept his promise. We chipped in to pay for a beautiful handmade pottery bowl, made by a local artist, Mr. Albright. The next day, we called Papa Shawn into the stone cottage. Dottie gave a little speech before the presentation, quoting Keat's: *"A thing of beauty is a joy forever"* and saying we all hoped this bowl would bring him as much joy as he had given us.

Shawn spoke to us, spilling out his sorrows, telling us how much we mattered to him as he tried to maintain the art of the dance in these days of war. Dance was to bring people together, but here, lately it was the opposite, which made his sacrifices meaningless. He ended by saying, "I love you all and now I know you love me back."

From then on energy flowed as it had at the beginning of the summer. Papa Shawn could not teach us enough fast enough to satisfy our thirst for dance. Shawn introduced us to the theories of Francois Delsarte, saying we must all read Genevieve Stebbin's *Delsarte System of Expression*. Delsarte developed a process of expression based upon the basic trinity of the intellectual (head and neck), emotional-spiritual (upper torso and arms), and the physical body (trunk and legs). These three areas were then subdivided, For example:

the upper arm expressed the physical; lower arm expressed the emotional-spiritual; hands expressed the intellectual.

The legs' values were similar: *feet, intelligent!* I guessed because of all those nerve endings and how they got our feet to go wherever. Shoulders were the thermometers of passion. The elbow, close or away from the body, was the thermometer of affection and self-will. The wrist was the thermometer of vital energy. It was from Delsarte that Shawn told us that moves from the center of the body were true and good; that movements initiating from the extremities toward the body were destructive and bad. "Every little movement has a meaning all its own" was not just a simpering song, but truth. We instantly experimented trying to fool each other.

Delsarte's early body-language system also applied to stance. It was new to learn that a strong stance in second position—torso centered over bent legs apart, parallel, weight even—that this was not the strongest stance. It would need a shift of weight before a man could take a step. Stronger was a narrow base, one foot at the arch of the other foot, weight forward, so that the forward foot could move instantly. Quiet strength was similar but with the weight back, ready but waiting. Both these latter positions presented a narrow target.

Shawn went on to discuss natural *recoil,* the body's initial reaction: positive or negative, in surprise, for example. This was in the *solar plexus,* occurring to a lesser or greater degree. Isadora Duncan used this knowledge before Martha Graham consciously integrated contractions in her technique. Where I had thought the eyes most telling, we saw hands constantly confessing inner states of being through the degree of openness of hand and thumb. It was enlightening but also humbling to dancers who move consciously with deliberation to learn we were just as oblivious to the obvious as anyone else.

Shawn used Delsarte lectures to lead up to Modern Dance. Although he said he understood the need to break away from older forms, he had not expected that his Denishawn dancers would initiate it. He mentioned Martha Graham, Doris Humphrey and Charles Weidman as provocative, but hurried on to praise Agnes de Mille for her wonderful *Oklahoma*! Everyone shouted "Oklahoma!" We all wanted to go to New York and audition for it. Shawn saw a new day for dance when the war would finally end. Americans wanted to dance their own styles as had Elizabeth Waters and Sybil Shearer. What we must not forget was the earlier work of a Russian, Michael Fokine , who had been disenchanted with ballet as early as 1914. Fokine's Five Principles of Modern Ballet:

1. No combinations from ready made steps. Expressions must fit the subject at hand.
2. Dancing and mime, etc., gestures have no meaning unless they describe the dramatic action. Gesture can never be mere divertissement.
3. Conventional gesture used only when the style of the ballet demands it. Gesture of the hand must be replaced by gesture of the whole body.
4. Groups and ensemble dance must be used expressively as a whole, not as decorative background.
5. There must be an unbroken alliance between dancing and other arts of music,

painting sets, costumes, that is equal in
freedom to each.

I wrote down all these rules as Shawn read them off.
In closing this lecture, he said a dance must have harmony
deeper than its steps, that all movements must have a living
idea. This was vital to modern dance.

Barton returned on leave to perform again in the
Jacob's Pillow Dance Theatre. John Lindquist retuned from
Boston to photograph him --and with Papa Shawn's
generosity, to photograph us scholarship students in dance
movements, too. Lindquist took group pictures and then
individual ones. This was regularly done outside on or near a
huge rock. In turn, each student chose his/her movement. I
hesitated a moment at my turn. "Come along now. You're a
dawnser!" called John. "Just dawnse!" I pushed off with all
my might into an arching jump.

There came a chance to dance in the Theatre again:
Barton wanted to see our *Gypsy*. We would do this at his
rehearsal. All the students were allowed to come and watch
Natasha and Grant and Shawn also rehearse, all unheard of.
Barton again danced *Pierrot in the Dead City*. It was a
reward for a summer's work. *Bravo! Brava!* Laughter and
applause rang out into this summer night on the Berkshire
mountains. Then it was time for us to entertain Barton. Out
danced Papa Shawn and me, romping through the various
dance styles while Barton's laughter egged us on. As we
returned for our bow, I carried a small purse of money
contributed by the students for Barton's expenses. Shawn
asked Barton to come on stage. There I was with Shawn on
one side and Barton on the other, my heart still pounding
from the dance. When it was the moment to present the

purse, I froze. Barton looked amused, then helped me out, "Is this for me?"

I nodded solemnly at which he burst out laughing, took the purse, put his arm around me as everyone in the theatre roared laughing. Mary joined us on stage for a final bow. Nearly swooning with joy, I knew this to be a moment of perfection. "Oh!" I thought. "If I die tonight, I know I shall have lived."

We all had one more chance to perform when Shawn included his *Sixteen Dances in Sixteen Rhythms* on the last performance of the season, August 28th. Virginia danced the *Gavotte;* Betty and Aldo, the *Varsovienne;* Ruthanne, the *Bolero*; I danced the *Barcarolle*. The whole school was included in *A Psalm of Grief and a Psalm of Joy* for the finale.

The next day, cold, inexorable reality hit me in the face like a wet flounder. My future. Everyone else headed to New York for classes and to audition for *Oklahoma!* Penniless, I had no one to turn to for seed money. The Civic Theatre was closed for the duration of the war at Syracuse. Then Papa Shawn led me into his office. Fifteen minutes later, I considered his proposition: that I take a teaching position during my senior year at a college in Georgia in exchange for my room, board and tuition. Brenau College wanted a dancer to initiate Modern Dance and direct a dance program.

"Me, teach? I don't know enough to teach!"

Papa Shawn assured me that I did. "Go from the known to the unknown. That's a rule of thumb in teaching. Teaching anything is the best way to make sure you know your field."

"Hello, Mother! Got a minute? Mr. Shawn got me this job teaching dance at this Brenau College in Georgia. Yes, Georgia. So I am going to transfer. I'm not sure it's accredited. Well, how else am I going to keep on dancing without any money or any help? I am twenty-one now, you know!"

CHAPTER FOUR

Fall 1943 - Spring 1944
  Brenau College, Gainesville, GA

The town of Gainesville, Georgia, looked pretty in the warm sun of early September, not at all the redneck, benighted place my mother feared I had wandered to while out of my mind. There was a town square with a fine old courthouse, a new post office and, nearby, the statue of a Confederate soldier. People were going into the Dixie Hunt Hotel and small shops along the square, all within walking distance of Brenau College. Sidewalks were laid out in hexagon patterns beneath magnolia trees dropping their pearly-pink blossoms. Pecan and oak trees towered over all.

The people I met lived up to their cordial reputation and there was little Yankee teasing; we were all in this war together. There were amusing differences: oranges sold by the pound; people had a Coke instead of coffee for breakfast. Grits, dry toast and crisp bacon were standard fare for us. Gradually I found what I had given up to come here.

Brenau College was not accredited but not for lack of scholastic stature. A recent tornado had diminished its endowment. Nevertheless, it was a small women's college with a faculty of only thirty-five. Panic riffled through me on learning the Drama Department consisted of one Mademoiselle Maude Fiske LaFleur, that there were only three of us students in Drama class.

Mademoiselle was a small, middle-aged woman with a high forehead and dark hair in sausage rolls along her hairline, She spoke with the self-conscious Shakespearean accent fashionable among provincial elocutionists. Her dark, shoe-button eyes would roll, then fasten on one of us as she gave rhapsodic readings of Sidney Lanier's poetry.

"What play had she selected for us this year? Would there be open auditions," I asked.

"Oh, my dear girl! We don't do pla-aays! We just do sceeenes!

For my academic credits, I had Miss Eva Pearce for Novel with the Great Books to read. Miss Eva epitomized Southern gentlewomen decorum, speaking firmly yet quietly and always courteously. Sometimes she would delicately smack her lips, then pronounce her response in precise grammatical expression. A large, quite round woman in her fifties, her gait was deliberate and dignified. I supposed she was fat, but with Miss Eva, it was as though she gained weight as she gained wisdom. No quarter was given in her scholastic demands, but her quiet warmth convinced us she wanted us to excel. There were times when I wanted to give her a hug but knew that would offend her sense of propriety. I also had an interesting Economics teacher, Dr. Stone. She was short but wiry, her gait slightly mannish. She was accessible to students, often smoking a pipe in her office as we argued. Dr. Stone and I were the *avant-garde,* from the outside world, both considered warily.

For my chance to dance, I had given up my Senior Honors at Syracuse, my ballet teacher, my dear sorority friends, and men! I was billeted in a cottage with other transfers. My senior privilege was being allowed my to go downtown by myself. Still I jumped at this chance, sure Papa Shawn would not steer me wrong. They now wanted Modern Dance and were giving me room, board and tuition to provide it. Revved up from dancing eight hours a day at The Pillow, it was physically impossible for me to slow down. I would have to be one snappy apple to pick up the tempo at Brenau College. My energies flowed into my dance classes, unaware that they were grassroots dance just beginning to sprout down South.

Outside of class, didn't they do anything interesting? Some kind of special student run project??

Well, in November, the senior class would hide the Brenau Spade and the juniors would have a week to find it.

Uh-huh.

Wasn't there some talent here?

Why not an all-student show?

Sarah and Jean, the other two-thirds of my Drama class, were for it, taking me over to the Tri Delta House to gather enthusiasm for a show. Talent came out from all over campus. We titled the show *'Round About Town,* determined to set the campus ablaze. Why not make it a Bond Show and raise money for the war?

To attend a Bond Show, people either bought a War Bond or bond stamps. Acting-president, Mrs. Heywood Pearce, gave the necessary permission. When I brought this good news to my boss, Miss Stookey, I was rewarded with a scowl and the warning that this must not interfere with my work for her. Under no circumstance were my classes to be turned into rehearsals for some little student caper. Dismayed, I assured her that I had intended to work outside my classes.

"You should have asked me first!"

"I thought time outside of my classes was my free time. President. Pearce is pleased about it."

"I am not!" Miss Stookey glowered back. "Ted Shawn wrote a letter praising you, but we both know this is your first year teaching. Do you even have any teaching methods?" I invited her to come observe my classes.

One look at Margaret Mantle Stookey and the thought occurred that she was singularly miscast for her position as Director of the Physical Education Department. ("We do *not* call it 'phys ed'") She was short, round and swaddled within a body much like the cartoon character The Little King. She was white; white complexion, white hair pulled back from her face and tightly rolled close to her head from ear to ear. Her rimless glasses and her straight-line mouth gave her a severe aspect. With short legs, her stride was more waddle. It was hard to imagine her in vigorous physical activity. Discourse with her was like trying to talk with an angry penguin. Brought up to be mannerly to my elders, I was respectful to Miss Stookey, concerned to have her displeased with me.

She was right; I did have to prove my ability to teach. Still, I had expected some support or guidance from her. Less willing to follow in blind obedience, now used to discussing issues of theatre and dance with my teachers, I expected the same here. No! That was arguing with authority.

My first class I literally had to chase my students to get them into a full run. Running fast and faster—backward runs—turning runs! They laughed, so pleased with how exhilarating it was that most of them were won over. I had no dearth of dance material. Shawn's motto, *Go from the known to the unknown* was a method to my own ideas. A music scholarship student, Travis Wylie, was my accompanist for Modern Dance and Folk Dance. Patty Harry, another upperclassman, taught Tap.

I called an emergency meeting for the show's cast. Promises were vague, the script still amorphous. No crew. I was going over all this nicely when the queer feelings I had had all day suddenly suffused in a wave of intense heat and I fainted. Taken to the infirmary with violent cramps, suffocating waves of heat, then quivering chills, I came down with amoebic dysentery. Hospitalized and delirious for days, I was out. Blotto.

Once I began to improve, I bounced back fairly quickly. Miss Stookey took my illness as a personal offense. But bless their little hearts! The cast had worked without me.

The night of our performance, the cast dribbled in at will, but the show did go on. *"'Round About Town"*, presented by the Defense Council of Gainesville, went up Saturday, November 13, 1943 at the Brenau College Auditorium. It was a variety show, the acts held together with a patter by my other Drama Musketeer, Jeanne Drain. Lynette Rosen sang *That Old black Magic*; Willie Williams poodle-doodled on her xylophone; a Russian Dance; my first ensemble choreography*, Stairway to the Stars,* a *Sadie Hawkins* number; *Creation,* original music by Louise Garwell, for my solo. College and townspeople had come to fill the auditorium, raising a respectable sum for the war. At the Defense Council party afterwards, President Pearce asked me to repeat the show for the Red Cross Drive. I was pretty pleased. Papa Shawn had been right; I had been forced to grow here.

Miss Stookey was not one bit pleased, saying she was not so sure she wanted Shawn to perform here next spring. I did not have her permission to repeat the show, saying I was neglecting my classes. President Pearce sent word that "perhaps Miss Stookey did not understand that this was for the Red Cross." The show went on. Substantial funds were raised. Papa Shawn's program was forfeited.

It was not until spring that I learned that this was also Miss Stookey's first year at Brenau. I took offense at being hated and went out of my way to be honor-bright and faultless in my teaching: absences, grade lists, credits, etc. I made it difficult to catch me in the wrong. But I was a neophyte in vengeance, unprepared for insidious plotting ahead by Miss Stookey. I was not used to being hated. I did not like to hate others. Righteous indignation was another matter.

When it was time for the Physical Education Spring Recital, Miss Stookey demanded every dance and/or "phys ed" student be in the program; then criticized them for inexperience. I was planning to dance *Romance* (our Jacob's Pillow woman's war dance). Miss S had a costume she wanted me to wear: bright red, so low in front a bra would show, plus a narrow skirt with a pouch of material at the diaphragm and a heart cutout in the back. Plus it did not fit me. Totally wrong for *Romance*. It was "wear it or you cannot do that dance." So I didn't.

There was one more worry. I was also a senior at Brenau, determined to complete my Bachelor of Arts Degree in Theatre. In lieu of a play, Drama seniors were to present a Senior Recital of monologues. I convinced Madame LaFleur to allow me a Senior Recital in Dance. The idea was approved by the Dean of Women, Miss Eva Pearce. When I explained that this was an academic requirement for graduation to Miss Stookey, she accused me of neglecting my classes. Therefore, she reasoned, she would split my classes, giving me twice the hours to teach. This filled my day until 5:45 p.m. The dining hall closed at 6:00 p.m. I kept my mouth shut about my evening rehearsals, but she soon discovered I returned to practice and took my keys, shaming me for using electricity during the war. She set the lock, as well.

Spring had sprung in Gainesville, and I was hot and sweaty after teaching; changing for chapel; changing to teach again, at least four times a day. Left alone, it was too much to walk by the swimming pool below the gym. At first I just went down a ladder and got cooled off. Next time it seemed nasty to put my sweat into the pool, so I took off my leotard and dipped in naked for a sec. Next I let go of the ladder and swished around. And then one evening, my body just took off swimming the length of the pool and back. Glorious! The big sign— NO SWIMMING ALONE!!—made it a guilt trip, but it was still delicious. And I could make it in time for dinner. One time I was at the far end of the pool when I heard a loud click.

Miss Stookey!!

Faster to swim or get out and run wet-footed? I swam like lightening. Oh where was she now? Fear was a tremendous accelerator, and I was by my locker, grabbing a towel with my chest heaving when I realized my hair was streaming with water. I yanked open the shower door, barely had the water running when I heard her calling. "Shirley! Shirley!! Are you still here?"

I kept silent until she pounded on the shower door. "Hello? Oh, Miss Stookey! Out in a minute. Just washing my hair."

Miss Stookey stood fuming, suspecting but so far finding no evidence of wrongdoing. Unless the pool waters were still undulating!

"Hurry up! And put your towel in the right bin!" She stamped out while I sank to the floor of the shower and let it play over me. Might as well wash my hair and get a hamburger at the Tea House tonight.

There was also to be an Indian Pageant with Miss Stookey directing her production of *The Story of the Sun God Sha-Ka-Ru, A Mystic Indian Mask.* Patty Harry (Tap) and I were to teach the dances from her cherished manual. Patty was to be Chief Lap-Sha-Ro, while I must be Princess Wa-Lo-Hi. Again every dance and phys ed student must take part, *i.e.,* every student on campus. Previously rehearsals had been forbidden during regular dance classes, with which I concurred; now classes were to be devoted to rehearsals for the pageant.

Locked out of the gym, I rose early to rehearse my recital dances in the dusky morning light filtering onto the auditorium stage. This would be where I was to perform. When Miss Stookey learned my recital date, she chartered the auditorium for herself. Travis, my class accompanist, was playing for me in my recital. Miss Stookey threatened to flunk Travis if she played for me.

I marched to my cast friends at Tri Delt, furious that Miss Stookey would involve others in her feud with me. While I was there, another Tri Delt ran in, saying she had just been told that anyone who helped me with my recital would flunk gym. Looks were exchanged. I was sent out of the house until called back.

Sarah, president of the Tri Delts, spoke, "Miss Shirley Traver will you do the sorority of Delta Delta Delta the honor of allowing us to present you with a Reception following your Senior Dance Recital?"

I caught my breath in surprise. But it would only get more girls in trouble. "I can't drag the whole damn campus into this mess. You girls can't put your grades on the line."

"Don't worry," Sarah grinned, "We won't have to. Can you see her getting away with flunking sixty-six of the smartest girls on campus for a nonacademic activity? And if she did, no students, no classes, no Miss Stookey! Here have a Coke and stop bawling."

Miss Stookey got the word: checkmate.

I thought about writing to Papa Shawn but was too ashamed at the mess I had made while trying to work for Beauty in the Face of War. I thought of his dance, *Prometheus Bound:* Prometheus chained to a rock for bringing fire to the people. Why was dance getting me in trouble again!

With Travis restored, I faced the Indian Pageant. One counterfeit Indian pageant would be enough for a lifetime. Patty and I shuffled students to portray Indian ponies and totem poles, to dance corn, basket, scalp, blanket and snake dances. Nothing like a swarm of Southern college girls faking as native American Indians in a fake pageant!

As time went by I asked my parents to come down for my Recital instead of Commencement. I also asked Mother to bring a gift for the Tri Delts, as I could not afford a respectable present. Although I had saved my parents tuition, room and board, I still received just my three dollars-a-week allowance as I had at Syracuse. Plus Dad always gave me money for my train fare. He had said, "You can always come home." even though he has not approved of where I had gone. They arrived to stay at the Dixie Hunt the night before my program.

May 19, 1944, at 4:00 p,m., Brenau Auditorium filled to the brim as my heart hammered backstage. Seven of my eight dances were Denishawn: *French Sailor, Viva Faroan, Barcarolle, Styrienne, Evolution of Prayer, A Line Study and*

Romance. Holiday for Strings was my original choreography. Halfway through the program, Travis played her piano solo, *Malaguena.* After intermission, as I was dancing the suspensions of *Barcarolle,* Miss Stookey made a point of loudly stamping her way out. At last the time came to dance *Romance.* Peggy Victor had made me a lovely, flowing water-colored chiffon gown that echoed the motions of the dance. I went into the scene, wistful and longing as I must say goodbye to my lover; then there was nothing else but the dancing. Owning the dance was the epiphany for me.

The Tri Delts offered a gracious and bountiful reception for Travis, my parents and me. Mother brought a handsome crystal vase as my gift. She said my program " lovely." Dad squirmed and said it was "All right." All that I could hope for.Euphoric, I was convinced the worst was over, that Beauty had won through after all. Two weeks to graduation.

The following Sunday, Miss Stookey called me over to her apartment. Sweet as a marshmallow, she hoped we could have a little chat. Over I went and rang her bell.

"Oh, is that you, Shirley? Come right in," Miss Stookey sounded positively cheery. "Come along. We're having coffee in here." *We* proved to be Miss Stookey and President Pearce.

"Good morning, President Pearce. Excuse my shorts. I had no idea you were here," I blurted out in surprise.

"Nor I, you." President Pearce cast an eye on Miss Stookey, and then smiled at me. "Catching up after your recital?"

"Yes. I was very pleased to have you come. Now it's exams."

"Well, now that is the reason I asked you here, Shirley. President Pearce and I were just talking, and it seemed a good time to have you here to straighten the record."

Wary, I looked from one to the other. President Pearce looked baffled, then attentive. Miss Stookey was enjoying a secret smile. "In fact, to keep to the point, I have made a list," she said, producing a yellow sheet.

"This is in no way an official meeting of any kind, is it Miss Stookey?" President Pearce stated.

"Oh, I leave that to you, President Pearce," she chuckled. "This is my list of Shirley Traver's offenses, and it is time for an accounting. Number one, constant insubordination. Two...don't interrupt as usual Shirley! Two, constant defiance of authority. Three, incompetence."

That brought me to my feet just as President Pearce interrupted. "Shirley, it is later than I thought so I will excuse you now. You will hear from me."

I uttered an anxious goodbye and started out of the house, angrier every step. I could still hear their voices. Self-preservation insisted I eavesdrop. Miss Stookey was talking back to the President. "That girl should be expelled!" I caught my breath, stunned.

Then I could hear President Pearce's voice rise and fall, sounding nearer. "You asked me here... breakfast... official confer... tomorrow...," It was time to scram.

This was something the Tri Delts could not save me from. Off I went to find Dr. Stone, my Psycho-centric Economics teacher, who insisted the human factor was primary in all economic consideration. Dr. Stone would be candid and to the point. She was in her office, just off the library, with eight books about her desk. She took one look and shook her head.

"What are you hauling at today, Traver?"

After listening, her eyes pierced into mine. "Well, I've no trouble standing up for you, but I ask you to think: Am I likely to do you any good? Most of the faculty here think I'm a Communist, you know."

"Well, they know you are honest," I contended.

"B'God, you're right. But I ask you to hold my uncertain powers until you need a character reference."

The next morning, I cut academic classes. As I tried to sort things out, Melba came in to do my room. The black maid was unusually quiet and, thinking it was because I was an inconvenience, I offered to go read on the porch.

"No, no, Miss Shirley. You no trouble," she assured me, then pursed her lips.

Melba was the only black person I got to know even a little in Georgia. I had failed to make the tiniest dent in the lack of equality between blacks and whites. All the help was black, of course, so I did have daily contact at the dining hall, for example, but the strictures of college life kept relationships service-oriented. I had intended to violate the separate doors at rest rooms, but found these gestures upset the blacks as well as the whites.

"What is it, Melba?" I asked gently.

She shrugged it off. "Jes candles is all."

Candles? Candles she had to buy for her church, or be shamed, but she could not afford . Could not let on she could not afford. We got to talking over the demands of ministers, husbands and bosses, and I found myself confessing my anguish over Miss Stookey.

"Why that's as bad as fer us!" she exclaimed. "Don't you let that no account woman do you!"

Shyly, I suggested that maybe I should light a candle or two for hope. Could she do that for me, since I could not do that in chapel here? Melba was not fooled, but she thought it might be done. I gave her a hug as I would our childhood cook, Anna. And for a moment we held each other. For a moment, I was safe in someone's arms, a gift I had not known I needed until now.

Besides this worrisome threat to my graduating, my teaching and exams, I had to answer a letter from Dr. Duggan from Texas. She was offering me a job teaching dance and getting my Master's Degree in Dance at Texas State College for Women. And again, except for my train fare, I was as penniless as I had been the year before. Then the call came from the President's Office to be there in one hour. There was no time left to ponder.

One hour later, dressed in my best, I was sitting on one of the teakwood settees in the parlor of Yonah Hall, the Administration Building of Brenau College. Waiting, I remembered Dr. Stone's final advice, "For God's sake, Traver, keep your trap shut until everyone finishes talking. Shut up! Even if you have to bite your tongue 'til it bleeds!"

"Miss Traver, the Board will see you now," the secretary stood aside to let me pass.

The first thing I noticed was that Miss Stookey was not there. The second thing was that I was not invited to sit down. With the American flag on one side of her desk and the flag of the State of Georgia on the other, President Pearce spoke first. Seated on either side, Miss Eva and Miss Ellen Winfield, Registrar, listened carefully. My superior Miss Stookey had brought a serious change against me. She was calling for my expulsion from Brenau College. Her list of my infractions was overlong, perhaps, but did not exclude examples of poor judgment on my part. According to the list, most chronic was my disobedience. If given a chance to complete my degree, I must prove my character worthy of being a Brenau Graduate. This was an unfortunate circumstance to the President's mind, for she had seen me use my talents well earlier in the school year.

Right or wrong, I was in trouble.

President Pearce asked Miss Eva if, after studying the list, she had any questions. Miss Eva put down her pencil, clasped her plump hands together and leaned forward across the large desk. "I have. Miss Stookey's list of your unpardonables includes the accusation that you have been swimming in the pool alone. Now I should like to have you tell me the truth about that."

"Yes'm," I answered, falling into the Southern way. "I did. It was quicker."

"Quicker? Quicker for what? You know we have a sign there forbidding *anyone* from swimming alone at *any time.*"

"At first I never did," I said. "Then Miss Stookey doubled my classes. It made it hard to get out of the gym and dressed for supper by six o'clock. It was quicker to dip in the pool."

"You say your classes were doubled. Why was that?"

The next questions came in a flood: How many hours was I teaching? When did I finish? Could I explain why so many students hated gym? How many sets of keys had I lost? Why had I refused to wear a costume Miss Stookey provided for me?

Gradually, always speaking slowly and clearly, Miss Eva took me back through the months, asking questions and waiting for full answers. I answered only one question at a time, keeping Dr. Stone's warning in mind. Gradually I began to console myself that at least my side was being heard. Finally Miss Eva nodded to President Pearce that she was finished. Miss Winfield next asked me about my scholastic standing. Thus far I was on the Dean's List and was expected to graduate with honors. President Pearce raised her head from her notes. She looked directly at me a long moment. I met her gaze, then dropped my eyes.

"You are excused, Shirley. We will advise you of our decision."

Anxious, restless, one minute I wanted company and the next I wanted to be alone. Time went into a suspended dimension as I waited for word, replaying my answers, then not wanting to think about it at all. Maybe no word for days! I jumped like I was shot when the cottage telephone rang. I was to report back to the President's Office at once.

It was twilight by now. A light breeze tossed my hair, ruffled my skirt as I returned to Yonah Hall. Lights were on, glowing in the empty marble entry. My heels clicked audibly on the stone floor. Taking a breath, I paused before the heavy door to the President's Office and knocked gently.

"Come in, Shirley." The voice told me nothing.

President Pearce alone was seated at her desk.

"There seems no purpose in reserving our decision until a later time," she said and then hesitated.

I wondered where I had stored my suitcase.

President Pearce pushed back her chair and came around her desk to stand facing me. Again she paused; choosing her words, then drew herself up and spoke formally.

"Shirley Traver, we shall be happy to have you complete your degree at Brenau College."

An "Oh!" escaped me before I could catch it. "President Pearce, I shall be very happy to complete my degree here at Brenau College."

For a long moment, we two women, a generation apart, looked toward each other expectantly. Spontaneously each reached out her hand for the other's hand in respect.

"Thank you, President Pearce."

"It is as it should be. Good night, Shirley."

There was a quiet walk away from the campus for me, a little weepy business in the dusk along the magnolia-strewn sidewalk.

Everything was anticlimactic after my trial. Thanks to the integrity of Miss Eva and President Pearse, I was free to graduate and received my B.A. in theatre.

It was necessary to change trains in Washington to get back to Harrisburg. Wandering around Union Station at 2:00 a.m., I realized this would be my fourth trip through my nation's capitol without seeing beyond the station. After checking the trains again, I went out to the street and called a cab.

"Where to, Miss?"

"Washington!"

"You in Washington, Miss."

"Show me all of it. Please drive by the Capitol...the White House..."

"And Lincoln's Memorial and Jefferson's. You payin', Miss."

At 2:15 a.m.. the June night in Washington was gorgeous. A recent shower made the streets of the city patent-leather shiny. With the reflection of the street lamps and the traffic lights, the light doubled, making it all surprisingly bright outside. Great buildings loomed up before me, massive, overpowering. Like a photo study in black and white, the lines were sharp, white marble glowed. Classic Greek columns, balustrades, expansive flights of steps, plazas, monuments and statuary created a dream in architectural harmony. Wide boulevards curved intersecting new directions, leading past gardens and the waterways of the Tidal Basin. We passed over arching bridges and reflecting pools on the way to contemplate the Lincoln Memorial. Each moment brought forth new splendors. It was a loveliness to last all the way home.

And through a reprimand for taking a later train.

CHAPTER FIVE

Fall 1944 – Spring 1945, Dance Teacher
  Texas State College for Women, Denton, TX

Who said I wanted an M.A. in dance anyway? I yearned to leave the female college scene and get to the dance scene in New York. After a summer's study at The Pillow then...then the same haunting guilt every time I saw lists of the war dead and missing persons. The same insoluble financial obstacles as before. My parent's opposition had not changed. It never occurred to me to ask them for the tuition money I had saved them and it was never offered.

What was offered was this fellowship at Texas State College for Women paying me $500 to $600 a year to teach dance while getting my Master's Degree in Dance. There was a performing Modern Dance Club—Mary Campbell wintered there, accompanying performances and classes. Shawn recommended it. All this hurried me into going backwards in order to go forwards. Besides, I did not have the guts to defy my social conscience for my own ambition.

Upon arrival, I learned that my job was a combination of five: dancer, dance teacher, grad student, but also undergraduate (changing majors from Theatre to Physical Education for a dance major), and to top it off, House Mother to students a year younger than I.

Graduate Studies:	Undergraduate Studies:
Anatomy	Principles of Education
Body Correctives	Fencing
History & Philosophy	Elementary School Games
of Dance	
Methodology of Research	Tap Dancing
American Literature	Folk & Square Dance

There were two beautiful hard wood, sprung-floor studios, one for shoes and one for barefoot, with plenty of bright Texas light. I was assigned teaching Modern Dance, Folk and Square dancing, and Tap Dance. I confessed my novice skills in tap to Dr. Duggan. She airily replied, "You will take my tap class the hour before you teach yours. You'll be fine." So it was. I learned buck, military, soft-shoe, eccentric, rhythm-buck and waltz tap dancing.

Rehearsals for the Modern Dance Club were daily, with an occasional Saturday afternoon off. With the schism between Ballet and Modern Dance styles very much in force, it was a surprise to have Dr. Duggan ask me to teach ballet to our Modern Dance Club. Ballet turnout was obnoxious to the barefoot modern dancer. Studying both seemed self-defeating until I remembered that was exactly what we did at The Pillow. A *barre* was set along one studio wall. On the basis that "I knew more than my students," I began with the plié and the Five Positions.

With my first month's pay of $66 burning a hole in my pocket, I asked for a weekend off. An Air Corps captain I knew in Harrisburg was now stationed in Coleman, Texas, and asked me down. It was a long bus trip, but Anatole was just what a girl stuck in a woman's college needed. As I was getting off the bus, Anatole shouted, "Stop! Stay where you are. I want to always remember you at this moment!" I laughed; everyone laughed.

Anatole was of Yugoslavian heritage, complete with continental courtesies that were a delight in small doses. Now he whisked me away in a white convertible to his quarters, his rank of captain allowed him to live off base. He was billeted in the home of a Texas oil widow who also had a room for me. The tour of the house began with the Texas Library, a room devoted to Texan artifacts and volumes of Texas history. Then we had a tour of her oil wells.

Anatole whirled me back to town for dinner, introducing me to the waitress as the love of his life. Next he stopped a jeep full of M.P.s, "Gentlemen! This beautiful girl I shall marry! Am I not a fortunate man!" There must be a shortage of women in Coleman, but as it was, the rush was delightful. Then Anatole took me to a treelined street, told me not to say a word. As we walked along, he began to sing to me—four whole love songs ending with *I Love You*—and then he kissed me.

The big event of the weekend was the formal dance at the United States Army Air Corps Officers' Club. That evening I was dressed in a white, flowing chiffon gown, wearing his sash of red flowers from shoulder across to my waist. The large clubroom was decorated with colorful streamers. Bursts of laughter were heard as pictures were taken. Then the jazz band began playing everything from *Laura* to *Dance with A Dolly with A Hole in Her Stocking,* and we went to town. Whatever Anatole's bluster, he was a terrific dancer. That is how we met, dancing, and from the first moment, we hit it off, fast, slow, waltz—whatever. He liked to walk on the beat, side by side, then pull me in for fast turns ending in a dip, then up into a reverse turning. As he tried to catch me off-step, he became more inventive. Soon we had the dance floor to ourselves as others stopped to watch.

At intermission, cooling off on the porch, Anatole was quiet and tense.

"Say my name. Go on, say it," he asked,

"Anatole Bosovic."

"And now say where I am."

"Coleman, Texas. Why?"

"That tells you all. I am going to get out of here one way or another. To Europe! I know the language! Wouldn't you think…"

A loud clanging interrupted him as an enlisted soldier came around banging a spoon against a pie plate. "Everybody in, sir. Entertainment beginning, sir."

There was some banter and 'thank you's' to the committees and introduction of commanding officers. A lieutenant sang a ballad. Next a patriotic selection from the band. Then a slim, unsmiling corporal was introduced as a concert pianist. As the young man exchanged seats with the jazz pianist, he paused to announce he would play the new *Warsaw Concerto*. The crowd stood listening, then gradually sank to sit on the floor, couples holding each other close as the passionate music poured over us. A lover of Rachmaninoff, I was touched by the urgent, rushing arpeggios, the dissonance in minor keys, envisioning the awful plight of the Polish people in the ghettos. Here, the French doors of the Officers' Club were open to the soft air of the night. We women could wear our pretty, bareback, strapless gowns in floats of rose tulle or silhouettes in blue satin, free from harm. The airmen, tanned, healthy, looked invincible in their dress pinks. *Sharp!* was the going word for military chic.

It was uneasy to sit here and listen to music while others suffered. I felt a deep obligation, unmet, hollowing down inside me. Eyes bright, I turned to Anatole, who held me tightly. As the final chord faded away there was a silence, then long, louder applause as the pianist stood, half-smiling in response. The jazz band took over and, though we jitterbugged or sailed smoothly through the crowd, there was a sense of borrowed time. Back at his quarters, Anatole offered me wine. He spoke of his grandfather left back in Yugoslavia. Then he got out his violin, playing it as he sang a Yugoslavian folk song to me. He told me again how he loved me, so I kissed Anatole. Kissed him because he was angry. Kissed him because he was handsome and brave. Kissed him to make up for the past kiss-starved year. Kissed him to remember how.

In my dance classes again, I could see there was work I could do. I rejoiced to find the knock-kneed girls with the pronated feet, the sunken chests and badly curved backs. Pilates exercises infiltrated my modern dance classes. I found verbal images got them to *move!* Walk on grass—now hot macadam—a sandy beach—a fence rail—in turquoise waters—through falling snow—run slowly—run in the dark—run in love—run backwards. Oh, yes you can! *RUN!*

It was a tradition for the Modern Dance Club to perform at the Annual Thanksgiving Assembly in the Main Auditorium. Wearing russet leotards and knee-length, beige skirts, we carried autumnal foliage in our arms as we promenaded down the central aisle with the college choir singing *Come Ye Thankful People, Come.* Our liturgical dance, *We Praise Thee, O God,* was choreographed with the dancers moving only on the voice patterns: two dancers took the soprano rhythmic pattern; two, the alto; two, the tenor; and two, the bass voice patterns. We also closed the program with our dance to The Doxology as the congregation recited it. Although there was no one here without war worries, we knew we had reason to be grateful. Singing and dancing opened our hearts, as is their way.

November became December without a single snowflake. Nature seemed out of sync in Georgia and now here, forgetting to give the Earth it's cleansing, its gift of purity. I must have groaned about no snow for the Phys Ed majors gave me a paperweight that snows for Christmas. Delighted, I shook it hard and disappeared into it. Then our Modern Dance Group danced on the Christmas Assembly. Jeanette danced to *I Wonder as I Wander*—such a wistful Christmas song. Jeanette was lovely dancing it. Tall people sometimes seem to get in their own way, but never Jeanette. She and Mary became dear friends..

My college was called the Department of Health, Physical Education and Recreation. To me, it was fizz-ed (Phys Ed) but I had to remember to speak of it correctly. There were a lot of fizz-ed majors looking for sports careers, and about twelve dance majors. As I had to make up undergraduate classes in fizz-ed, I was often with the majors. I had to be a good sport when they delighted in making me "it" in Elementary School Games. Now these girls could run! Then they would have me for Tap or Folk, but few took Modern Dance as an option. Being nearer their age and used to the informality of teacher/student relationships at The Pillow, where all used first names, we got along fine. There was a small group that liked to hang around. Dr. Duggan noticed and asked me to discourage this.

Crossing the snowy lawn at twilight after the lo-o-ong train trip from Texas, coming home to Harrisburg for Christmas still held its magic. First the welcoming hugs, then the arms-length appraisal. ("You want to shower first, dear?") Then we had the traditional chicken noodle casserole in the strawberry breakfast nook. Back in my third-floor bedroom, I slept deep and dreamless.

But wartime in Harrisburg was far more warlike than Denton. Servicemen were everywhere. Sentries were posted at all strategic bridges, particularly the longest stone-arched bridge in the USA across the Susquehanna River. Convoys held up traffic. Gas, sugar and butter coupons were more precious. My dad would go to the railroad yards early mornings in hopes of getting oranges from Florida before the Army took them all. Nana gave up quilting, and she and Mother knit socks and mittens. Mother and I rolled bandages for the Red Cross. Pat and I danced with the servicemen, waiting to be sent abroad. Aunt Pummie was in London, worrying about Uncle Herb, who was a Coca-Cola colonel on the Continent.

My family did not *want* but had to use ingenuity to survive. Dad's business had trouble getting machine parts, help and meeting deadlines to supply linens to hospitals and the services. Surprising to me was the number of parties and Christmas events in clubs, parish houses, Army bases—all over. Phyllis was home from Stephens College, where she was determined to learn how to fly. We all went to Christmas services, grateful our Pine Street Presbyterian Church had not been bombed as had so many in Europe. At our greeting, Reverend Smith asked me to stop by sometime.

We had this running argument over dance, so I stopped by his church office one afternoon and the damnedest thing happened. Proudly I told him about our Thanksgiving service and dancing The Doxology. He replied he was by no means ready for any kind of dance in his church. Reverend Smith invited me to look at the church from his office window above the organ. Looking out this window, I could see the entire majesty of the church with all its Gothic arches and appointments. It was impressive. I said so and rose to leave. Abruptly Reverend Smith said, "Kiss me goodbye."

It was awkward. However, used to giving my elders an air kiss, I made the gesture.

Reverend Smith kissed me full on my mouth.

Oh God!

"Shouldn't you remember your wife?" I stammered.

He didn't know. Was I sorry? he asked.

As I backed away, it was more confusing. He said he could see I was sorry he'd kissed me, but that he would like to be the one to marry Anatole and me when the time came. Driving home, I got angrier with each mile. Why had I not been like Myrna Loy and smacked him on the spot. It was my family's church. I told no one.

Back at TSCW, I looked at my schedule and groaned: Standard of Measurements, History & Philosophy of Dance, American Literature, Kinesiology. I also had to give lectures on Health and Hygiene. I was chosen to teach *Processes Of Elimination*. I wrote to Papa Shawn (who had never been fresh with me!). He answered immediately from his winter quarters in Eustis, Florida:

January 14, 1945

Dear Shirley,

 I know your impatience with the full
education program, But your decision,
whichever way you make it, will bring much
that is hard to bear. If you decide to hit New
York for a stage career, the unpleasant things
would not be the same things—but just as
unpleasant if not more so.

 However, if you have the courage, and
the determination, and feel the hunger to
actually dance professionally strong enough,
then why don't you give a year to it and see
how you make out? It means endless visits to
agents and managers, auditions with a lot of
riff-raff, who will probably get the job
although they don't dance as well as you do
because they know the right people, and if you
get a job, long weeks of rehearsals, and maybe
on dances that you do not like, and then the
show will flop and it will all have to start all
over again.

 And yet there is always hope, like the
pot of gold at the end of the rainbow, that you
will hit the right thing—dances you enjoy,
good salary, good run. Only you can decide—
but be sure whatever you choose—there are
just as many difficulties and things you dislike
in one place as another. Life's like that.

 I know in the field of education, you
couldn't be in a better place nor in better

hands than you are now. But if you feel like
taking a crack at Broadway next season, come
to The Pillow for the summer, make your
contacts with the various dancers who come
there that gives you an inside track. Every
single girl or boy who came there last
summer, who tried for a job in New York,
eventually got placed this season.

And be assured that my interest in you
and belief in you is just as strong as it ever
was.

Yours,
Shawn

With his letter, Shawn enclosed a postcard of himself
as the Thunderbird and his annual Christmas letter, reporting
his yearly activities. Again, he was struggling to raise money
for the next season at The Pillow. With a better spirit, I faced
exams, taking them and giving them. All written tests
required a pledge of honesty. All physical activity subjects
required a demonstration of skill. I asked my modern dancers
to incorporate an idea into an original solo based upon
sixteen counts in any rhythm. They were to use changes in
level, contour, tempo, rhythms and dynamics. After the
original panic and protest, the results were revealing. One girl
became a ball in a pinball machine. Another became Mary
Magdalene. Then there was the girl who started at the back of
the studio and trundled back to her seat. In fairness to the
other students, Bobby Sue had to dance or flunk. I gave her
the choice of meeting me an hour before dinner or retaking
the course next semester.

"Five o'clock."

She nodded, miserable and resentful. Bobby Sue had an overweight body, knock knees, pronated feet as illustrated in my Correctives Manual as an example of deteriorating body condition. She hated her revealing leotard, the class, and likely me. Dance had destroyed her self-esteem, the opposite of its purpose.

At five she appeared, hangdog and sullen. "Must I change, Miss Traver?"

"Yes, Bobby Sue." Minutes later, she dragged back into the studio, glowering at my determined smile. "Okay, Bobby Sue, we're going to start you off with the same movement theme you presented in class. Your run, of course," I explained to the baffled girl. "So choose six numbers between one and twenty, okay? Write them on the blackboard in any order you want. This is your dance."

Constantly making Bobby Sue decide where she would start, which direction for the first seven steps, how fast for the next five steps, then how to use her arms on the following three steps, I persuaded her into constructing a line study with two reverses, three half turns, two diagonals and a final pose. I banged on a Chinese drum to keep her tempo, cueing her changes with accents. Finally, Bobby Sue did her sequence accurately, knew it and almost smiled.

"Terrific, Bobby Sue! Hey! You're dancing. Want to try it with one of my wrap skirts? OK. Just so you know you can dance whenever you want to, right?" Next class, Bobby Sue did borrow my wrap skirt and performed her dance before her astonished classmates.

Having Mary Campbell there to play for classes and for the Modern Dance Group made a tremendous difference in giving our work substance. She taught us musical structures, explained odd time signatures that changed and played with dynamics to clue us when a steady beat got boring. Always asking if this is what we meant or might like to know. The respect she gave Jeanette and me, and the students lent stature to our fumbling choreography.

Our next performance was the Annual Redbud Festival.

At Brenau there had been this feverish Fashion show, the models chosen by popularity, which hurt feelings. Here in Texas, every girl could be a Princess. Families spent Real Money on their daughters who would be Redbud Princesses, all one hundred and three of them in gleaming white satin gowns. President Hubbard officiated at the Coronation of the Queen. We dancers were part of the entertainment for Her Majesty. We danced to *Slavic Moods* by Tchaikovsky; Jeanette danced to Kreisler's *Liebesfreud;* and I danced *Viva Faroan.* In a unified effort, dancers, singers and college orchestra joined in a finale of *Waltz Themes* by Johann Strauss.

As a reward, Jeanette and Mary took me to Dallas for the first time, introducing me to avocados and cilantro in a Mexican cafe. Next we went to Justin's where I bought my cowgirl boots. I instantly adored wearing them. Heck! Texas was not so bad! I was even getting used to the twanging cowboy music. It was the weird bugs that frightened me. Never a bug girl myself, I now jumped over all kinds. Scorpions were the worst. One evening late, I heard loud screams from our Travis House bathroom. Running in, I saw Candy, naked, flat against the far wall of the shower, screaming and pointing at a scorpion wiggling his stinger, slowly moving toward her. There was one of my girls, terrified! I ran off to run back with my tap shoe in hand and bravely stepped close enough to smack that scorpion dead.

He wiggled in death throes as we both watched, still in horror. Finally it seemed safe to help Candy inch around it and wrap her safely in a towel.

Work was so intense; there was no time for fun. "Outreach," the Recreation staff called it. Yammering about being isolated I got seven square dancers to go along with Irene, our square dance teacher, to a local Denton square dance. It was exciting to be with the public at a genuine Texas dance. Live music! I could feel the vibrations zinging through me. We eight gals formed our square for the next dance, *Little Susie.* This square has many turns and reverse turns that keep you thinking as you dance. It all made for smiles and laughing.

There was a stag line of sorts. I was pleased to have a cowboy come tip his hat to me, asking me to dance. Away we went! Even though this dance was new to me, he was such a good partner I didn't miss a step. We were going on to the next dance when Irene came over and nodded to the six other gals waiting on the side. It had been my idea to come and now I had spoiled our square. I thanked my cowboy but had to return to our all-women square. The dynamics changed now, back with all women, being watched by the stag line. We didn't stay much longer. I waved goodbye to my cowboy, but he looked away.

The Modern Dance Group was preparing for its Spring Tour, reviving old choreography and creating new suites of dances. One revival from repertory was *How Dear to My Heart,* dances to childhood poems. Why? Because our tour would take us to grammar schools. So, at age 22, I found myself dancing as a key in *Chopsticks,* a solo as *Pooh,* and a duet to *I Have a Little Shadow.* Next we were earnestly choreographing a suite of American negro spirituals without questioning our right to do so: *Let My people Go, Go Down Moses, Swing Low, Sweet Chariot.* Racial equality was not discussed. Mary composed a *Color Suite* with varying dynamics for each colo*r* that gave us the opportunity for our own original choreography. Next, a provincial theme was mandatory.

For this we set dances related to the *Heritage of the Southwest*, again with music composed by Mary. If we could be negroes, certainly we could be Indians, Spaniards, pioneers and, of course, cowboys. Our choreography was based on research and respectfully, thoughtfully designed. For me, there was a cliché quality to our choreography that bothered me, although I had to admit I was the least sophisticated about the West. I became the Cowgirl who "rode" a bronco, nearly getting tossed off. (Me? Who had only tried an Eastern saddle on a horse that had its way?) I got lots of help being taught the standard gaits of horses, starting my ride with a rack to a trot to a lope, but at a gallop, my mount rebels, sunfishes, twists and tries to knock me off. Only one hand is allowed to hold on; the other swings in counterbalance with my body's responses. I barely managed to stay on—then trot off. Apparently I was convincing enough for a rancher to approve. The kids loved it.

After our spring tour throughout flowering southern Texas, I got another weekend off to be with Anatole. My body floated away from the daily tensions. I caught myself smiling. this time in San Antonio. Such luxury: the hotel, the parks, the shops along the river where Anatole bought me red espadrilles; the food! The dancing together at night in love. When I got back to Denton, there was a telegram for me from a Syracuse theatre friend, Ken Abbott, who was now Ali Hakim in *Oklahoma!*

"Come on up to New York and I'll get you in the show!! Send pictures!"

Oh! OOOH! OOOOOOOH! My wildest heart's desire just fell from the sky!

One of my House daughters, Diane, was photographer for the campus press, *The Lasso*. She jumped up and down with me. I changed into a dance outfit and we ran to the roof of the Ad Building, the highest place on campus. There I posed on ventilators and balanced on the two-foot cement ledge of the four-story building. To get a shot against the sky, we decided a jump was necessary. Balancing on the ledge, I jumped into the sky just as the cast iron bell in the roof tower loudly bonged the time. The sudden volume of sound went vibrating through me midair. For an awful moment I did not know where I was. Diana ran to reach me; we collided and clung to each other as the great bell kept tolling, then stopped, leaving us as two tuning forks in the sudden silence.

"Oh, God! You scared the hell out of me, Miss T!"

"Me, too!" I gasped. Laughing, shaky, we held onto each other on our way back to the stairs.

The problem came when Dr. Duggan laughed off my glorious offer. "You are not free to go, you know. You signed a contract for two years."

"But it's Broadway! You could let me out of my contract, couldn't you?"

"No."

Anguish: Mary saying "There will be other chances for Broadway." A visiting famous artist saying, "Forget education! This is your chance! Go!" Ken wiring, "When can you come?"

Should I follow the Dance? Or keep my word? Why were they at odds? Could not Falk's personal integrity through artistic integrity be reversed into artistic integrity through personal integrity? I wanted to climb a tree to think, as I had so often done as a youth. There was none suitable. So I went over the fence at the pool, climbed the diving tower and sat on the highest diving board. Studied the water, shimmering in the twilight below. Stood and bounced on the board. Looked up at the sky. I swore not to go down until I had decided. Every rationale came back to a question of my self-respect. Finally, resentful, self-sorry, I let my body weight pull me back down the ladder, step by heavy step, knowing I must stay. Seeing my dancing career floating off into Time, I gave a loud aching cry.

April 12th, President Franklin Delano Roosevelt died. We were rehearsing our Spanish dances that Thursday when Dr. Duggan's secretary came into the studio with the news. It was a great loss to the world, leaving us vulnerable, no longer protected by his great spirit and intelligence.

May 7th Germany surrendered. At first we were paralyzed. Next, jumping for joy. Grabbing each other, running out of buildings, shouting, jumping in clusters and running to the Ad Building for more word. I could stop grinning only to laugh more with others. Glorious! Tears of gladness. JOY! Impromptu marching and singing! *God Bless America —Yankee Doodle— America the Beautiful*. TSCW was having its V-E Day! After this mass, gladsome hysteria, I found I wanted to be out by myself, to simply look across our land. I wanted to feel the bare ground of my country sure it would feel different now.

I put on a clean, cotton dress and went out beyond the campus to the start of the western plain. There was the Earth, open as far as the eye could see. The handful of earth was warm. The sky, clear blue. My mind soared further, around the globe to Europe where other countries must be rejoicing with us. Now Japan *must* stop! I sat there wondering.

New word arrived from Ken, saying although the current opening for *Oklahoma!* was not possible for me now, he would keep in touch about any others before he went to Hollywood in September. My hopes soared again until I remembered I had signed for next year on that dratted contract. Although she could rave about Martha Graham or La Meri and other dance stars, Dr. Duggan primarily looked to professional dancers to inspire dance students to become dance teachers. My *Oklahoma!* problem was irritating. Then, urprisingly, Dr. Duggan herself suggested a way out of my dance crisis.

"Well, if you are determined to dance on stage, why don't you just get it out of your system in the *Starlight Operettas* in Dallas this summer?"

Dr. Anne Schley Duggan Knew Everyone and started the mechanics leading to auditions being extended to our campus for dancing jobs in the Operettas. There was plenty of appeal: professional dancing, nearer to Anatole, money and freedom from this academic sweathouse. Other dancers from our Modern Dance Group were interested too. Carl Randall, the choreographer for the coming *Starlight Operettas* season, came to audition us himself. He was slim, trim, with dark wavy hair and a natty mustache. Taking his cigarette from his mouth, he smiled with a jaunty air and performed a few tap steps across the studio floor. After we demonstrated our skills in tap and then modern dance, Mr. Randall smiled, but said we must wait for word until after the Dallas auditions. Dr. Duggan, impossible to satisfy in rehearsal, now sang our praises. We were then told the employment terms, should we be chosen. Two weeks rehearsal without pay followed by two weeks at half-salary to be followed by full salary at $32.50 per week for the following eight week performance period. *The Great Waltz* would open the season on June 16th. Mr. Randall parted, telling us to keep our hopes up.

I sighed aloud. "One more week of waiting."

Dr. Duggan laughed, "Shirley, when are you going to learn not to take people literally? You and Nina are both in. The rest is simply a formality. Get your grades in so you are free to go."

Sure enough; the contracts came just before Anatole, who had news of his own. He was being transferred to Ft. Worth. Close to Dallas where I would be dancing! Before the weekend was out, we were jubilantly engaged to be married.

CHAPTER SIX

Summer 1945
  Starlight Operettas. Summer Theatre in Dallas, TX

Heart high, I signed in for the first general call of the *Starlight Operetta* season, joining the gathering number of performers, stagehands, musicians and costume dressers on the open-air stage. Eyes darted here and there, as people looked for fellow thespians and out of curiosity. Laughter and snatches of song could be heard. Nina and I went to the girls' dressing room where we met our dresser, Mona, and other dancers. One, Carolyn George, had danced here last summer. As we were getting the backstage dope from her, there was a thunderous BOOM! BOOM! BOOM! on the tympani. Scooting back on stage, we watched a small parade of men in business suits marching down the center aisle. One was tall and slim, one was short and fat. One was short and slim, and the last man, sturdy.

Tall Charles Meeker welcomed us all and, as business manager, introduced his companions. Carl I knew from our auditions. The plump, moonfaced man wearing the bifocals gave a bounce and a smile—Giuseppe Bambochek, Musical Director. The short, sturdy man was Director José Reuben. His sharp eyes went everywhere as he clenched a cigarette holder in his teeth, angled quite like President Roosevelt's. As he was brushing his hand over his receding hairline, Mr. Reuben began to speak to us. Gesticulating, he told us we all worked for him first of all "in this impossible thing of producing an excellent show every week for ten straight weeks." In mime, Reuben scooped up a part of the crowd and placed them figuratively to Mr. Bombochek "for song."

Another group to Carl "for dance." Pulling another group to his chest, Reuben claimed the principals for himself. Then snatching each group back and compressing them together, like forming a popcorn ball, we would meld into "one grand operetta! You see? *Voila!*" He flung his arms open and gave us all a grand smile. Everyone applauded.

Carl took the dancers with him to the old Fairground Theatre where we would rehearse the first days of each week alone. Thursdays would be crowd scene days on the main stage for blocking; dress parade and dress rehearsal for the rest of the week. Carl told us we must pick up the new dances early in the week, for our dance time would be interrupted from then on. Smoking constantly, Carl introduced his wife, Fanette, a diminutive, dark-haired French woman, also a chain smoker. While Carl held his cigarette snug in the corner of his mouth, Fanette would take a long drag off hers and emit a big puff skyward. She was there to help rehearse us and to perform when needed. We must be ready to dance in many styles. There would be some opportunities for special solos and duets, but most of the choreography would be for an ensemble of four boys and fourteen girls. While principal and supporting roles were cast in New York, other auditions had been held in Dallas. There would be no time off. Equity rules allowed only for meal breaks. (Oh, Anatole!) Dancers were to supply their own makeup. Ballet slippers would be provided. Swimming at noon in the Fairground pool was allowed but no tan! Ever seen a tanned ballerina! Now who brought practice clothes? Get ready for some publicity shots.

For two weeks, rehearsals were set for morning, afternoon and evening. Then we would rehearse days and perform:

STARLIGHT OPERETTAS
SEVENTY NIGHTS OF GLORIOUS ENTERTAINMENT
PRESENTED IN A SETTING OF NATURAL BEAUTY
UNDER THE TEXAS STARS!
The Great Waltz Blossom Time Countess Maritza
Maytime The Student Prince Three Musketeers Cyrano
Anything Goes Gypsy Love

My training at Jacob's Pillow, with its variety of styles and techniques, was more helpful than recent Modern Dance. Usually there was a ballet in each show, but the more recent operettas demanded tap and some jazz. The system demanded that we perform *Countess Maritza* at night while rehearsing *Blossom Time* during the day, so we could then perform *Blossom Time* the next week while rehearsing for *Cyrano,* and try to forget the dances from *Countess Maritza!*

At our first dress rehearsal at night, we all had a surprise, nerve-wracking, for the dancers in particular. A light curtain was used to indicate the down stage edge of the stage. Lights faced us during the acts; then faced the audience for scene changes and intermission. Coming from the darkened wings, often moving fast or spinning, it could take a dancer's eyes a moment or two to define the edge of the stage. We got used to this and braved the June bugs, but there was one other chronic problem: how to keep singers from moving into our dance space. Often singers and dancers were on stage with the leads, supporting them with song and dance. Singers, once down stage, had great resistance to returning upstage out of the way. We would practice in a given space protected by Carl only to find it diminish by half in performance. When we complained, Carl told us, "Kick them out of the way! They'll learn!" They didn't.

Thursdays were the most tedious as José set his group blockings. I often made the time pass by watching José set the various flow patterns in time and space. Throughout my theatrical life, I would never find a director who could block crowd scenes quickly or without major changes. The best conceived plan fell before a costume change, a forgotten entrance of a minor character, or the size of an exit. Move one peg and it jostles the next. Singers, for example, would not move through a musical retard. Often scripts included the direction *they chorused* by the ensemble at large. Repeating the words "rhubarb rhubarb" helped simulate crowd sounds. People who had no trouble chattering backstage could barely mumble as the hero cried out, "Men! Are you with me!"

Our first show was *The Great Waltz,* the ultimate romantic operetta. With music by the Elder and Younger Strauss it offered sweeping, swooning melodies for passions of defiance, despair, courage, faith and, of course, love. The leads were Dorothy Kirsten and George Britton, first class opera stars. Miss Kirsten was beautiful, her blonde hair swept up at the sides with ringlets down her back, her bare shoulders in her glamorous Viennese gown. Singing, she became song. Could a voice be clear and mellow, pure yet rich? To sing like that! Both Dorothy Kirsten and George Britton stayed on for our second show, *Countess Maritza.* George sang the popular *Play Gypsies, Dance Gypsies,* after which we danced a long, furious czardas with stamps and heel clicks, spins galore. Exhilarating! New leads came for each show including such singing stars as John Brownlee, Martha Errole, Melton Moore, Marguerite Piazza, and Frank Hornaday. I wished my Strauss-loving Dad could have seen and heard this show; then he would see that my life was not only decent but beautiful too. My theatrical fantasies were coming true. Each week brought new excitement. New costumes would be shipped in from Brooks or Eaves costumers. It was true they had been worn before, but I decided this brought luck from their previous dancers.

I loved my work. I enjoyed living in a big city again, taking the trolley through the streets out to the Fairgrounds, being apart of life away from schools. There was just one annoying problem; Dr. Duggan had gone on ahead and arranged a room for Nina and me through a Dallas friend. I was furious at having her interfere in my private life. I refused until Nina pleaded with me to try it; her parents would not let her stay here without me. I made the best of it. It was economical, had kitchen privileges and our paths rarely crossed with our landlady, a night nurse.

When Anatole came to see *The Great Waltz,* I danced it especially for him. He praised the show but as we walked the Dallas streets later, we seemed to be talking on two different levels. He was being sent all over the country interrogating WWII prisoners and hoped to get abroad. Anatole stopped walking to face me.

As soon as Japan fell, he had his plans. He was going to complete his interrupted studies in International Law. He had his father's financial backing for this under one condition: that he not marry before completing his degree. Only two weeks ago, we had telephoned his parents with the rapturous news of our engagement.

Proud, of course, I would not stand in his way. But was not strong Love to find its way, too? During the run of *Blossom Time,* the operetta rumored to be based on the life of Franz Schubert and his broken love affair, Anatole's letter arrived. It would be three years before he would be free to marry me. He had not the right to expect me to wait, despite his love for me, tra la la. One more war-torn romance. I shared my love lost with Schubert, but I put no candle in the window for Anatole.

I thought about changing my first name. *Shirley.* Shirley Temple stole my name back when I was a child. It bothered me then and still did. Yes, she was talented and adorable, but too many people joked over the similarity. It was tiresome. Sherry? Hmmm.

Turning Rostand's grand poem, *Cyrano de Bergerac,* into a musical seemed heresy to me until opera star John Brownlee's performance gave the show heroic stature. This was also an ambitious show for the dancers, four big dances in differing styles: a Court Dance for the Cardinal; the Pastry Shop Ballet; a Spanish dance; and a "battle dance" for the boys, using broadswords. Carl had great hopes for the ambitious Pastry Shop Ballet, but in rehearsal, it soon became hilarious. This was a prop dance with us carrying pies, cakes, and trays of cupcakes aloft as we danced. Spinning, leaping, bowing, the cakes must not suddenly take flight. While these props were being readied, we practiced with paper pie plates that fluttered away unpredictably, pulling us off-course and making a shambles of rehearsal.

We got silly. Carl got cross.

The quantities of pastries were considerable and it was not until opening night that we had the real props in hand. Made of *papier mache,* they were lighter than real pastries but looked delicious as real cream puffs, cup cakes and pies. Some were glued onto trays; some were loose for serving to Cyrano and his cavaliers. Early in the scene, there was room to dance, but as the soldiers arrived wearing swords, pathways were clogged and the ballet became a comedy act. Carl was irate while the dancers were laughing hysterically, comparing our desperate improvisations.

Before the next show, Carl gave the singers a blistering, with full support of José and Bambi. That night the singing chorus made room. By the fourth performance, respect for the pastries was eroding backstage. Dancers threatened to throw pies at the singers who played toss-and-catch with the cupcakes and juggled the cream puffs. The inevitable pie tossing and cake crowning ensued, leading to the Cupcake Battle backstage. I stayed out of it until a cupcake bounced off my head. I hurled it back. Some of the dancers and singers were put on probation, the rest of us given a dressing down for childish, unprofessional behavior. This was true, of course, but few of us were contrite; it had been too much fun.

The prop man had no sense of humor about it at all.

Musing over it all later, I laughed over how silly it was for the prop man, a full gown, stolid adult, to be so serious about his prop cakes and pies. Yet theatre made us all do odd things in order to seem true on stage. Even the most blasé, most egotistical artists had to demonstrate a conviction in their work or no audience would believe them. True fakes. Or should it be fake truths? Whatever, people had no trouble with the basic principles of theatre.

Seeming and *being* began to seesaw in my head. It was fundamental that there had to be a reality, a thing or person to *be* the show. Real *papier mache* and real raisins on fake cupcakes. Real people for the acting, singing, dancing: in motion. Ha! It was my medium of motion that made theatre a re-living of life. In the theatre, I could be two people at once, the character and myself. Sort of.

Pretending to be or act as I thought someone else would be or act could only be second-guessing. The best verisimilitude of time and life was little more than a clear echo from the original, always second-hand. Could anything as alive as theatre be ultimately reduced to a frivolous, time-warped conceit? What real good was it all if it was not true? Wasn't it insidious to present pretense as truth? Or did it all fall under the general apology of Entertainment? Was it all just divertissement, psychological pap for the worn or empty mind?

If I were devoting my life to theatre, away from the commerce of the world, would I be dedicated to anything more than glorified lying? Would that make that part of my life fake? Exactly what I was fervently dedicated to avoid? Why did I want to be in Theatre instead of Real Life? I had always thought theatre far nobler than grunging away in everyday business for money. Had I been kidding myself? Vainglorious?

Tangibles were real. What about intangibles? Aha! Without intangibles, the thinking, problem solving, the emotions, momentums, the only tangibles on Earth would be Nature's. But then I was a tangible and intangible, too. Surely dancing was the most of both at once. So why, when theatre and dance had been part of man's heritage since man began, was I staying up questioning all this?

I wanted to be true.

I wanted to be seen as true.

To offer truths of being through dancing.

But just *where* were these silly or serious truths?

A magical place called Being in Motion.

But that was not enough to define the ongoing way life appears and dissolves in time.

I thought of Miss Ruth in performance: flesh and blood but also with a mystical spirituality. Iridescence! No, that was Miss Ruth's personal shining.

Evanescence. Evanescent?

That was the closest I could come to describing the particular characteristic of the performing arts. Dancing, the most consuming of person, threw the most away into the airs of time. For a marvelous moment, that extravagance struck me as positively heroic. Let others spend their lives over Things. I was back with Havelock Ellis: *Dance is life itself.*

Life as dance was evanescent.

But was not everybody's life?

The next day I went to dress rehearsal early to have some space to myself. After putting on my white satin, long-sleeved blouse and black trunks over my suntan net tights, I wiggled into my tap shoes and clicked out onto the empty stage. I practiced our routine and then began to improvise. The luxury of the full stage was irresistible, so I whipped off a fast tripping step all around the stage. Then I kicked off my shoes and went sailing away in great split leaps. Space, space, beautiful space.

What a wonder of the world is Space. Mysterious that it is invisible until defined by objects. Amazing that all sizes can fit in any old shape and it was allowing, impervious. And yet specific: this space, this stage. I dropped down and sat leaning back on my hands. In a moment, the warmth of the sun on the boards came through to my hands. I turned to look at the wood. It always intrigued me how moving things in space mattered. Time-space-relationships. A tree became a board that became a stage that became a ship, a market, a castle, a garden, whatever. And then people would put on pieces of fabric that would make them move one way or another as other people watched. And though the Earth turned, the space was still there! So space was not evanescent.

Evanescence. I liked the word, its mystery, its danger, its demands. Maybe it was not meant to be wholly understood. Like flight, maybe it died when interrupted or commanded to be still to be analyzed.

Right now it was fascinating to consider how it happened that we as dancers were gypsies, then musketeers, soon to be snappy tap-dancing dollies. That fully alive as all this was, there was nothing left of any of it anywhere and there was always room for more!

Evanescence must be what allowed the Present to become the Past, which then allowed the Future to be the Present.

Time? Calling it time was a man-made concept for our convenience. Could it be as simple as Action! What was a better simile for this changing force? Action is an evanescent tangible and true! Really true. Oh, wasn't I smart to be a dancer!

There was a price. A big price, in that choosing a life of action instead of things, there would never be anything left of any of it to put like a bright pebble in my pocket.

(But what of the shadowy leftover images? Kirsten singing, her head held high. Carolyn caught in a lift. Carl's eyes everywhere. Anatole playing his violin. Fanette spitting out a watermelon seed. Bambi's cheeks wobbling to the beat. Nothing could stop the images coming; nothing could stop them from watering away. Films? But they too passed.

Life simply is not meant to be kept.

Freedom to act was all that was available with each moment. I held my breath, watching myself stay alive second by second. My insignificance was overwhelming, then alarming. I jumped up, poised and alert. I must not just stand here as pristine moment after pristine moment went by.

I burst out running, arms wide, covering the whole stage. Then stopped with a jolt, my hands to my head. What was I doing? Putting a burden of decision on every second?

Voluntarily or involuntarily, that is what we seem to do.

The image of *The Hundred Petal Rose* came to me, another symbol of Infinity.

"So, what are you looking at so hard you didn't hear me coming?" Walt, one of the tenors, asked.

"Oh! Hi, Walt. The…the air, I guess."

"God Almighty! We don't have to worry about the air now, do we?" he teased.

"How would you like a sock in the biceps?"

"Oh, tough are you? Just try!" Walt flexed his biceps, tempting me and grinning.

So I socked him. Hard.

"When are you going to hit me?" he laughed.

So I used both fists but broke out laughing. "Oh, thanks, Walt. I just had to feel something solid."

We went out for watermelon after the show.

As the season went along, I was given acting opportunities. After the tarantella in *Firefly,* I was the girl Frank Hornaday sang to while he held me in his arms. It always looked so romantic, but the experience itself was disillusioning. As he sang, he showered spit over me. From my viewpoint, all I could see was dental bridgework. I could measure his nightly degree of passion by the marks left on my arm. Walt had no need to be jealous.

I was given a speaking role in *Maytime* as well as a dancing one. After a Waltz Clog, I became Maria, the fiery gypsy fortune teller in a red gypsy dress and dangling gold earrings. Melton Moore, as Rudolfo, sang his *Gypsy Song* to me, after which I told his fortune. In Act II, dancers had a wild Cancan complete with cartwheels, splits, flashing petticoats and bloomers. Next we had a major Spanish Dance, featuring Fanette. In Act III, more gypsy dancing, and in Act IV, we became models, parading in bouffant, off-shoulder gowns.

Both Carl and José coached me in my role as Maria. Melton could not have been nicer. Why then did I lose my voice right after dress rehearsal? It would take a frog to understand me! Fruit juice was no help. Sleep it off. No luck. No luck next day. As José did not run the scene again, he was unaware of my problem. I did whisper it to Melton. He gave me a hug, saying he would fill in for me somehow. On I went in my Gypsy Maria swagger, ready to mime when I heard this loud, clear voice shout out, "Gold! Gold! Much gold do I see in this hand!! Good fortune shall be yours, my good friend!! And soon!"

Thank God that voice was mine.

Reprieved, I danced my Cancan as never before. I thought I was cured. But no! My anxiety attack lasted the full week; luckily, so did my bold recovery. For our last show, *The Three Musketeers,* Carl set a version of *Swan Lake* with guest artist Jeanne Devereaux as Swan Queen. It was a beautiful ending to a marvelous summer. And there was a coda.

I became engaged to Walt. I even took an engagement ring for the first time. So exciting! However, the night before our last show there was in operetta vernacular An Untoward

Incident. Our nurse/landlady came home to find Walt and me on her bed fully clothed but with our shoes off. I was instantly banished. I apologized for abusing her hospitality, but when she called me trash, treated our love as dirty, I became offended. I grabbed Walt's hand, he grabbed our shoes and we strode out into the night. Another dancer took me in the last night. When I was allowed to retrieve my things, I left a long letter, saying we were a decent man and woman planning marriage.

With little time between Dallas and returning to TSCW, I asked to bring Walt home with me. My parents refused to let Walt come! I was engaged to a sailor after ten weeks? What had happened to Anatole? I defended Walt, saying he had fought in the Navy, managing to survive three years of the war and now we wanted to be the new Alfred Lunt/Lynn Fontaine on Broadway.

"You always say you want me to be happy, but then you get mad when I tell you I am!" I ran upstairs to my room to find it all turned around. My parents had been billeting various Air Corps officers while I was gone, with the understanding they must leave for the few days I would be home. But it did not feel like home now. And what could I tell Walt?

I took Dad's car and drove up to the Harrisburg Country Club to sit and think in the late August sun. I bumped into Ben Burns, an old school friend. We had not dated but always had some earnest chat at parties. We sat in the grillroom, sipping our cokes. Ben was now a resident naval officer in Obstetrics at Jefferson Med in Philadelphia.

"Everything is an emergency at Jefferson. Strange to find this quiet order here in a civilian weekend at home. Look at this place? Same as always," Ben mused.

"Yes, it's the tempo that jolts me, too. Theatre is quick. Like your emergencies in a way. And civilians have a narrow range of movement. Mostly vertical, arms moving from the elbow," I agreed.

"That's funny. I'm not used to seeing all these healthy people moving about and you find them all out of shape. That's what happens when you are deep in your own world," Ben went on. "Well, they don't know what we think and don't care."

"They care what doctors think, don't they?"

"You'd be surprised. Even sick, people pretend they aren't. Don't take their pills. I spend more time trying to get people not to be afraid than anything else."

I told Ben that I wanted to put off having babies so I could dance, bringing its values to the world. Walt and I might join the USO for a time. How long did he think Japan would hold out? Had he any news of schoolmates in the war? Our friend Fred got it on the Arizona right off. One high school sorority sister, the tiny one who was our mascot, joined the WAVES and was killed on Okinawa. Others were still in danger in Europe.

"Oh, God! I worry about holding my balance while my friends are off dying!" I felt obscene to be alive and started to weep.

"Come on, Shirley, pull yourself together. You'll have to make up your mind about how you going to handle your guilt. From your reaction, I gather you've been nursing this neurosis for some time."

"Neurosis? You think I am neurotic!"

"Sure. Don't be offended. What intelligent person isn't these days? You can't deny being obsessed with this. I don't think you need professional help…"

"Oh, thanks a lot! I worry about bringing Beauty to the world, and you say I'm psycho!"

"Shirley. I did not say 'psycho.' You're an intelligent girl. Face your fears. They don't seem to be physical, but I can tell a fear when I see one."

"I don't believe in being afraid of anything," I shot back. "It's waste of time."

"Well, make up your mind. If you have a good reason to dance, just do it. If you can't feel good about it, find something else where you can. I'm not on the front lines either."

"At least you are in the Navy. I look selfish when I want to give with all my heart."

"You care what others think? It's tough on idealists: you either have faith in what you're doing, or you conform. Since when have you ever been a conformist?"

"But I'm trying to conform to my ideals. Dancing for or with people is one of the most beautiful things in the world. How is that nonconformist?"

"Any idealist who continues to be one as an adult automatically is a nonconformist. Shirley, you need instruction about the real world. Everything's relative."

"Relativity? Einstein's?"

"Not really," Ben laughed. "Time as related to people".

"I know a lot about time/space/relationships," I said confidently.

"Do you? What do you know?"

"Well, that's what dancing is all about. Exchanging places through space in different tempos…"

"No, no, that's dance talk. Dr. Burns' relativity means everything is different to different people because of where they are, what they think."

"Well, I know that."

"Well, if you do, you don't apply it. Look, medicine and dance are both dependent upon the common man who knows little about either. I need patients. You need an audience. We are both dependent on the workings of the mass mind. They will need me before they will need you."

"But they need dance, too. It's preventive medicine," I protested. "Dancing together is the lilacs of the soul."

"I may agree with you, Shirl, but they don't know they need dancing and take their lilacs where they find them, as God given. They do not care about medicine or dance."

"That's one more reason we must bring them to them."

"Do you like strangers to tell you what you need? What to believe? I think you should face the fact that our common man's relativity to dance is minimal to the point of being nonexistent. If that's why you are dancing or teaching, I think it's the wrong reason, Shirley. Are you crying again? My God. Never knew a girl to bawl as quick as you."

"I know. I hate it because everyone thinks as soon as I cry I've lost all intelligence. I can think weeping. It's thinking about something that makes me cry. It's just hard to accept that what I know is wonderful is worthless to the people I want to give it to. Holy cow! It's bad enough that it only exists in time and space!"

"It isn't good mental health to swaddle yourself in this rapture of bettering mankind through dance—or anything else for that matter. If Jesus couldn't do it, what makes you think *you* can?"

Although Ben had spoken softly, reasonably, his words were harsh to hear. Trying to do good, I was now shown as vainglorious and incompetent at once. But he made sense. I did not want my life to be one big conceit. Oh, how could I be so educated and still so ignorant about daily living others just get on with?

"War does not make it morally wrong for you to devote yourself to your profession But...look at me! You do not have to take on the whole world."

"But Ben, even if I wanted to be professionally selfish, I know I would still need to dance for people. I have to give to someone. Look, you've learned how to deliver babies. Don't you want someone to have a baby, so you can?"

Ben struck his forehead. "You want to be a heroine!"

"Don't you want to be a hero?"

"Damn right!"

CHAPTER SEVEN

Fall 1945 - Summer 1946
  TSCW Redux and Starlight Operettas

September 2, 1945 World War II officially ended with great relief and celebration throughout the world.

The next week my plane descended onto the bracelet of amber lights of Love Field, Dallas's civilian airport. Arriving ten minutes early, I saw Walt before he saw me. He was there at the counter of the coffee Shop. I took three steps toward him and froze.

I shut my eyes and then stared again.

I started to back away when Walt saw me and ran out to meet me. It could have been a stranger who hugged and kissed me at that moment. I tried to revive my feelings for Walt but knew clearly I could not marry him. How could I tell that to this nice man I had sincerely loved? Was it a summer romance? I tried to be gentle returning his ring. It was a shock to Walt...shame for me. Love's willful way.

This unhappiness marked the beginning of a year of angst at TSCW, as well. I had at last begun my professional dance career and was now a member of Chorus Equity to prove it. I should be in New York! I was twenty-three! Instead, on top of my usual classes, I had to add practice teaching at one of Denton's schools and coaching the Tapperettes, plus getting my thesis subject approved and writing it. All this for $810.00 a year salary. And I missed Jeanette, who had taken leave to go to New York.

Dr. Anne Schley Duggan was the Advisor of Faculty Academic Projects. I submitted the outline of my thesis to her. It seemed logical to me *to dance* to qualify for my M.A.

in Dance. As my minor was English, I developed a program titled *Dance Illustrations of Literary Forms*, planning to choreograph dances based upon works by Emily Dickinson, James Thurber, Conrad Aiken, Ezra Pound, William Saroyan and a Psalm. I would choreograph and perform all the dances. Also write up all technical and artistic aspects of a dance program, plus an evaluation.

No.

It was unheard of to submit a practical dance event instead of a scholarly research paper with conclusions in written form. As I argued my case, Dr. Duggan said to write it up and submit it to the Thesis Committee, which she chaired. My outline was rejected as lacking in detail. When the second was rejected as too detailed, I told Dr. Duggan's secretary I thought Dr. Duggan was being unfair.

I was in our locker room, changing for class, when Dr. Duggan marched in scowling, waving a letter.

The letter I had sent to my nurse-hostess about marrying Walt.

"Fair! YOU! How fair was it of you to abuse my reputation and embarrass me before all my Dallas friends! Such despicable behavior! You are a disgrace to the Department! Don't tell me about fair, you immoral slut! And watch it! I have an insult file for people like you!"

She slammed out the door, leaving me shocked and mortified. Before I could pull myself together, I heard Mary sound a chord on the studio piano. Tears of rage stung my eyes. I wiped them away furiously. I had no time for this. I galvanized all my strength and ran into the studio calling out to the class, "Follow me!"

121

After ten minutes of nonstop running various ways, a student protested, "How come... this class is... all... running..., Miss T?"

"Stamina!" I yelled back, leading them into running turns.

The irony of all this was that I still was a virgin

Dr. Duggan and I were embattled from then on. When it was time to teach The Doxology to new Modern Dance Group members, she had me demonstrate the slow kneel and found fault with it six successive times. By my third demonstration, I knew she was trying to get me to break. I just obediently continued to perform it perfectly until the students grew restless and Dr. Duggan realized her harassment was obvious.

It was also obvious that my thesis idea would never be approved. I chose instead contemporary ballet as a field I should know more about when I went to New York. Although Dr. Duggan had the final say on thesis subjects, each candidate had an advisor. I finally asked mine, Bonnie Cotteral (Stunts and Tumbling) to come with me when I resubmitted this new outline to Dr. Duggan. As she frowned over it, I spoke up.

"It is mid-December. If this outline is unacceptable, I see no reason to stay at TSCW." My respect for my contract was wearing thin.

"The Christmas program—" Dr. Duggan was caught off guard.

"Why, Shirley, what would we do without you?" a surprised Bonnie interrupted. "I think this outline is just fine, now don't you Dr. Duggan?" It was reluctantly approved.

Mary Campbell and I were both going home for Christmas. Our train from Dallas was two hours late. This was the first Christmas after the end of the war. We soon realized we civilians should not be taking up space veterans earned, but it was too late. We missed connections in St. Louis, where Union Station was literally carpeted with servicemen coming from all directions. Misinformation sent us awry. Mary fainted from the crush. A Navy lieutenant gave up his place in line to help me get her to the snack bar for tea. I battled our way to the ladies room for a breather, changing from my skirt to my frontier pants and boots. Hours later, we were carried on a swell of humanity toward an arriving train only to be separated. I found a space in an aisle to sit on my suitcase. As the long, overloaded train tried to pick up steam, I tried to look for Mary. Squashed together, I could not move until I followed the harried conductor pushing his way through the train.

No one would let me into the next car until I explained my worry over Mary. Did she even get on the train? By then the conductor was too far ahead. The only space was on the armrests of the seats. So getting more help than I wanted, I stepped from armrest to armrest, calling out "Mary Campbell! Mary Campbell!" Guys helped me yell and we finally found her in a seat four cars back. She waved "Okay." By the time I got back to my suitcase, I was "Tex". My train was fourteen hours late. And Mary was going on to Maine!

My new thesis outline approved, I made a New Year's vow to try to get along better with Dr. Duggan. By exam time, another problem arose. Besides taking dance classes as well as sports, the majors also had to make a circuit of the curricula as coaches. My tap dancing coach was a motherless girl named Jack. Her father, a rancher, had wanted a boy and raised his daughter as a boy. She had a boy's haircut and the walk of a horse rider. But under her gym shirt she also had a bust and her manners were gentle, if not shy. She was one of the majors that hung around. Coaching Tap had seemed a nightmare to Jack, but she plugged along and mastered teaching a buck routine.

At our mid-semester faculty meeting, Dr. Duggan started intoning about having only the right kind of personalities as majors in the department. The Department was getting national attention now. It was time to screen new majors to include only normal, high-spirited women, eliminating any of those applying that manifested masculine characteristics. This included those Majors mistakenly enrolled now. Midterm, she continued, was a discreet opportunity to grade these disoriented students wisely. She looked straight at me.

I looked behind me to see only a straight-faced Bonnie. Then I began to burn. I opened my big mouth and asked flat out, "You mean flunk her?"

Concrete silence. Not a word from the other dedicated Health, Physical Education and Recreation faculty. I was promptly dismissed to go to rehearsal.

Of course I did not flunk Jack. She told me how Dr. Duggan had tried to convince her to change to a business major "to help my Dad at the ranch."

"Do what *you* want, Jack," I said.

Carolyn George, my sister dancer from *Starlight,* had enrolled at TSCW the previous fall and was a great plus to our Modern Dance Group. On our spring tour, we did *Nutcracker Suite,* with Carolyn and I the only two *en pointe.* It was rewarding to just dance, but I lost a great deal of research time. My overloaded schedule told me I'd never finish writing my thesis by June. But spend summer in

Denton? Scheduled for teaching, too? I called Ralph Meeker, Director of *Starlight Operettas,* and was hired for the coming season. I would finish my thesis somehow in Dallas.

Carl Randall, Bambi Bambochek and José Ruben were returning to carry on as last summer. Carolyn and I were joined by another TSCW dancer, Kitty Higgenbottom. Our pay was raised to $37.50 a week, far better than TSCW paid. And this season I made sure to acquire my own single quarters. Soon we were dancing as Casquette Girls sent from Paris to New Orleans to marry settlers in *New Moon.* Again gorgeous music filled the air. *Wanting You* and *One Kiss* sung by Lucille Manners and Arthur Kent spoke for yearning hearts everywhere. Because of my training in Spanish dance, Carl featured me in his choreography of *Capriccio Espagnol.*

After the other dancers set the scene in a café, I sauntered in provocatively, posed with one foot on a chair while the men dancers competed to light my cigarette. After rejecting this man and that, I danced my solo. The two worries were getting the cigarette lit on time despite the summer night breezes; the other was managing not to travel on my sixteen *fouetté entournant* finale. (Yes, the very ballet skill that had floored me at Nijinska's class). Waltzes, polkas, tarantellas, tap routines and ballets flew by in the shows. The only choreography approaching Modern Dance was in my favorite show, *The Cat and the Fiddle,* music by Jerome Kern. Movie star Allan Jones, who played Victor, closed the first act with a love song that sent him dreaming. Carl experimented with freer dance movements as we flowed to Jones, then away, as visions of his love.

Midseason, I thought I had died standing up.

All this while, I had followed my strict schedule of rising early to work on That Damned Thesis (TDT), and writing my thesis backstage in our dressing room at lunch and dinner breaks, as well as at home after the show. There was a Walgreen's Drug Store near the theatre where I would get a tuna fish sandwich and a Coke for a quick supper. One evening, I hurried back from the drugstore to sign in, forgetting my overstuffed zippered case with my TDT in it. Too late to go back. I could hardly concentrate on the show, for I knew I could not replace my research notes in Dallas. I took out my distress in my dancing, using almost violent energies to express my anguish, upstage away from the audience.

When I raced back after the show, the case with TDT was gone!

Stolen!

Why? It was no good to anyone else.

Dr. Duggan was going to win after all. That was all my degree meant to me now—a determination not to be prevented from finishing it.

I sat down on the curb and just bawled.

As I sat there, one of the guest actors came puffing up to me "Hey! Hey, now. What's the matter? Can I help? Why were you acting like that on stage tonight?"

Oh, it was Eduard Grant, a supporting actor in *Cat and the Fiddle*. "No one can help," I blubbered, wanting him to go away. "My thesis is gone."

"Well, I'm sorry, but it is no excuse for that kind of behavior on stage. You can't just use your role as a vessel for whatever you're feeling at the time."

"I didn't think anyone would notice upstage."

"Notice! My dear girl, you are noticed. Come on. I'll take you home."

But he didn't. Eduard took me first to the Baker Hotel for a drink and a late supper. Then we went up to his room where he listened to me unspool all my wretched recent history, my frustrations over *Oklahoma!,* and my current defeat. Then he told me how my dancing had caught his eye; that he wondered how ambitious I might be. He said earnestly, "You'll make it if you want to. I am sure of it."

Eduard called downstairs for drinks. Worn out, I did not pick up on the compliment and sagged into a chair. Eduard took off my sandals, then my blouse, and I slid between the smooth sheets. Umm! So lovely. When Eduard joined me, a heavy rain began pouring sheets of water down the windows. Lightning bolts cracked the sky. As the thunder rumbled ever louder, we turned toward each other. So lovely!

The next day came, no TDT returned.

Day two?

Nope.

Day three?

No.

Four?

No!

Day five. Someone brought TDT back to Walgreen's!

I went into Neiman Marcus and bought a black cocktail dress.

I also went into a Dallas bookstore to check recent dance sources.

There was a new book on my subject! Just out was Winthrop Palmer's *Theatrical Dancing in America: The Development of Ballet from 1900.*

Although I could not possibly have used this book as a source for my completed research, it would be enough to give Dr. Duggan an excuse for another delay. It was already into August. I called Bonnie, who was "not quite sure." It might be a problem. I junked the early dance years, changed my viewpoint and the title to the *Development of Ballet on the Concert Stage of the United States of America between 1940 and 1946.*

Romantic and Classical Ballets, Folk Ballets and Modern Ballets were analyzed for the years between 1940 and 1946.

In this way, I reported all new ballets in the repertoires of any and all ballet companies I could find in the USA. Choreography was defined in three major classifications: Ballet, Folk and Modern, to define the dominant style of the choreography. Conclusions:

> American dancers and choreographers influenced the classic ballet companies. (Example: *Les Ballet de Monte Carlo's* Folk Ballet, *Union Pacific,* has an American folk libretto but a Russian choreographer, Leonide Massine.) The ferment for more contemporary ballets is growing in the United States. (Example; *Ballet Theatre's Lilac Garden* choreographed by Anthony Tudor.) Dance in all three forms is becoming increasingly part of American culture on the Concert Stage. An American audience for Ballet is shown increasing between 1940 and 1946. The conclusion drawn is that the time is rapidly approaching when there will be a distinct *American Ballet* on the Concert Stage of United States of America.

It helped to dance Johann Strauss's deliriously delicious waltz on *A Wonderful Night (Die Fledermaus),* then tear off lickety-split into *Perpetuum Mobile,* to stamp out another czardas in *Gypsy Love.* Jose´ offered me another speaking role in *Rose Marie,* but the deadline for That Damned Thesis was up the last week in August. Ralph Meeker gave me permission to leave *Starlight Operettas* without penalty.

Two bound, printed copies of my thesis were required. When I presented Bonnie with my finished version before it went to the publishers, she asked me about my dedication to Dr. Duggan. I replied it was my privilege; that I would not select Dr. Duggan.

"Oh, but all the Masters Theses are dedicated to Dr. Duggan, for all her guidance and wisdom," gently insisted Bonnie.

I had made it a point not to involve her or Mary, or anyone else, in my battles with Dr. Duggan. They could observe tension, perhaps, but nobody asked to know more. That was the way I wanted it.

"I will only say this, Bonnie, that if my thesis is not acceptable without a dedication to Dr. Duggan, I refuse to offer it. You can take the damned degree. I no longer want it."

"Why, why Shirley I ...this has never happened. You..."

"Nope. Gibraltar will crumble first."

"Dear!" Bonnie flustered. "I suppose I can ask President Hubbard. Dr. Duggan is not on campus now."

Dr. Hubbard honored my right of dedication, Bonnie reported, incredulous. I knew it had taken this fifty-some, old fizz-edd teacher some courage for this, so I dedicated my thesis to her. I had been passed my Orals in May. And I did go to graduation after all. Dammit! I had earned this degree for one reason or another. *Education* was a dirty word now but a believer in ceremonies, I marched proudly out into the Texas August sunshine in my black gown with its new red lined hood, a Master of Arts.

M.A. How could two letters contain so much. I vowed never to work for a woman again.

Flying home, I finally changed my name. No longer Shirley, I was now Sharry. Sharry with a soft A as in Sharon. Sharry Traver.

And freeeeee!

CHAPTER EIGHT

Fall 1946
  New York, NY

At last I had earned the right to be here in the Greatest Theatre City in the World. Hot damn!

Free from encumbrances!

Fat with dreams.

An edge of danger, financial danger perhaps, but for now there was $100 ($90 of it safely pinned inside my bra).

It so happened that my Aunt Marie (Pummie) was still in Manhattan. Telling me I must look successful, Pummie had cajoled me into buying a cream wool dress and red kid shoes at Lord & Taylors: that took $30. She was subletting an apartment in Sutton Place with a vast view of the East River. The wide differences in city living became clear to me very soon, as we tried to find a place for me. A friend of a friend gave us a decent address: 350 West 85th Street.

"It's pretty far from 42nd Street," I ventured.

My Aunt turned to me. "You do *not want* to live on 42nd Street! And do not keep answering everyone who speaks to you. Always look like you know where you are going in New York, even if you don't."

Stanford White had designed the apartment house on 85th Street, A step inside and we found ourselves in a Gothic courtyard bedazzled with balustrades, friezes along the ceiling, a medallion of Medusa, glaring from a wall. and a dry fountain gargoyle. Wrought-iron lamps provided a gloomy light. We creaked up to the sixth floor in an elevator lined with antiqued mirrors. Mrs. Hodges, the landlady, showed us to my room, my third of a room actually, for I was to share this space with a stranger and an oversized fireplace. The furniture had been shoved in with little regard for convenience. Pummie and I shrugged and I took it.

"Good luck, Pansy Eyes!" Pummie gave me kiss on the forehead as a blessing. "Write to me in London." And off she went.

In an overzealous burst of nest building, I sought to surprise my roommate by rearranging the furniture on the third day. We could always put it back. And so we did! Rose Goldberg taught me the difference between dividing a room and sharing it. Rose was a native "New Yawka." She had black, wiry hair, wore pounds of orange makeup, heeled pumps, and tight short skirts. She surveyed my collegiate wardrobe with disdain. The more courteous I was, the more foul language she used. We both fascinated and repelled each other. One night she came home late and upset, waking me with the overhead light. When I protested, she launched forth a scathing tirade about "bitches" like me who had everything while she…Rose broke down in sobs despite herself.

A sap for anyone's tears, I went over to her. At first she abruptly turned away, but as her troubles came tumbling out, she turned to me. She was right. I had had it easy compared to her. Married at sixteen, knifed by her husband when pregnant, then divorced. Recently recovered from polio. Now worried about having cancer, as her mother and sister had died of it this year. As I listened with a mix of horror and compassion, she went on about hating her job at the Shanty Shack. Eight hours a day on her feet with jerks for customers.

"What is a Shanty Shack?" I asked, unfortunately. Rose started to answer, then with a look that put me back into enemy camp, she wailed and threw herself on the bed, having nothing more to do with me.

Before the week was out, there was another slice-of-life experience at Mrs. Hodges. Dottie Spence, my Jacob's Pillow writer friend, and I were chatting in my room when pregnant Donna stumbled in, moaning in labor. While Dottie timed the pains, I telephoned Donna's doctor. "Bring her out here right away!" he insisted.

Here was Rosemont, Long Island!

The three of us took off in a ball of frantic motion and anxiety to the subway, to Penn Station, to the L.I.R.R. In the dark and the rain, we got off a station too soon. While Donna howled in pain and fear, we found a cab to take us the rest of the way to what looked more like a mansion than a hospital. "Where the hell have you been?" scolded the doctor.

After the baby was born, Donna gave her baby away. She was more worried about losing her job as a cashier at the Empire Hotel.

I was awakened one morning by Rose getting dressed in her deliberately noisy way. I knew she resented my staying in bed, but now I was resenting her having a job. Even at a Shanty Shack, cheap burger stands littering the city: Rose was filling a basic need for people, whereas I was needed by absolutely no one. Rose slammed out the door. Quiet. No need to get up.

Until now my every waking moment had been spent cleverly creaming my dancing into my jobs, studies and love life. After working years to get exactly here, suddenly there was…nothing. Oh, I learned the hard way not to trek to casting offices until afternoon. (Don't Go Away Mad—Just Go!) My Equity card gave me audition information, but there was none this week. My rent was due in ten days. I had only

134

$28 left and this 5'6-1/2" brown-haired, blue-eyed Caucasian female with no more than a raisin-cookie bosom and an apple-hard bottom lying on a cot.

I thought of my last audition for *Showboat* at the Ziegfeld Theatre. Learning that Pillowite Charlie Tate was dance captain, I asked to see him and was allowed into the semifinals. There were eight jobs and at least one hundred girls auditioning, all beautiful and talented. Most wore their hair in a ballet bun; some pulled it into a ponytail. A few let their hair hang long and soft about their faces. Some wore ribbons to match their leotards. Some wore net opera hose, or pink tights. A couple of dancers were barelegged like me. Most girls brought ballet and toe shoes, but one girl brought tap shoes, too.

"Is there tap dancing in *Showboat*?" I asked, alarmed without mine.

"I don't know. But I got caught at an audition without mine once, so I always bring them along. Do you know if they want short or tall girls?"

The audition was filled with traps that eliminated dancers right and left. First a dance combination was shown to the dancers *en masse*. Next six girls were called out at a time, without having had a chance to practice except in their heads. Those who passed were held for new combinations. I was washed out the second run-through with a bored "Thank you!" (No head shots or resumes for dancers in 1946; not even names until cast)

Now was there enough of me to be enough here? Holding my breath, I got hotter and hotter. I whipped into a little ball and snapped the covers over my head. Gone.

A long minute, I was not there. As it got hotter, involuntarily my legs braved the nameless fear at the bottom of the bed. Shame flushed through me. Tears filled my eyes and ran down into my ears. I took a careful deep breath, forced my body into a nonchalant position and exhaled. Relaxed. And Fear was gone. But that had been Fear. For all my faults, fear had seldom been one of them. Intent on what I was doing, I was often unaware of dangers. "She's too dumb to be afraid," my sister Jane had snorted with disgust. Did it help to now know Fear?

I jumped up, dressed, banged my way out of the dim, dark courtyard, walking into a shaft of sunlight. I paused and felt its warmth on my hair. Good! If the indifferent sun could find me down here among all these buildings, surely some one in New York could too. I treated myself to a full breakfast at Rikers Diner. Filching a deserted copy of *Variety,* I read that Ken was still in *Oklahoma!* I sent a note wishing him well, including my telephone number.

From this, a phone call, a first lunch at Lindy's to catch up. Ken was married now and had a two-year-old daughter. He had been working in radio and theatre since leaving Syracuse. And he got me another chance to audition for *Oklahoma!* When Ken learned that I had not seen the show, he arranged a seat for me before the audition. Agnes de Mille quickly became my favorite choreographer. She was also my Great White Hope, for although she used classic ballet, she did not always require *pointe* work. When I saw the dances, I was thrilled: I could dance that!

A few days later, Vladimir Kostenko, dance captain of *Oklahoma!,* gave me a private audition backstage before the matinee at the St. James Theatre. Ken introduced us, then left. Mr. Kostenko did not choose to give me any dance combinations from the show. Instead he gave me a very strict classical ballet *barre* and center technique including a classic ballet variation. I failed.

I signed up at Ballet Arts to study with Agnes de Mille, but she was too busy to teach. When I learned Thalia Mara had ballet classes at Carnegie Hall, I worked happily with her. I knew it was important to keep on with ballet not only for its strengths but also because most show auditions demanded its skills. Otherwise, I no longer yearned to be a ballerina. Modern Dance appealed to me far more for its originality and the subjectivity of its themes. Modern Dance held out artistic freedom and a dare to me ever since Martha Graham had given a concert at TSCW. Although I was then working in Modern Dance, I was shocked at the dimensions in range of technique, intensity and personal styling she and her company demonstrated. Martha proved she could reveal the private person in public without the "emotional massage" so abhorrent to my Syracuse Creative Writing teacher. Martha Graham loomed far above me.

Through Aunt Pummie's friend, Bob Bergh, I met Gertrude Shurr and took some modern dance classes with her. Gertrude Shurr had studied with the Denishawns, Humphrey-Weidman and Martha Graham. She had danced in their companies. Gertrude's class for me was a mix of old and new modern dance technique, adding contractions to floor work and new falls. So far no one had taught me contractions. Gertrude assured me no one mastered contractions in one lesson.

Where I used flex/extend, Gertrude used contract/release.Where I bent at joints, she wanted the torso to cave in contraction. And her release was not a relaxation but a hyperextension. "Look around," she suggested. "Try

Martha's class. She'll teach you contractions. Or try Humphrey-Weidman on 16th Street."

Class at the Doris Humphrey and Charles Weidman Studio was next and it felt marvelously at home. Once you started moving there, you did not stop dancing until class was over. There were no long demonstrations or explanations to cool your muscles or interrupt the flow of motion. You learned by observing the company members who knew H-W technique and from Charles' constant corrections and comments. More, it was dancing, not just mechanical exercise. Elevations ran through the class; not just saved for the end. There were exciting suspensions, rebounds, off-center turns and balances; less floor work. I liked Charles himself at once.

There were also auditions given by the Choreographers' Workshop, a newly formed association of choreographers planning works at the 92nd Street Young Men and Women's Hebrew Association (YMHA/YWHA.). One of the choreographers, Tally Beatty, chose me, but after working with him a short time, I wondered why. A black man, Tally's style of movement was then what dance historian Curt Sachs classified as *convulsive* in his *World History of Dance*. There were many pelvic thrusts (the very kind my father described as vile). My only former experience with this style had been the master class with Asadata Dafora three years ago. I tried valiantly, but Tally improvised choreography at rehearsals, making it difficult to know what moves were *in* and which *out*. In Tally's floor work with fast rollovers, there were these convulsive contractions before successive motions. There were also explosive jumps in bent body positions. Tally would get going at a furious pace of excitement (without a dance belt, which distressed me) and just dance. He was not interested in teaching his technique; just doing it.

While scouting out dance, there was an immediate need for a survival job, one to feed and house me, that would still free me for class and auditions. In order to drag out time between my skimpy meals, I walked on Riverside Drive until I got a hunger headache. Then my Lipton's Instant Noodle Soup, toast and milk, or Nescafé would taste marvelous. Feeling flush on a sunny day, I would go to Rockefeller Plaza where the atmosphere was always exciting. Then off to Howard Johnson's across Fifth Avenue on East 51st for a hot dog on a toasted roll (15c), a cup of hot coffee (10c), a dish of peppermint ice cream (15c), and still have a dime for the tip—all for 50 cents. Delicious!

My first job was working for a publisher from 6:00-to-10:00 p.m., but I quit because the books were trash. Next a job in a mailing house where I had to keep circling the huge assembling table fast enough to elude the advances of Irving, the night manager. One-on-one was not good enough. All my education was worth nothing in the marketplace. I took my thesis to Walter Terry, dance critic for *The Herald Tribune,* for advice. He was very cordial, adding he was already planning a similar book. So nothing came of that and I decided not to take dance time to chase publishers.

My Dad had sent us all to college so that "you never have to be a waitress or work in the Five & Dime." These jobs were avoided, but they did fit into my free hours after class. I finally lucked into one that would give me supper. For $13 a week, I was counterman ("Should I change that to read counterwoman?" "Jess fill in the card, doll.") My uniform was too long but an apron helped. From 4 P.M. to 10 P.M., *The New York Times Café* needed me to fill sugar bowls; slice 'n dice butter chips, make fast ham 'n cheese sandwiches, or scoop up dollops of mashed potatoes or cheese macaroni at a steam table that literally curled my hair. As most of my fellow workers were Puerto Ricans, I probed for some remnants of my Spanish classes. This brought forth a torrent of Spanish I could not handle.

Behind the steam table was a huge walk-in refrigerator with a thick insulated door. This was constantly opened and closed. Told to gather all the sandwich fixings and stack them in the frig on my second night, I took them in and kicked the door shut. After feeling like steamed carrots, it was pleasantly cool in there as I went to work, chilled as I finished and went to leave and could not. Push-pull, screw, find handle, say magic word—nothing worked. Neither string nor scream helped. There was a small glass window, 5"x7", that my coworkers constantly passed and, needing nothing in here, heard nothing. Slabs of red raw beef, piles of blue glassy-eyed fish and yellowing nude chickens surrounded me. I jumped up and down, irate. Finally, the chef pulled open the door.

"Ha! So here you are! Hiding out?" My baleful look and the chill of my arm as he grabbed me changed his mind. "Madre de Dios! Chico. Tea! A mug of tea, pronto!" I ricocheted home for a hot shower. Gamely returning the next day, I found there had been a flash-fire on the fast food grill. No *New York Times Café*.

Dottie found me a new room, a fifth floor walk- up on 63rd Street that cost ten dollars a week. That saving let me spend what was left of my *New York Times Cafe'* paycheck to try the *Martha Graham School of Contemporary Dance* on Fifth Avenue. I took the beginner's class and found it a mixed blessing to have Martha herself as our teacher. The tension in the studio was palpable.

My person condensed to lead. When we began to move, it was in a seated position on the floor, one foot *on the walk* (toes touching, heel lifted) lined up with the body's sagittal line, the opposite leg with bent knee, inside thigh to the floor in back; rather like a swastika in 3-D. Isolated moves, starting tiny and increasing in size, were to initiate in abdominal contractions of the *solar plexus*. With serpentine eyes, I followed whomever I was facing, doing my best to contract and release in the standard Graham sequence. If a good number of us "lost" our contractions, Martha stopped the class to give excruciatingly specific corrections. This was help directly to the point, but her searing inspection was unnerving.

This was the period in Martha's work when she used (or developed) one of her benchmarks: the yearning body contraction, arms along the body, palms open, the head oblique to the side; a wanting movement of desire. There were kneels into side falls and side contraction to recover that developed into a half-turn kind of roll around-and-up to kneeling position. Most of the class time was spent on the floor. Eventually we did stand and warm up the feet before going into sideway prances with lifted knees. Next came the triplets, running down-up-up, down-up-up that must be as fleet as a windblown leaf. It was a simple exercise, but its perfection was elusive. From a basic running step, action progressed to stag leaps, the forward knee bent in flight. My poise was restored in the elevations, but I left Martha's class feeling like a constipated accordion from all the contractions and the tension. I let gravity pull me down the stairs, mulling over the power and gut strength of Graham's Technique. My aching innards felt sucked into an internal vortex for hours. What an Amazon Martha was! What a marvel. Her class did help with Tally's piece, but he dropped me anyway. He was right; I was not fast enough with his convulsive style, but he could have told me instead of not mentioning the next rehearsal. I should go back to Martha, but she was *down* and *in,* while I was *up* and *out.*

At Chorus Equity, I learned that Michael Kidd was holding auditions for *Finian's Rainbow.* The show had been the talk of the summer and many dancers were eager to work with Michael. His success with his ballet *On Stage* made him popular in theatre too. At the audition, Michael did not sit out front with an assistant doing the work. He himself was there showing dance combinations, cheerfully joking with dancers he knew. The audition was even fun. I made it to the finals!

"Don't call us! We'll call you," they tell you, so you wait, hope fluttering like a flag in a gale. My postcard finally arrived:

Dear Miss Traver,

Sorry we can't use you in Finian's for reasons other than dancing,

You gave a good audition.

James Gelb Stage Manager

Three great chances to get into a Broadway show and I failed all three. Dreading it, ashamed, I went over to 8th Avenue to the Unemployment Security Office to register. Dancers had told me plenty: "All those grabby guys giving you the once-over." "Don't dress nice—they'll think you're lying." "They hate theatre people, 'cause they know they can't find you a job." "It takes six weeks, even if they believe you." "Don't ever go alone!" "Whatever you do, don't lie.

My boyfriend did and now I gotta feed him." "You can work part-time, but they love to cancel you."

They forgot to tell me about the smell. Subways were greenhouses in comparison. It took only one minute there and I reversed, heading back to my New York sanctuary, Rockefeller Plaza. One thing I missed in New York was SPACE. Space inside, where the dance studios were no match for the beautiful, glossy floors of TSCW studios. Space outside, where here everything was tight together. The Plaza at 59th Street was a joy but not as spacious to walk about in as handsome Rockefeller Plaza. Central Park beckoned, but everyone warned me never to go alone, if at all. No, it was Rockefeller Plaza, where you could see the sky without turning upside down; where people seemed to hurry more politely; where there was an airy space in an island of time no matter what time. There was a constant cheerfulness there. The opportunity for fun, ice skating even if you didn't. And the fresh flowers or shrubs and flags, so faithfully provided. Most of all, there always was room for me.

The next day I was back at the one-hundred-year old, oily, grime-and-filth of the Unemployment Office. Filth! Now I knew what it was. The stench was not just gym-locker smell but ancient, bad bacterial smells, a suffocating mixture of fetid breath, city stench, stained clothing and urinals, all heightened with some aromatic odor-killer that didn't. On my way up the stairs, I passed a side room with a door with the sign: Sell your blood $5 PT. I shuddered at this blasphemy. Giving blood was a good thing, selling it a sin. Upstairs the floor made gritty, blackboard scraping noises as old derelicts and cloth-swaddled women shuffled in line. I breathed as shallowly as possible. Then patiently, I repeated answers to repeated questions. I waited for a replacement of the rude civil servant who left in the middle of my history. It takes time to be poor. Looking around a bit while waiting, I thought now I know what people mean when they say: "There, but for the Grace of God, go I." Here without the Grace of God was now Sharry Traver!

On the way down the stairs, with three more weeks before I could even qualify, I hesitated by the sign, then entered the room. Maybe some of my blood was needed to save the rest of it.

"Only take men, Miss! No sense wasting your time."

"Why?" I demanded of the man in a white lab coat. "Why is a man's blood better than a woman's? It's all red, isn't it?"

"All right," the man sighed. "Come on, take the blood test." Every one coming back down the stairs stared at me.

"Here," the attendant returned and was holding out a card. "This gives your blood type—O Positive. And here, take these." He handed me a small green metal box.

"What's this? Ferasol?"

"Iron pills. You're anemic."

"I can't..."

"Believe me. Take the pills."

Not even my blood, my very life's blood, was good enough for New York City! I was literally worthless. I just might vaporize any second. On the long way back to my room on East 63rd, some base primitive momentum kept my feet following each other to the house, up the five flights to my room, where I dropped on my bed, just a Thing.

I put my hand over my heart and felt it beating like a tympani. What a good brave heart it was to keep me dancing anyway! To my surprise, a tingle of excitement thrilled through me. C'mon! Your life's not in danger, I told myself.

But I felt hollow and alert. When I swallowed the iron pill, it rattled all the way down, like a button tossed into an empty jar. Was I becoming evanescent! Jumping up and down, I pounded my thighs and smacked roses back in my cheeks and then gave myself a good wallop on the behind. Better mad than sad!

Got to sleep imagining I was in a four-poster bed with an angel at each post: Ted Shawn, Ruth St. Denis, Agnes de Mille and Pummie..

Time to join the AFL. Experienced dancers told me to check in at the New York Hotel Trades Council on West 47th Street. I promptly agreed to pay dues from my salary and was accepted for the position of hostess by Mr. Ralph, Maitre d' of the Great Northern Hotel on 57th Street, just east of the Russian Tea Room. Mr. Ralph was a short, middle-aged Frenchman; his black hair parted in the middle and slicked down. Wearing a dark suit, he was formal and officious, showing me the dining Room, grille and kitchen. My hours were from 5:00 p.m. to 9:00 p.m. I might have a light snack before work and then supper with the staff in the grille after the dining room closed. Told to wear something dressy, the cream wool dress and red kid shoes were acceptable. I knew how to be gracious to patrons and in two weeks was getting used to having a decent supper when Mr. Ralph fired me.

"Why?" I wailed. "What did I do wrong?"

"Jesus! Don't cly!" begged Mr. Ralph. "You nice girl. You find something, eh? You have one week!"

My last night, Jean, one of the waitresses, came up to Mr. Ralph and said, "Whyuncha giver a chance waitressin'?"

"Oh, would you, Mr. Ralph?" I pleaded tearfully. Helen had her hands on her hips. Phil's arms were folded; and Texas, too, was glaring at him.

He threw up his hands. "It's clazy! Hokay. Try! Jess don't cly!"

Mr. Ralph's eyebrows beetled watching me learning to carry a tray overhead. While Helen taught me course timing, Jean alerted me to ready orders, and Phil taught me French service. Texas taught me how to carry five martinis on a tray without spilling them. The pastry chef saved me Napoleons. The Chef, however, liked to put a live lobster on my shoulder, and the bus boy kept whispering "Chica! You be my gel?" I studied our new hostess, Frances, in her black crepe dresses with a spattering of sequins or gold clips. Dangling earrings and baby doll shoes lent a certain way of walking. The clothes. The sex.

I still got paid and fed, and the job did not interfere with classes or auditions. Jack Dempsey owned our hotel. On payday, for me at night, I had to go up to Mr. Dempsey's penthouse office. It was a chance to look out over the city sparkling all around me, so near, so far.

Now New York was putting on its Christmas glamour, lights of all colors, blazing day and night in constellations of all sizes, just everywhere. The famous Christmas windows at Macy's, Lord & Taylor's and Saks Fifth Avenue gave us an old fashioned Christmas, a toy-land Christmas, and futuristic Christmas fantasy. Rockefeller Plaza had its glorious tree creating a noble beauty for everyone. It was my first Christmas away from home, Carolyn George's, too. I called Carolyn, asking her to come to my room for a Christmas breakfast. We were both wistful, but after enjoying our Danish pastries and coffee, we were laughing over our New York dance adventures. She told me about class with Mikhail Oboukov, Alexandria Danilova, and about the School of American Ballet (SAB). Carolyn wanted to join a ballet company. We promised to do better getting together.

Working Christmas Day at least gave me a chance to be part of festivities some place. The hotel looked beautiful. Everyone was cheery underneath the fluster of special *entrees*. It was a late night but I had bought myself a present to have when I got home: the *Autobiography of Frank Lloyd Wright*. Architecture had always been an interest since studying ancient Greek and Roman history. Also my state Capitol building back home fascinated me in all its marble splendor and spaciousness. Ayn Rand's *The Fountainhead,* with its hero's defiant sense of integrity, had sustained me in my contest with Dr. Duggan. I had just left Sanford White's medieval courtyard. And everywhere I went in New York, from the grandeur of Pennsylvania Station to the crummy Chock-Full-o' Nuts coffee shops, there was architecture.

Reading Wright's book was both inspiring and one of the smartest things I did to get a perspective on all modern arts. Just to follow the thinking of the man was a privilege; to share his tragedies was humbling. His vision and resourcefulness gave new definition to the creative spirit; exciting to watch his ideas develop into solid structures. The passion and warm-heartedness of the man shone through his arrogance and self-destruction. With all Wright's grand ideas and extravagance, he never lost sight of the human dimension.

Frank Lloyd Wright shook me up good and proper. My days had fallen into a rut of classes, waitressing, running up and down stairs and carrying things. I was in an obedience cycle, doing nothing creative on my own initiative. When I managed to save $100, I quit my job. I was not going to be one of the millions of clothespin people following orders from day to day.

"You qwvit? You have show job, yes?" Mr. Ralph beamed broadly. There was no way I could explain to my hotel gang without offending them. They all had my full respect. It just was no longer for me.

"What'll ya do when your money runs out?" Jean demanded.

"Get another job, I guess,"

"Not here, you won't," Helen snorted and kept folding napkins.

"Thank you for all your help. You all saved me, you really did. And Helen, you're probably right. I'll be broke again but I can still stop by to see you,

Helen snapped a napkin at me with a rueful smile. "You won't be back. Show people. You're all nuts!"

When I picked up my last paycheck, I took one last look over the sparkling city from the penthouse. I was right to start over.

148

CHAPTER NINE

Winter 1947
  New York, NY

My new freedom was exhilarating. I felt as though I had just bought Manhattan and was looking to see what I got. What an inventory! I walked all over with my brisk city stride and a sappy smile on my face. In crowds, I delighted in slipping seamlessly between people without breaking my pace. Or I dawdled, meandering down Fifth Avenue, surveying the shop windows as though I had never seen these things before. I did not have things or fashionable clothes, so I mentally purchased whatever struck my fancy and did not owe a cent. I stared at the buildings like a hick without caring if people had to dodge me. I wandered into new coffee shops for a *cappuccino;* had a great pastrami sandwich at the Stage Delicatessen; got all the way downtown and took the Staten Island Ferry, enjoying the wind and the waters, watching the crew, and sighting our heroic Statue of Liberty. Oh!

And, oh, the colors everywhere, of everything, of everyone! Not a mishmash, but a color for each and every thing and every one. Bright primary colors in cars and clothes and food. Lots of subtle colors in buildings and hues in the faces of people. Isn't COLOR wonderful! I ran to the museums—the Met, the Whitney, the Museum of Modern Art—and came away stunned with the power of the individual artist. I felt physically expanded while mentally admiring or being confused by what I saw.

In class I took a "go-to-hell" attitude and danced for my own sweet self. No more 'Simon Says' obedience. No more imitating the company dancers. I let my hair hang down and flow with the movements, wore an old sweater. I got my dancer-self back again. I smiled so much, Peter joked, "What's come over you? Are you in love?"

A member of the *Humphrey-Weidman Dance Company,* Peter Hamilton taught its modern dance technique at the Studio, alternating with Charles. About 5'6", Peter was young and handsome with blonde hair long enough to fall over his blue eyes. He had a strong, spare dancer's body with reserves of energy that never ran out. Although a demanding teacher, Peter smiled at us a lot, unlike most dance teachers. It made us work to get better technique to please him as well as ourselves.

Ada Reif, a terrific dance class accompanist, could improvise the precise musical quality the dance dynamics required. She played her best for Peter's exhilarating classes.

When Ada was not there, Freda Miller often accompanied class. With neither there, Charles or Peter walloped the rhythms for class on a snare drum or tom-tom. Both were excellent percussionists, cueing us with accents and changes in volume. There was no *barre* or mirror in The Studio. We danced barefoot. Class lasted one hour and a half. We refined our basic skills in the class warm up, which was set and without interruption. It began with deep breathing, a signature aspect of the Humphrey-Weidman Technique that carried all through the vigorous exercises.

To warm up the feet, Charles used a Denishawn version of ballet's *petit battement,* dividing the class in half to take turns. It had a little, polite gesture at the end. Then we went into movements fully involving the body; a variety of body bends that developed from simple to integrated successions. Then there were the suspended leg successions. More of the class went on the diagonal from USL to DSR.

This included the floor traveling "modern dance split" with back leg bent, which progressed from chest lift to forward stretch (and alternate). There was a vigorous hopping series: one bent leg forward, side, back; straight leg front, side, back; and then again, with the "pick up foot" (bending the hopping leg). There was a series of balances: count one step out in attitude, bend to floor, return to attitude, and change sides; four counts the first time, then three, two, and one, making sure to hold balance. The catch came by having to relax over the standing leg and then pull up strong, balanced, before the alternate side.

Many moves in H-W were off center and I loved that. A series of alternate off-center turns or spins were done in *plie'* on the diagonal. Charles also had a sequence of fast, low turns with a quick one-foot stop that led in a circle around the studio. Leaping variations went into barrel turns. Floor work included exercises with increasing and decreasing dynamics. Falls included a spiral fall. The dance phrases put many H-W factors together. Where ballet arms moved through set positions, here the arms moved from momentum. Balances were not still, but floating suspensions. *Momentum* and *flow* were vital characteristics of H-W technique, one move melding into the next without perceivable transitions. Repertory or new dance inventions were taught toward the later part of class.

The Studio Theatre was now very busy with rehearsals following classes. Doris was there, working with José Limón for a January 5th performance. No longer working at night, I could go. The very size of José and the space he consumed were impressive, but to me he seemed earthbound in *Lament for Ignacio Sánchez Mejías*. The women dancers, Letitia Ide as the Figure of Destiny and Meg

Mundy as the Figure of a Woman, were slight beside him. Frederic Lorca's poem was not familiar, the readings difficult to understand, but pain and remorse spoke through the dance. Modern Dance was exciting because it was personal and could speak of the human condition in any aspect.

Most evenings, I went my backstage rounds seeking replacement jobs. *Street Scene* had recently opened at the Adelphi, too soon for replacements. With what I thought was encouragement from the dance captain, I paid my way into *Annie Get Your Gun* with Ethel Merman, choreography by Helen Tamiris. The high spot was the Indian dance, *Wild Horse*, performed by Daniel Nagrin. There was nothing demanding for the girl dancers but a cowgirl line dance and later ballroom dancing. *Agnes de Mille's Bloomer Girl* was in town, then going on tour. Now I was in New York, I wanted to stay. I had the impression that road companies were lesser productions than Broadway, until I talked with Ann Dunbar, another Jacob's Pillow friend.

Ann, a lovely girl with long honey-blond hair, asked a pointed question. "Do you think the demands of a show are different on tour? It is the same show that was just on Broadway, right?" Ann had been in de Mille's *Carousel.* "You have to watch out for your back with de Mille. She loves backbends."

Ann also convinced me now there would be few if any auditions until spring, that I had better take any job I could get. So, the next evening, I checked backstage at the *New York City Center* where *Bloomer Girl* was running. Standing backstage, waiting to speak with the dance captain, a Bloomer Girl came walking my way and it was Carolyn!

"De Mille is working on a new show and she's shuffling dancers in and out of her shows all over the place. I thought I might do *Oklahoma!* but here I am in *Bloomer Girl*. I've only been in two weeks. I love the show. Nanette Fabray is so funny." Replacements? Some dancers were trying to decide about going on the road. Carolyn promised to let me know of anything.

Days went by. No word. Late one January afternoon, going home after Thalia's ballet class, I passed the City Center stage door again. No point pounding on the door at 4:30 p.m., but my feet took me there anyway. To my surprise, the doorman let me in.

"Would the dance captain be here now?"

"Yep! She's upstairs, practicing or auditioning. You go up them stairs. Third floor, you'll find her and some others." Fragments of music and voices led me to a rehearsal room where about twenty dancers were trying out dance combinations in a closed audition. An older girl with brown wavy hair, wearing slacks and a dark sweater, turned to me.

"You here to audition?"

"Yes. Uh, if I may."

"Are you Equity?"

"Yes."

She told me to warm up while she worked with the boys. Excited, I began to take off my slacks, then remembered in dismay that I did not have on a leotard. No, I was in my Independent Dancer mode and had gone so far as to wear white TSCW shorts and an old sweater to Thalia's class. No tights. My long hair was only restrained with a barrette. All the other girls were in the classic auditioning attire of black leotard, tights and slippers with their hair in ballet buns.

No time to worry about it as I joined in learning dance phrases from the show's choreography. Then came the lifts and along with the other girls, I ran to jump into the arms of a total stranger, sure I would be caught. In one, a very strong preparation was needed for the boys to catch us just above our knees and hold us high against their chests, so we could arch far back, arms open. Next, with no comment, the dance captain demonstrated an unusual turn—actually a spiral of turns in one place, but on three levels: high off-center *attitude* turn, down onto knees with circling back bend, on up to original position and arm circle. This was done swiftly. Seeing our eyes big, she gave a little Mona Lisa grin, then repeated the turn. Now we were next. I thought of her image and tried to produce it. Finally we were asked to turn swiftly and fall on our knees, without tipping forward. Then she asked whether any of us had any modern dance training. It was as good a time as ever to speak up and mention my modern dance experience and knowing Carolyn, too.

It had been a fair audition, I thought. It had been easier to concentrate in that setting than on a stage, taking turns with many others. I felt pretty good about it. Maybe the captain had "seen me," as Louis Sullivan had seen Frank Lloyd Wright. But no postcard came after three days. No message for me when I swallowed my pride and stopped backstage again. Outside in the cold January chill, a great gust of wind swirled dust around me. I deflated like an old balloon blown along a dirty street. Sullen, leaden with inertia, I stubbornly waited for the next hard wind to shove me along. What did it matter? I was just one more little bit of clutter on the streets of Great New York City.

Back to class; the daily bread of class. Funds were getting meager again but classes sacrosanct. I went dutifully to find life had a present for me. Doris Humphrey came to teach class, filling in for Charles. Here was the Priestess of

Modern Dance, one of the original Four Pioneers of American Modern Dance, right here in The Studio. I respected and had a growing affection for Charles, awe for Doris Humphrey. Tall, pale but handsome, she came to face the class with mixed emotions. She was fully dressed, reluctant to actively move, but as her intelligent eyes appraised our warm-up, Doris became genuinely interested in us. She began to make small corrections as we were in motion but when we got to the off-center leg development suspensions, she clapped her hands smartly and stopped the class.

"What are you doing? Don't you know that a true suspension never stops?"

Briefly she reiterated the H-W theory that the rise and fall of the body constantly affected movement. She removed her jacket and demonstrated, hand to chest as it rose and fell. Breathing to lift the chest, holding the air to allow the suspension was vital. Breath control was also important in the follow-through fall, which must pour and not collapse. Doris demonstrated the wrong and right use of the shoulder/arm/hand sequence in off-center suspensions. While the height of the extending leg was important, the height of the suspension was more so. The emphasis was on the rise above gravity. And again, most important, we must remember that a true suspension never stops.

"Delight in delay!" said Doris Humphrey.

She demonstrated lifting her upper body, shoulders, arms and head in a harmony of motion. Her face was lifted as her arms moved overhead to crest, floating a long moment before descending softly to her side. The action was expansive in size, emotional in the curving motions, and the suspension heroic in going above center. Doris's beauty touched us all. As she demonstrated again, she spoke,"De-light in-n-n de-la-ay... De-light in-n de-lay."

As she hummed the word *in,* retarding the passing of the peak of the suspension, Doris's whole person seemed to float. Then came the resolve, with just a germ of momentum to pulse the motion on. As the class sought to make this technique our own, Doris kept coaching us. This was not a sappy, wishy-washy sentimental movement! It took vigorous strength. The soft, full descent took control in timing. I caught on that the suspension went full circle. There was the slightest hint of impetus felt in the upper chest and back that carried up to "break" the hands open at the crest. As a cup filled above the brim spills over with one more drop, I felt a fountain flowing up from inside that spilled over, and I could not keep from smiling. Heretofore, my suspensions had been intuitive; now Doris gave me an insight that cleared away excess and supplied the specific technique. At our loud applause as class ended, Doris smiled brightly, but only for a moment.

After class, I learned Doris no longer attempted to perform; arthritis had acutely affected her hip. What a tragedy! This was my only class with Doris Humphrey, but it was the one I would have chosen. Just as Natalie Krassovska had given me my *grand tour jeté,* Doris gave me my suspensions. She was around The Studio now, working with José. Pauline Lawrence, José's wife, was also there working on costumes. That same week, Doris returned with a box of practice clothes to give away. One by one, she tossed her things into the class. Catching my eye, "Here!" she said, tossing a pair of black trunks my way. The trunks were the old-fashioned kind; flimsy rayon with no elastic at waist or leg; just a cotton string that tied center front, but they were a treasure to me. Then what should I do with them. How could I—*I!* dare wear Doris Humphrey's trunks! I finally decided I would wear them for luck opening nights and prayed there would be some.

Back home, I stopped by the hall table for any mail. No notes about calls. No letters for me. One manila postcard face down. I idly turned it over. And gasped.

Office of John C. Wilson
10 Rockefeller Plaza
New York, 20, N.Y.

Dear Miss Traver;
      Please come back stage Friday night before the show around 8:15.
      I'll introduce you to the business manager and we can discuss rehearsal time, etc.
      Sincerely yours,
      Emy St. Just

I inhaled in shock, slapped the card to my breast and ran furiously up my five flights like a rabbit to its den with the last carrot. I placed the card by itself on my bedspread to read it over again. *Bloomer Girl* wants me! I've made it. Friday night. Oh Lord! Today IS FRIDAY!

Thrilled, I joined a cluster of dancers backstage at the City Center and followed dance captain Emy St. Just back to the audition room where we all signed our contracts: $50 a week for rehearsal; $100 per week for performance on tour, travel paid. Then I popped into the girls' dressing room.

Carolyn saw me in her mirror and jumped up. "Oh, I was hoping you made it. Emy just told me tonight. You'll love the show." Then a pretty blond girl came in the door. Betty Jones!

"Shirley! Are you coming into the show? Ruthanne is in it, too! And so was Winky, but now de Mille wants her for a new show, *Brigadoon.*"

Emy arranged it for the dancers to see *Bloomer Girl* from the house. We were eager to see what we had signed on to do. The story concerned a rebellious daughter, Evelina, who agrees with her Aunt Dolly's ideas about freedom for women and emancipation of the slaves at a period just before the Civil War. Her father wishes her to marry a Southerner to improve his manufacturing business. All the singing was fine, the costumes ante-bellum and beautiful. But where was the dancing? Not until Act I, Scene 3.

The dancing Bloomer Girls marched onto the scene at Dolly Bloomer's paper, *The Lily.* All in bloomers, they ridiculed women's place in the home in *"It was good enough for grandma, but it ain't good enough for us!"* Further on, Daisy, Dolly Bloomer's maid, had a solo, singing and dancing a strip tease down to her pantalets in *T'Morra' T'morra',* Opening Act II, there was a charmingly beautiful waltz, featuring one girl and man. A danced parade of protest, and then what astonished us all, de Mille's *Civil War Ballet.* It was a modern ballet that dramatized the Civil War, treating each dancer as an individual at that time while advancing the action of the show. Usually dancers take bows *en masse* at curtain calls, but here the four foremost dancers had the first bow on their own.

Emy said she would let me know when to come to rehearsal, but days passed without hearing a word. *Waitngwithoutknowing* was one word I hated. I studied my *Bloomer Girl* souvenir program: film people who wanted to get back to the stage developed the show. Lilith James became fascinated with Amelia Bloomer, who fought for freedom of speech, from slavery, and from confining clothes. James's husband, Dan, came up with an idea for an historic musical. He took the idea to Nat Gladstone as a film possibility. Gladstone was looking for material for composer Harold Arlen and lyricist E.Y. Harburg, who also wanted to work in theatre again. Writers Fred Saidie and Sig Herzig, fictionalized events compatible with Amelia Bloomer's time. Actual historical events were not incorporated into the story, but the time period was historical America before the Civil War. John C. Wilson, director, became co-producer, auditioning players with only Arlen's singing on tape. Celeste Holm, David Brooks, Margaret Douglas, Joan McCracken and Dooley Wilson signed on as leads. When Wilson played Arlen 's tape of *The Eagle and Me*, he won Agnes de Mille over to choreograph the show. Lemuel Ayers signed on for scene design; Miles White for costume design.

The original dancers were chosen by Agnes de Mille from her association with dancers from *Ballet Jooss,* her previous Broadway shows, *Oklahoma!*, *Carousel,* and from Chorus Equity auditions. With her new husband overseas in WW II, de Mille wanted to do a serious ballet about women during a war. Assured she could, she agreed to take it on and set right to work. When the producers encouraged de Mille to stress the exultant aspects of war, she protested and arguments over the Civil War Ballet continued through new versions by de Mille and threats to cut it by her bosses. Then

Wilson firmly told her it must go. With the support of Harold Arlen, the one boss on her side, de Mille pleaded that the dancers be allowed to perform the ballet once, on opening night. With full costume and theatrical lighting, the dancers danced out their stories. The ballet was a stunning success and stayed in the show. *Bloomer Girl* opened in the fall of 1944 and ran 654 performances on Broadway. I learned all this and more from the Official *Bloomer Girl* Program while anxiously waiting to rehearse. Monday. Tuesday. Wednesday of our one week rehearsals and nothing. Then another postcard came from Emy.

> Dear Miss Traver.
>   Please come to rehearsal 12 o'clock
> Thursday.
>   Wear something to cover your knees.
>   Emy St. Just

I crumpled to the floor in a heap of relief.

At our first rehearsal, we learned the saucy march *Grandma,* but I was not to be one of the floor scrubbers. Nor would I be in the waltz, to my regret. Then Emy beckoned to me, saying, "I want to teach you to run on your knees. Emy had decided to leave *Bloomer Girl* and was giving her part to me!

Emy told me she had taught another girl, but Agnes was not satisfied with her. Now began the half turn drop to the floor onto the knees, then the run on my knees directly down stage. How far? The depth of the stage. It was important to cover space, not wobble in place. The body must be held erect from head to knee. At my sober expression after a few tries, Emy consoled me, saying I would have a big petticoat under my skirt to cushion my knees. Then she warned me against running up my skirt and being stopped. When my knees would get too tender for this, I would have to run on my toes in a sitting position, low, close to the floor. After I tried that and fell forward on my hands, Emy gave her little Mona Lisa smile. "I know. It's harder, but sometimes you will have to use it."

We turned to the next challenge: the high, off-center *attitude* turn that spiraled down to the knees and up again. The turn was preceded by a breaking out from a tense stand, with a desperate run forward into a backward run into the turn, which must be seamless. There were two revolutions, first the *attitude* and second the turn drop to the floor, my body circling in a backbend on my knees to rise up again to circle the sky with my hand. It was a gorgeous dance phrase when Emy danced it. I watched her every performance the days before I was to take over.

There were new leads, too. Pat McClarney for Evelina and Arthur Maxwell for Jeff, as well as other dancers. All in all, we had seven rehearsals and only one run-through on stage with the orchestra. I asked Caroline about Emy. She was Dutch and had been a member of the *Kurt Jooss Ballet i*n the Netherlands. The company left to escape the German invasion, going to England, where Emy met Agnes de Mille, who brought Emy here. I could see why she could dance the *Civil War Ballet* with such passion. And now, why she decided to let it go.

"I 'm still surprised she gave it to me. Not to another dancer in the show."

"She asked me about your modern dance. I told her what I knew, dancing in Texas," Carolyn said. "Emy told me you were the only one she could find to do it."

CHAPTER TEN

Winter 1947
   New York City Center

"Saturday, February 16th, 1947 at 2:30 p.m. I shall make my debut on Broadway!" I announced this to the world at large on my way to the theatre, completely unconcerned that the world cared not. Now my dream of dance and the truth of my life were one.

I signed in. From then on, each demand was as a labor in a folk tale: if I accomplished each demand with skill, I would be changed from an impoverished nobody to an Acknowledged Professional Dancer in the Supreme Theatre of the World. I went in early so I could warm up and put on my makeup without distraction. It was five months since I had performed. It was so good to be wearing the satiny makeup again. Home! Home! I was home again. Then to the dresser, Margaret, who gave me my Bloomer Girl costume: white pinafore ruffled blouse with black tie, yellow-and gray striped skirt and matching bloomers, spats, black leather belt. And I had new black ballet slippers. What a thrill to tell the clerk at Capezio's "Just charge them to *Bloomer Girl,* thank you!"

Emy called the new dancers on stage to check makeup. "No eye shadow?" she asked me. "Only mascara. My eyes are too deep set." She said not a word about the dances. As the others left the stage, I took a quick look about then went dead center stage to certify this paramount moment in my life. The curtain was open. Thousands of empty seats rose in tiers from floor to the vast upper reaches of this great golden theatre. Seats that were waiting for people expecting a good show. My air bubble floated from heart to head, then plunged to my feet as ushers entered the auditorium. I fled.

Back in the dressing room, Carolyn showed me the correct way to wear my long hair parted in the center, then curved over each ear then tucked into a black net snood. At the first note of the Overture, we ran down to join a cadre of sixteen Bloomer Girls.

Act I, Scene 3:

The main parlor of a bordello with Victorian red wallpaper and drapes, potted palms, an exotic screen. Now this is the home of *The Lily,* Dolly Bloomer's political newsletter. Evelina enters to join Dolly and sings *Good Enough for Grandma.* The Bloomer Girls march to the song, taking militant poses or imitating: Grandma's dreary chores, cooking, sewing, scrubbing. Evelina sings a protest:

> *She had no voice in government and bondage was her fate...*
> *She only knew what love is, from eight to half past eight!*
> *And that's a Hell of a fate!*
> *Look twice before you step on the fair sex of the Earth*
> *Beware our secret weapon, we could stop giving birth!*
> *Take that for what it's worth!*

On the way back upstairs, Betty, asked, "How'd it go?"

"OK, I think, but next is the Fashion Show and I haven't even seen my costume."

"Oh, brother! I hope you've worn hoop skirts!"

"No!"

Out of the bloomers into long white stockings and pantalets. A fancy headdress—a crown set with jet beads and a white feather bird on each side, covering the ears. Attached to this crown in back was a flow of white organdy piped with black velvet. A white organdy chinstrap held this on. There was also a jet-beaded necklace to clasp quickly. Then back to Margaret in wardrobe.

"Name!" demanded Margaret.

"Traver!" First a hoop skirt. I stepped into it, hitched it to my waist only to have it fall to the floor like a collapsed drinking cup. Margaret hastily pinned it and handed next a huge petticoat, then the dress, a black velvet gown. It was beyond a doubt the biggest dress I had ever seen, movies included. Almost off the shoulder, the dress descended over the hoop to the floor in three grand layers, each with a deeply scalloped edge. The top layer had white *fleur-de-lis* scattered through a field of black velvet covering the torso from shoulder to knee. Centered in the bodice was a V of white organdy crisscrossed with black velvet piping. Below this black velvet skirt was a second layer of lime green scallops, and below that the third layer of white taffeta scallops extending to the floor. The black velvet sleeves, inset with white organdy cuffs, flared extravagantly from the elbow to a long black velvet train. It was magnificent. It also weighed seventy-five pounds.

I had not previously worried about this ante-bellum fashion show, but now I was trying to maneuver to place without being able to see where to place my feet. A dancer, also in a glamorous gown, who entered before me, whispered, "Don't forget to bell your hoop!"

"What?" She was gone. Then Carolyn floated up in a pale pink confection. "How do you bell a hoop?" I begged.

"Easy," she smiled. "Just swing it forward and back as you walk." Then she, too, was gone on stage.

"And be careful not to step back through your hoop as you curtsey. You'll trip," warned Patty. "I did and had a terrible time getting up again." Her warning shook me but saved me, too. Lester, one of the sons-in-law, was to escort me down three steps I could not see. Then moving forward to perform a grand curtsey, I stepped to the side and avoided entrapment. Managing to rise without staggering with the weight of the dress, I paraded and circled to place with a haughty smile. Next Evelina modeled a dress, came forward and dropped her skirt to reveal bloomers!

End of Act I, and a backstage *entire act,* as sixteen hoop-skirted women tried to get off the stage while stagehands tried to get on.

Act II, Scene 1

The scene is a village park, the action an informal mix of dancers and singers, promenading after church with Evelina singing *Sunday in Cicero Falls,* a song about hypocrisy. The singing becomes a fugue, but it is interrupted by a parade led by Dolly Bloomer for *Women's Right*s and against slavery. Dancers were now in fancy band uniforms with matching hats. Carolyn and I were partners, entering with high prances into cartwheels, rejoining hands to go down in splits and then rise together still attached.

Act II, Scene 2 takes place in jail. Pompeii sings his *Railroad Song*; Dolly sings *Satin Bows and Silver Shoes* to Evelina, also in jail.

Act II, Scene 3:

This is *The Lily*'s version of *Uncle Tom's Cabin*, played in an opera house. The chorus sings the story, offstage. A dancer dramatically dances Liza crossing the ice. Then with little Eva resting on a couch, Daisy as Topsy sings and then dances to *Never Was Born*, cakewalking with hitch-kicks in a buck rhythm. In a flurry of warning trumpets, a slave trader drags Uncle Tom (played by Pompeii) to the block to be sold.

Backstage I was putting on Emy's costume for the Civil War Ballet. When it fit well, I took that as a good sign. The costume was that of a countrywoman, two full white petticoats, one ruffled; no pantalets or bloomers. The full skirt was double, the underskirt a soft orange, the overskirt, black. The deep orange bodice extended to a V over the skirt. It had a double collar of yellow and orange and three-quarter sleeves. I wiggled and stretched. I could kick to the moon in it. Putting my hands on my knees, I prayed not to run up my petticoat. John Begg and I searched for each other to practice our lift. We hugged each other quick and hard. "Merde!" John whispered for luck.

"You, too!"

I was practicing my kneels when a stagehand shouted, "Heads up!" and the whole stage went bananas. I was blocked twice trying to get out of the way and to my place down stage right in the dark. There had been no tech rehearsal for us replacements. Then I heard the drum beat! I couldn't miss my cue for my first performance! I pressed forward desperately in the dark. From somewhere, Margit grabbed my hand and pulled me behind her. "Here! Here! OK?"

"OK," I panted, heart pounding.

The prologue to the *Civil War Ballet* takes place before the curtain. The Drums of War are beating. Standing down stage right in a green spotlight, Scott, a Union Soldier, stands with one hand behind his back as with his other arm, he swings his Union Army jacket in circles over his head 32 times in a call to arms. Other soldiers, in twos and threes, rush in behind him, followed by the wives and sweethearts bidding farewell. The men rush off. Margit, *The Girl in Rose,* anxiously helps Scott put on his Union jacket. They embrace and he runs off to war with Margit and I waving last goodbyes. Eight women are left standing, backs to the audience, as the drum beat continues eight more times. The curtains part to reveal a dark, devastated countryside under stormy skies. We each walk stalwartly into the lonely, frightening days of the Civil War, each taking a particular place.

As the music begins with the theme from *Grandma* in a minor key, Margit as the *Girl in Rose* stands downstage right, feet together and holding her skirt out to each side for moments. She steps out into an arabesque, arms circling, searching, one way, then the other. As she starts the third arabesque, she breaks out weeping, and runs off.

With one fist pressed against my other hand, elbows sharply bent, I face upstage during Margit's dancing, sustaining my control until its force turns me to drop to my knees. Arms extended wide, palms open, I run the depth of the stage on my knees, contract and collapse into a side fall; contract again to lift my body up onto one arm and beat the earth blindly with my free fist. I rise into a fast, tight circle in *relevé* that then opens into a wide run that carries me all the way upstage left, my fist in my hand again for control.

As I stand facing upstage again, other women by ones and twos have their dance phrases to express the loneliness and terror of being left behind, not- knowing. Again the anguish builds up in me, and I turn to rush forward in a fast pleading run that pauses, suspends, then runs backward into the desperate off-center attitude turn that sweeps me down onto my knees to continue spiraling up into a stance facing upstage. Then one arm describes an arc across the dark sky. Dramatically, this spiral turn carries me from the heights to the depths of despair, on up into a sustaining courage.

Now Cecile, The Woman in Black, comes slowly forward, her body in labor pains. She drops to the floor into a birthing sequence, first alone, then aided by other women. The ballet continues until the music cues the return of the wounded soldiers, forlorn in disrepair. At the sight of them we all freeze, staring. There is a silence. As I see my lover, I throw back my head, my body in a deep contraction as I stamp the floor in joy and then fling myself forward into John's arms to be carried high in the lift. All the women rush forward with me into the lifts except The Woman in Black. As she learns she is widowed, other women come to comfort her, and then I, too, before exiting stage right.

Intensely I watched the reconciliation between Margit and Scott from the wings, waiting for my cue to return. Then I remembered I was to hitch up my black overskirt to reveal my brighter orange skirt, but where-oh-where were the hooks! Frantically I stuffed wads of my black skirt into my waistband and prayed it would stay as I reentered with syncopated jump-steps of joy. These led to a hyper-extended strut of celebration among us all that climaxed with the women lifted, arching far back, held cantilevered on the men's chests as they turned. All joined hands in a community circle that broke open to lead Scott and Margit and me, one behind the other, stage center where we danced *grand pas de basque*. I felt like a great bell ringing as we leaped side-to-side as the curtain fell.

Then came a rush backstage to get in place for the joyous *Coda*. This carried the celebration across the stage before a beautiful, blue sky with cirrus clouds and sunshine. I led it with a prancing plié/relevé walk with Agnes's "angel arms." Instead of using the arms raised and the shoulders going up and down, Agnes used the shoulders going forward and back repeatedly, like wings. Scott carried Margot on his shoulders as we went back and forth to the music of *The Eagle and Me*. On the last phrase, "*I gotta be freeeee...,*" we paused, open arms and stance wide. And when the music continued with "*...the eagle and Meeeee,*" I poured into my pinwheel turn and beat my wings offstage, transported.

In the final scene, there is a reprise of *When the Boys Come Home*.

With Jeff and Evelina united, the entire cast sings the finale.

Margit pulled me beside her in the front row. Pressing my hand, she cued me to move forward with her, Scott and Cecile, for our curtain call. As I bowed, the applause sounded like a thousand butterfly wings. I tried to sing along but could not stop smiling. Oh, bless Agnes de Mille! Emy! Papa Shawn! In my rapture, I clasped Margit in a grateful embrace. Then it was Scott and Cecil with us all laughing and shouting, "We did it! We did it!" In moments the stage was cleared. It was all to be done again tonight.

"I'm not taking my makeup off between shows. When we go out to dinner, we don't bother," said Caroline. "Penn Central okay with you?"

Dinner? Oh! Well, why not? Waiting for me at the stage door I found Dottie, Irene and Eduard, all beaming. Eduard asked me to dinner, graciously including Dottie and Irene. Carolyn passed by and pointed in the direction of the Penn Central Hotel. I hesitated. Eduard gave me a hug, "Go on," he said, "This is your new life. Go with your dancers."

Before the evening performance, Emy told me my flying hair was not good for the ballet. Did I know how to put my hair in a bun? I thought I was finally rid of my waitress bun, but it was a small price to pay. She said nothing about the dancing. I wrote her a note, thanking her for my beautiful part.

Packing my trunk for the tour, I kept singing and laughing. "I just have to dance!" Grabbing my Kleenex box, I tossed "white roses" to my audience until I caught a glint of green in the air. Five twenty-dollar bills! How could I have forgotten I hid them? With my new paycheck, I now had $200 smackers!

"Oh, Daddy! Daddy! You see! I did it! I jumped over that old brick wall!"

No one in the family came to see the show. Pummie was still in England. Daddy did send a wire: "We knew you would do it." Not sure how he meant it, I decided to take it as, at least, backhanded recognition of my work.

What new challenges to my dancing were next?

172

PHOTO 1
Shirley Traver, 1927, Five Years Old
Paxtang, Pennsylvania
Underwood Collection

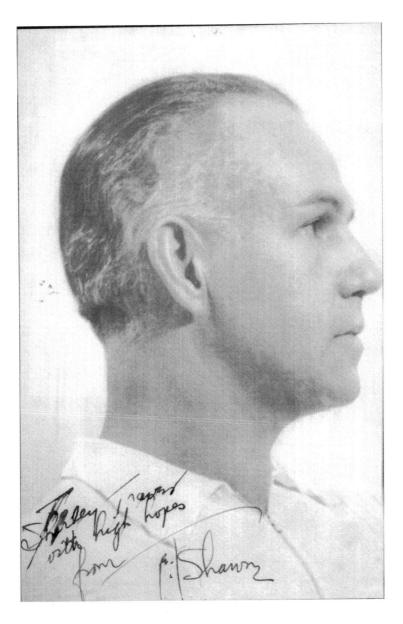

PHOTO 2
Ted Shawn, Jacob's Pillow
University of the Dance, Lee, MA, August 1942
Underwood Collection

PHOTO 3
Ruth St. Denis at Jacob's Pillow
University of the Dance, Lee, MA, August 1942
(Tommie nickname)
Underwood Collection

PHOTO 4
Barton Mumaw as Pierrot at
Jacob's Pillow Dance Festival
Lee, MA, August 1942
John Lindquist Photograph
Copyright © Harvard Theatre Collection, Houghton Library

PHOTO 5
August 1943: Jacob's Pillow Dance Festival, Lee, MA
FR: Virginia Bosler, Ruthanne Welch, Jean Tachau,
Marian Kirk BR: Geni Whitlow, Betty Jones,
Shirley Traver
Lindquist Photograph
Copyright © Harvard Theatre Collection, Houghton Library

PHOTO 6
Shirley Traver on Roof of Administration Building
Texas State College for Women, Denton, TX, April 1945
Photographer Diane

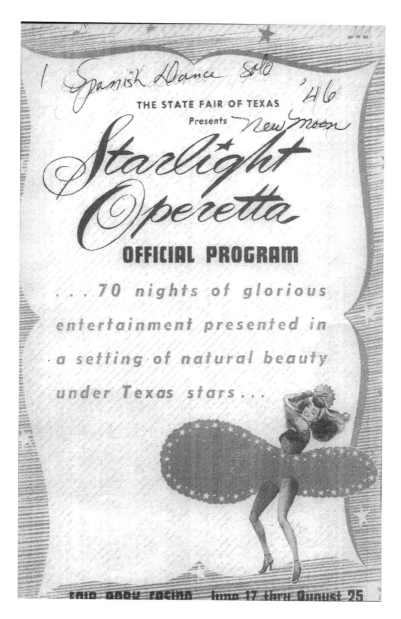

PHOTO 7
Starlight Operettas Program for 1945 Season, Dallas, TX

PHOTO 8
Shirley Traver as Cancan Girl in *Maytime*
Starlight Operettas, Dallas, TX 1946
Photographer Thomas Cone

PHOTO 9
Shirley Traver as Gypsy in *Maytime*
Starlight Operettas, Dallas, TX 1945
Photographer Thomas Cone

PHOTO 10
Bloomer Girls in Act I *Bloomer Girl*
in performance at Biltmore Theatre
Los Angeles, CA, June 1947
Gisella Weidner, Carolyn George, Margit Dekova,
Jean Kinsella, Sharry Traver, Susan Stewart
Photographer Jerome Robinson

PHOTO 11
Sharry Traver in *Bloomer Girl*
in performance at Biltmore Theatre
Los Angeles, CA, June 1947
Photographer Jerome Robinson

PHOTO 12
Hubert Dillworth (Bill)
singing *Eagle and Me Bloomer Girl*
In Performance at Biltmore Theatre
in Los Angeles, CA 1947
Photographer Jerome Robinson

PHOTO 13
Women in *Bloomer Girl Civil War Ballet,*
Biltmore Theatre Los Angeles, CA
Betty Jones, Gisella Weidner, Carolyn George,
Cecil Bergman, Sharry Traver
Photographer Jerome Robinson

PHOTO 14
Bloomer Girl Civil War Ballet, Biltmore Theatre
Los Angeles, CA, June 1947
Carolyn George, Cecile Bergman, Ruthanne Welch
(Far Right: John Begg)
Photographer Jerome Robinson

PHOTO 15
Celebrating War End in *Bloomer Girl Civil War Ballet,*
Los Angeles, CA, 1947, Biltmore Theatre
Sharry Traver, Scott Merrill, Margit Dekova & Dancers
Photographer Jerome Robinson

PHOTO 16
Coda to Civil War Ballet in *Bloomer Girl*
Biltmore Theatre in Los Angeles, CA 1947
Frank Reynolds, Jean Kinsella, Scott Merrill,
Margit Dekova, Sharry Traver
Photographer Jerome Robinson

PHOTO 17
House Divided, Charles Weidman as Abraham Lincoln,
Spencer Teagle as His Voice
Charles Weidman Dance Company,
Mansfield Theatre, NY, April 1948
Photograph by Fred Fehl
Courtesy of Gabriel Pinski

PHOTO 18
House Divided Charles Weidman Dance Company
Mansfield Theatre, NY, April 1978
Emily Frankel, Peter Hamilton, Sharry Traver,
Charles Weidman, Betts Lee, Marc Breaux, Nick Vanoff,
Felisa Condé, Carl Morris
Photograph by Fred Fehl
Courtesy of Gabriel Pinski

PHOTO 19
Lynch Town, Charles Weidman Dance Company,
1978 National Tour
Sharry Traver, Betts Lee, Emily Frankel, Felisa Condé
Underwood Collection

PHOTO 20
The Courtship of Arthur and Al, Pose on 1978 Tour
Beavers: Emily Frankel, Sharry Traver, Felisa Condé,
Jack Ferris, Charles Weidman, Carl Morris, Betts Lee
Underwood Collection

PHOTO 21
The Owl Who Was God
Charles Weidman Dance Company
Mansfield Theatre, NY, April 1978
Sharry Traver, Betty Osgood, Felisa Condé,
Carl Morris, Betts Lee, Marc Breaux
Photograph by Fred Fehl
Courtesy of Gabriel Pinski

PHOTO 22
Weidman Dancers & Accompanist on 1978 National Tour
Betty Osgood, Emily Frankel, Betts Lee, Freda Miller,
Accompanist, Sharry Traver, Felisa Condé
Underwood Collection

PHOTO 23
And Daddy Was A Fireman
Charles Weidman Dance Company
at Baltimore Arts Museum, Baltimore, MD, 1978 Tour
Betty Osgood, Marc Breaux, Sharry Traver,
Charles Weidman, Felisa Condé, Nick Vanoff,
Emily Frankel
Photographer Unknown

PHOTO 24
Posing Outside The Music Box Theatre
During *Ballet Ballads,* Sharry Traver, Katherine Litz,
Margaret Cuddy, Ellen Albertini
June 1948, New York, NY
Underwood Collection

MAXINE ELLIOTT'S THEATRE

Six Performances Only

Sun. Eve., May 9; Mon. Eve., May 10; Wed. Eve., May 12; Fri. Eve., May 14; Sun. Mat. & Eve., May 16, 1948

Under the Sponsorship of
American National Theatre and Academy
THE EXPERIMENTAL THEATRE INC.

presents

BALLET BALLADS

Written by John Latouche   Composed by Jerome Moross

Produced by Nat Karson
Directed by Mary Hunter
Choral and Musical Director—Hugh Ross
Associate Conductor—Gerard Samuel
Choreographers—Katherine Litz, Paul Godkin, Hanya Holm
Pianists—John Lesko, Jr. and Mordecai Sheinkman
Production devised, designed and lighted by Nat Karson

SUSANNA AND THE ELDERS

Choreography by Katherine Litz

THE PARSON .... RICHARD HARVEY
SUSANNA (The Dancer) .... KATHERINE LITZ
SUSANNA (The Singer) .... SHEILA VOGELLE
THE CEDAR FROM LEBANON .... SHARRY TRAVER
THE LITTLE JUNIPER TREE .... ELLEN R. ALBERTINI
THE HANDMAIDENS .... MARGARET CUDDY, BARBARA DOWNIE
THE ELDER (Moe) .... FRANK SEABOLT
THE ELDER (Joe) .... ROBERT TROUT
THE ANGEL .... JAMES R. NYGREN

The Ladies and Gentlemen of The Congregation   The Singing Ensemble

The Scene: A revival meeting. The Parson takes his sermon from the story of Susanna and The Elders as found in the Apocrypha.

PHOTO 25
Susanna and The Elders in *Ballet Ballads*
The Music Box Theatre, New York, NY, June 1948
Courtesy of Gabriel Pinski

PHOTO 26
Susanna and The Elders in *Ballet Ballads*
The Music Box Theatre, New York, NY, June, 1948
Foreground: Sharry Traver, Margaret Cuddy,
Katherine Litz (seated), Ellen Albertini
Underwood Collection

PHOTO 27
Dancing on Stage in *Willie the Weepier* in *Ballet Ballads*
at The Music Box Theatre, New York, NY, 1948
Dancers Surround Paul Godwin as Willie
Underwood Collection

PHOTO 28
Dancing on Stage in *Davy Crockett*
at The Music Box Theatre, New York, NY, June 1978
Barbara Ashley, Ellen Albertini,
Margaret Cuddy, Sharry Traver
Underwood Collection

PHOTO 29
Ballet Ballads Rehearsal with Annabelle Lyons,
Hanya Holm, Jerome Moross, John Latouche,
NewYork, NY, May 1948
Underwood Collection

PHOTO 30
Final Pose of
If This Isn't Love Dance in *Finian's Rainbow,*
46th Street Theatre, New York, NY, 1948
Margaret McAllen, Anna Mitten, Sharry Traver,
Kathleen Stanford, Erin Harris, Eleanor Gregory,
Harry Rogers, James Tarbutton, Gene Wilson,
James Flash Reilly, Roger Orthadiene
Photographer William Hawkins

PHOTO 31
Margaret Cuddy, 1948
Underwood Collection

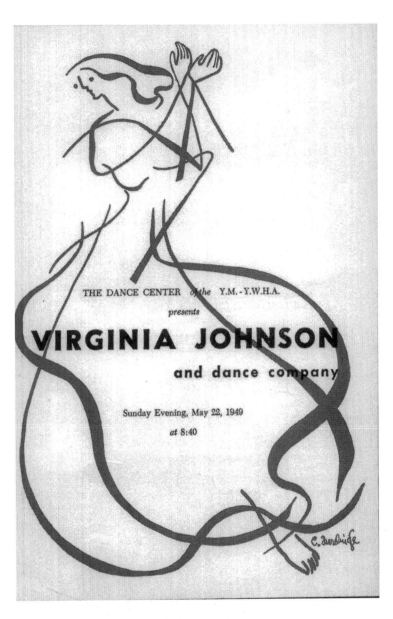

PHOTO 32
Virginia Johnson Program for *The Invisible Wife,*
92nd Street YMHA/YWHA, New York, NY 1949

PHOTO 33
Sharry Traver as Mother
James Nigren as Son in *The Invisible Wife*
Courtesy of Dance Magazine, August 1949
Photographer Otto Fenn

PHOTO 34
Margaret Cuddy, Bob Patchett, James Nigren
The Invisible Wife
92nd Street YMHA/YWHA New York, NY, 1949
Photographer Max Wallman

PHOTO 35
Sharry Traver as Wife & James Nigren, *The Invisible Wife*
92nd Street YMHA/YWHA, New York, NY May 1949
Photographer Max Wallman

PHOTO 36
Woman Working, Sharry Underwood
Boston, MA, Fall 1950
Lindquist Photograph
Copyright © Harvard Theatre Collection, Houghton Library

PHOTO 37
Woman Waiting, Sharry Underwood
Boston, MA, Fall 1950
Lindquist Photograph
Copyright © Harvard Theatre Collection, Houghton Library

PHOTO 38
Woman Loving, Sharry Underwood
Boston, MA, Fall 1950
Lindquist Photograph
Copyright © Harvard Theatre Collection, Houghton Library

CHAPTER ELEVEN

Winter 1947
  Bloomer Girl On Tour

Taking *Bloomer Girl* on the road was a massive undertaking. It took several railroad cars for the sets, lights, props, costumes, luggage, etc., and two more cars for the whole cast, stage crew and musicians. It was equal to moving a real house, a town park, and a jail along with several families. I made sure to be on time when the train left, but I had no idea where we were all going. We didn't go very far at first, just to Bridgeport, CT, where the realities of touring were enough for some to have second thoughts. Not me, though. I was still feeling enchanted.

Bringing our huge show into the limited stage of Bridgeport's *Lyric Theatre,* the technical adjustments were so many that only the principals had a chance to check spacing before the show. As I was checking my own entrance in the semi-darkness, I stepped into a coil of rope by the pin rail just as a stagehand somewhere gave a mighty yank, tightening the rope about my ankle and flipping me upside down. Visions of being left behind with a sprained ankle, I screamed bloody murder to stop him from sending me all the way up into the flies. Finally back on two feet, I fled to the dressing room in the theatre's furnace room. There we had to prop our makeup mirrors on steam pipes dripping scalding water. Margaret, who had just had the costumes freshened for the tour, was a nervous wreck.

In performance that night, the dancers had to change many steps from the horizontal where there was no space to the vertical space n order to keep in time to the music. Place twenty running, jumping, spinning dancers on this stage without a rehearsal and heroic and hilarious dancing was inevitable. From then on all stages were ranked as better or worse than Bridgeport. Fortunately, that was a one-nighter.

New Haven was next with a longer stay and a more accommodating theatre. We could concentrate on performance, not mere survival. Audiences were filled with Yale men who came backstage after the show. Groups of townies and show people flowed together into adjacent bars and restaurants, a typical touring pattern that kept us from being an ingrown society. With such a large cast, someone always knew a local to get the fun started. My lonely nights were over. It snowed in New Haven, enough to call me out for a wintry walk, so I accepted a graduate student's invitation to tour Yale. Proudly he took me to the Yale University's Art Gallery, pointing out the famous paintings of Gilbert Stuart, Charles Peale and John Copley. Then he brought me to John Trumbull's famous painting, *The Declaration of Independence.* Looking at this vivid picture of these very smart, visionary men stirred up my sense of patriotism. Was not our *Civil War Ballet* a touchstone to these same ideals? I remembered the war painting of Gettysburg in my Pennsylvania State Capitol. Quietly many aspects of my life came together.

At noon, my new friend took me to lunch at the Yale Commons. This huge room was like a feudal Great Hall, able to seat hundreds of students. Waiters carried huge tin trays through the noisy, crowded room, serving family style. It took a moment or two before I realized I was the only girl there. It was a boisterous ceremony among males *en masse,* and I felt quite female, even a little vulnerable among them.

Back at the theatre, rumor was rife: Agnes was coming to check the new dancers and the dances. No! Agnes herself was not coming after all. She was sending one of her best dancers who had been in *Bloomer Girl* as the Woman in Black, Betty Low. For a replacement? Last minute rehearsal? No one knew for sure and stage manager Ward Bishop was not talking. After dancing our very best, we found a notice on the Call Board: Rehearsal! ALL DANCERS Tomorrow 10:00 a.m.

Next morning, Betty Low ran all the dances, one by one, making her comments and corrections. Her manner was proprietary. Again and again, I would learn the de Mille *Civil War Ballet* had a special place in the hearts of those who had danced it. This fourteen minute ballet was never rated as just one more dance in a Broadway Musical, but equated with ballets set for the concert stage. It could be performed on its own. Although each role had the weight of a legacy, de Mille had been keeping it alive, shifting various choreographic phrases or exchanging dancer's roles. It was unnerving. New dancers, we were still in our two-week probationary period. Would I get tossed out as the girl before me?

Into the rehearsal, my heart froze. Betty called out Sue Stewart, Margit, Scott and me. That only made logic in the ballet's relationships if she decided to give my role to Sue. This proved true. Sue was to learn my dancing "so that Sharry can understudy Margit as *The Girl in Rose.*" I was being chosen to understudy the lead dancer.

My shock was so visible, everyone laughed. Trembling with euphoria, I then began to learn Margit's beginning solo, while John Martin learned Scott Merrill's part. Quickly we went on to the *pas de deux,* switching partners, adding Sue to our trio phrases. I worried that Betty might change her mind, but it was still true the next day. I thought performers already in a cast stood the best chance of promotion over newcomers. To their credit, not a dancer had a begrudging word or attitude toward me. Perhaps my bewildered delight took the sting away. So Sue learned from me; I learned from Margit.

Margit Dekova was a beautiful girl with refined cameo features and long, silky titian-red hair. She had danced with the *Ballet Russe de Monte Carlo,* meeting de Mille through that association. Margit had gone into *Oklahoma!* as a Postcard Girl. Here her role changed from that can-can girl to romantic ingenue. Margit and Scott are featured as Lovers in the Waltz, which ends with a kiss. Her role as sweetheart continues through the ballet. I never saw Margit give an indifferent or uneven performance. She was consistently excellent, technically, dramatically. I was in her debt for saving me opening night in New York and now as she graciously taught me her role as *The Girl in Rose.* Once, noting my sober intensity, she smiled. "Probably you will have a chance to dance *The Girl in Rose,* but don't count on it often. I'm pretty healthy and I intend to stay that way."

It was true; Margit danced no matter how she felt; and so did we all. In Hartford, Connecticut, a gastrointestinal blitz hit the cast. I had danced through menstrual cramps, sprained ankles, bleeding razor blade cuts, aching heart and hunger, but this unpredictable affliction seemed the worst. Our dressing room was on the fifth floor at the Civic Auditorium, a long way from the bathrooms. (How did my foremothers manage with all these layers of clothes?) It helped to learn it was an open secret: everyone moaned, laughed and just got on with it. A blend of colognes hung in the air for days.

As the dances became more imbedded, I began to realize that the way de Mille staged her dances each dancer had an opportunity for character development. For me, it was to go from girl to woman: first as the sassy Bloomer Girl in the 1860s, conforming to my peers. Although modeling my great gown, I join in political protest against slavery, parading in public, defying the law. With the outbreak of the war, my lover and son are taken from me and life is no longer a daring game, but fearful. I must find the strength to survive for others as well as myself. And, oh, the joy when my husband and son both return when the dreadful war is over! This growth of character made every dance new each performance.

Then I fell in love with my role. As I became more secure and plunged deeper into my part, I went overboard, carrying realism into actual tears. I forgot my lesson about "emotional massage" and wallowed in the dramatic universality of it all. As I was dancing away with joyous tears one performance, Scott stared at me with perplexed concern that turned to disdain. My boiling over was not seen as Greater Truth, but indulgence. One glance like that cured me forevermore. `As the shows rolled by, apparently I regained Scott's respect. We became good dancer friends.

Up through New England and on to Montreal in Canada, we went. There Carolyn and I took the tourist route, skating, sleigh rides up Mount Royal, drinking hot chocolate and eating divine food. Little by little, I was forsaking my sacred habit of only-tea-and-toast before a performance. I found that you could actually consume a regular meal two hours before signing in at seven o'clock and still dance just fine! Imagine, going to an excellent French restaurant with soft lights and delicious food never before tasted, next a little piquant sugary something and bitter coffee. Then walking the snowy streets with the lamplights gleaming softly on our way to His Majesty's Theatre to dance our gift to beautiful Montreal.

Although the Company paid our transportation, we paid for our room and board, usually at modestly priced hotels. In Toronto, however, Caroline and I stayed with a Canadian family, friends of my fellow Texas teacher, Irene Moll. It was a family of five sons from fourteen to twenty-five. They thought it was very glamorous to have two American *chorus girls* stay with them and flirted and fussed over us. This was a taste of English family life in Canada to compare with Quebec's French Canadian ways. Our hostess had formal English tea for us with delicate floral-patterned china teacups and buttery crumpets with honey. Through this association, I later taught a Modern Dance Master Class at Magill University here in Toronto and found I still loved teaching. We also took ballet classes with Boris Volkoff, director of his *Volkoff Ballet Company.*

I had to admit I missed the boys' attentions back on the road. The company had been quietly searched for good male companionship and been found wanting so far. Most of the men were married; most of the women were not. The choice was between sticky affairs with married men or platonic companionship with the gay cast members. Rumors of this liaison or that were constant gossip but more as news than criticism. While it was considered scandalous to be in a man's hotel room at any time—and worse at night—in my parents' society, just where else was there to go after 11:30 p.m.? How many Waldorf or Bickford diners could we stand? *Ghosting*, sharing a room illegally, was common, as much to save a dollar as for romance. Gradually, I melded into the same logic: if I had my self-respect, it was nobody's business what I did when or where. Actually, what I dared were late night bull sessions over theatre and dance, and gossip with a kindred soul. I was not interested in any entangling alliances. Occasionally, wives would come and visit when we had a week or two-week run. They were allowed backstage, usually knitting or reading, but checking out all the singers and dancers. All wives were suspicious; they had reason to be.

I got two surprises when we played Rochester. Friend Sox Tiffault, the pianist for our Syracuse U. student musicals, came to see the show. He was bowled over by *Bloomer Girl,* particularly the ballet and the music for the ballet. We had not seen each other for three years, but it felt as yesterday. He was married, with a baby, still composing, wanting to be part of professional theatre. We kept going from place to place as they closed up, talking and walking, while he kept missing trains back to Syracuse. It was dawn when we said goodbye.

And I found a telegram for me back at the hotel.

My mother and my father were coming to see Bloomer Girl tomorrow! Tonight!

The pretext for my father was a visit to his cousin Maude in nearby Fulton, N.Y. As long as they were this near, they could come see the show. I could not but smile ruefully. Now that it was a period show, I would not likely disgrace them. (Of course, it had not helped that from Dallas, I mischievously sent my father a picture of me as a cancan girl addressed "To my Favorite Sugar Daddy!") Well good. I'll dance my feet off!

When my parents arrived, I was so happy to see them I forgot to be standoffish. Dad gave me his bear hug and it felt so familiar from so long ago, I wilted. Mother was gently affectionate with a kiss to my cheek. She looked at me with such longing, my eyes flooded. Over an early dinner, there was news of my sisters. Jane was expecting her second child in April. Phyllis and Luke might be assigned overseas again; perhaps Japan. Pummie and Herb still in postwar Europe. Nana my dear Nana, was very frail but having good care, which made this trip possible. When I looked past my mother's smart navy hat with the veil and her Davidow suit, I saw her weariness and worry.

"Nana would love the costumes. I'll give you a program for her, all right?"

When we met after the show, I could see it had been more or other than they had expected. They seemed respectful of my work for the first time. I thought my musical mother was thrilled for me. For my father, it was "All right." In turn, I felt adult and equal in stature to them. But there was a difference; they were *civilized,* and I was *theatricalized.*

I loved the trains; the opportunities to mix it up with band members, one-on-one conversations, dining on the train as small town lights went winking by and you wondered what was going on there. There was the trains' roaring vocabulary of noises, as from a big black beast. Then Ding! Ding! And a wailing klaxon the wind blew away. On an even run, the train seemed to be tap dancing, stuck in a time-step. Or it went whooshing to a sudden hiccup kind of stop, throwing everyone forward in heaps of humanity. Stops sent us to hunt for a local paper, but turned into a snowball fight that began to get serious. Cards of course, with shouts of triumph or moans. Dreaming. Writing scrawly letters. And one I got from Sox in Cleveland:

> Shirley—don't let anything interfere with your
> dancing. If you could see yourself—to realize

how wonderful you really are. And surely, as prejudiced as I am, others can't help but realize your talent. There is so much to your dancing that can't be put into words—or at least I find myself incapable of expressing it. To me, its intangible, yet the most expressive thing in the world. With my eyes as they are, I could never have picked you out by your face, but I still spotted you immediately You stand out—your dancing has personality and a individuality—something the other dancers didn't have.

I treasured Sox's letter and was very grateful for it. His opinion meant a great deal, particularly since I could not see myself dancing. Dancing always started from inside for me, and still did, no matter whose class or choreography. It was good to have an observer's opinion on hand and to re-read it the times no one needed me.

When we arrived in St. Louis, we were picketed!

How could *Bloomer Girl* possibly antagonize anyone? There was nothing vulgar or indecent. Women's Rights? We've had the vote now for years. We were picketed for having a racially mixed cast in 1947 America? In St. Louis? It would have been silly, if it were not so sad. There were two black men in our cast, Hubert Dilworth, who played the part of the slave *Pompeii*, and Arthur Lawson, his understudy who played *Augustus*. Hubert, for some reason nicknamed Bill, and I had become friends, and I took his being picketed personally.

Bill had been a painter before turning to professional singing. He had sung on the Circuit, including New York's

Town Hall, Carnegie Hall and at Juilliard. Bill just left *Carmen Jones* for the role of Pompei because he wanted the chance to sing *The Eagle and Me (I gotta be free)!* and *I've Got A Freedom Song.* How often he stopped the show!

It was troubling when Bill said he and Art were not surprised. There had been problems touring already, most bothersome having to sleep in the theaters when they could not get hotel reservations. Why did not the advance men see to it? "They try. Never the best, but at least decent places. Then we show up and suddenly there is this *misunderstanding* and we're out. No place to go. I tell you, Sharry, Art and I do appreciate a good bed when we get it."

"Doesn't this make you want to leave the show and go back to New York?"

"Many times, many times. But the show's a way of speaking out, you see."

The next time I had to cross the picket line, I stopped to glare at the white people sullenly parading by the stage door. About to tell them off, Harry, our lighting hand, pulled me into the theatre. Taunts and foul language followed us. "Doesn't help to stir them up more," he said.

St. Louis was full of surprises. Just before a matinee, an usher brought me a small package backstage. It was a bottle of Tabu perfume. From Captain Myers? What! Really! What was he doing in St. Louis? Captain Joseph Myers was one of the U.S. Air Corps officers that billeted with my parents during the war. He had taken some family pictures over a year ago. A note with the perfume invited me to dinner. When I greeted him at the stage door, I got a stronger hug than I wanted and a kiss I barely managed to deflect. "Uncle Joe, how come you are in St. Louis?"

"Just to see you!"

And he was! Over dinner at the Chase Hotel, Uncle Joe proposed to me. Marriage! I laughed, sure he was teasing, but no. He was getting divorced, took my hand and fervently pleaded with me to say *yes*. It was sad. And infuriating! He thought all he had to do was ask me to leave the show and marry a man old enough to be my father!

We were picketed again in Kansas City for the same reason. Bill kept singing his *Freedom Song* for the same reason. Some local dancers came backstage, asking us out for a bite and dance talk. They were embarrassed about the picketing, saying it was just diehard Southerners. There was another problem. My knees.

For four months I had been running the depth of various stages on my knees in the *Ballet*. Petticoats helped but the Kansas City stage was set in cement at the Kansas City Civic Center. By Thursday of the first week I could no longer endure the pain. Even my scooting in a squat was little help. Fearful of hurting my knees permanently, I sought a doctor—who of course told me not to run on my knees. He did assure me no permanent damage had been done… yet! Architects should be made to jump barefoot a hundred times on cement before being allowed to design a stage!

While cursing architects, I remembered Frank Lloyd Wright had built a church here in Kansas City and set out to find it. Wright's Church of the Future was in a suburban neighborhood. At first glance, it was somewhat disappointing, having nothing about it in my experience to suggest a church. But of course that was the point. Opening my mind, I found the shallow, sloping roofs pleasing, sheltering without the stiff verticality of conventional churches. The entry led down from the top of the stairs into a rounded space, airy and rather like being inside a hollow egg.

The uncluttered, simple space allowed breathing room, freedom for private spiritual meanderings. No artifacts with inherent admonitions. Then inevitably came my urge to move in wide open, floating ways through the aisles. This meant lingering until no one else remained, but it was worth it. I felt very close to Frank Lloyd Wright.

On we went and found there was a theatre much worse than Bridgeport. We had a one nighter in Joplin, Missouri, in a theatre so small it took the crew all day to squeeze any sets into its tiny proscenium-arch theatre. This was also our most hilarious show. During the show, there were emergencies on the moment as principals found props missing and hoop skirts in traffic jams. We danced everything in place. There was barely a foot of space for the beginning of the ballet before the curtain. The eight drumbeats started and went on to nine...ten...eleven, on up to 36 drum beats before the curtain finally opened on the Garden Scene. We dared not look at each other or our control for our sorrowful ballet would be bankrupt. I imagined Agnes watching to control myself, but I totally lost it leading the coda into a solid brick wall. We backed up like so many dominoes. Blackout was the only exit.

In Wichita, I finally got my chance to dance *The Girl in Rose*. Margit was ill, but in the theatrical tradition, she waited until the very last moment before giving in to it. Thus I did not know I was to dance for her until I signed in. Scott was looking for me and we practiced the lifts. Sue took my part. Carolyn, Sue's. Others filled in for the waltz and Grandma. A fresh new energy surged through the dancers. My heart quite melted down within me as I put on Margit's costume with the sunbonnet hanging down the back. The soft peach color and the circular skirt over the ruffled petticoat made a more romantic costume than my sturdy countrywoman's costume. Now I must dance as a young girl in love and vulnerable.

As The Girl in Rose, I say farewell to My Soldier. Then, facing where he has gone, I stand in profile, holding my skirt wide to each side until a sob builds within and I break, weeping. I pull myself erect, again skirts held wide, then step into *a picé arabesque,* arms circling, searching one way, then another. I repeat part of this, but run off weeping. After the women have their turns dancing, I come back as the men return. There is the frozen moment until I hear Sue's stamp and rush into the arms of my Soldier. Here in the *pas de deux,* Scott helped me by dancing as though we had always been partners. Our lifts went high and full, side to side. He turned me to face him. Shyly, I reached up to take off his cap. He bent down to kiss me. Overcome I turned away, crushing his cap to my breast. When he offered his hands to me, I dropped the cap and gave him my hands as though forever after, and we joined the communal circle. As others formed smaller circles, I ran circling the stage to take the whole world into my arms. This led into the belling grand *pas de basques* with Scott and Sue behind me. *The Coda,* me riding high on Scott's shoulders before the blue cirrus-cloud sky, with the singers singing "I gotta be free!" was absolute bliss.

Margit got well overnight, but at least Sue and I had our chance to dance these roles. Sue Stewart was from one of the New Jersey studios that bred ballerinas for national companies. Sue had been in *Bloomer Girl* a while and was looking for something new. She had a beauty similar to Gene Tierney's—dark hair and eyes, high forehead and cheekbones. Directed energy in all her dancing made Sue project well over the footlights. We soon became friends.

After dancing my romantic lead, I suffered and cherished an aching euphoria; a blend of unrequited and theatrically requited "love." My moods ricocheted from one extreme to another like spring fever. I was positive our dancing was affecting people everywhere we went. I was proud to be a dancer. Everyday life was as vivid as performing. No intimate detail escaped me; from lines becoming curves in buildings, to the texture in hotel napkins; the walking pace of Western men and the expressions of the women, the colors of different flowers. What magic is color! It was as though I must gobble up the museums, the galleries, the shops, and also put away a four course dinner with wine! Sassy, a shameful period of practical jokes boomeranged into an intellectual hunger, reading Thomas Wolfe, Santayana and Dos Passos, one right after the other. What I needed was a real love affair.

As summer exploded around us, it was a joy riding on the Observation platform at the end of the train. There I could sing out loud as America rolled by, .When the train pulled to a stop by a water tower, the cast spilled out onto the track into vast wheat fields. In moments the dancers were flouncing through the ripening wheat. I fell out flat in a bed of tawny wheat, noting above the monumental dome of blue. But just where did that blue begin! High above the Earth? Just above me down here?

In the breeze-blown wheat, John lost his glasses. John was myopic. His glasses were so thick, he seemed to be wearing binoculars. He was my Returning Soldier, and although our lifts went well, I felt sure I must seem like a bundle of laundry flying to him. It was disconcerting to feel that he did not see the joy on my face at his return, so I imagined he was a boyfriend, running one night into Eduard's arms, next show Walt's, etc. Now blind, John frantically begged everyone not to move and to find his glasses at once. The search became a frenzy as the train hooted. The conductor shouted "Allllaboooard!" Our laughter turned hysterical as the last three dancers had to race the train to guide John onto the last car steps before its speed left them all behind, *with his glasses.*

Wheat fields turned to dry plains and suddenly, right out of the desert, immense mountains stood against the sky. Colorado! We played Pueblo, then Colorado Springs.

Greg McDougal, one of our dancers, took me horseback riding in the Garden of the Gods. The world could have been created there—eons of time made visible. The raw, massive motherstone bones of the world loomed high around us. Off the trail, there was a huge fractured rock with a narrowing passage…to oblivion? Rock configurations bespoke ceremonial grounds. The warm desert-red color was benign, the size and shapes of the rock walls, forbidding. We came across an elder Indian and a young boy who danced for visitors but had no chance to see a performance.

On to Denver, where the elevation we could stand in Colorado Springs grabbed us every time we had a jump. At first we didn't know what was the matter and thought we were getting out of shape. Learning we were dancing a mile high took the fault away, but we all collapsed after the ballet. By the time we were adjusting, it was off to California!

Learning that our train would pass over the Royal Gorge, I set my alarm so as not to miss it. Rising in the dark berth, I tiptoed through the sleeping cars to the dining car to see out the window. I pushed open the door and came upon several porters and waiters sleeping uncovered on the dining car floor. Of course my coming disturbed them, and a couple tried to rise as I retreated mortified. "Breakfast in l'il while" faded behind me as I struggled back to my berth, shocked again at the conditions for blacks in my free country. I had always thought there was an extra car for staff. No wonder they could get passengers up early; they never really slept.

As soon as we arrived in Los Angeles, I caught the first bus to Malibu and ran right out into the Pacific Ocean. The tide was out but the great ocean breathed in huge swells that swept my feet off its sandy bottom. Instinctively, I raised my arms to let them breathe with the motion, forgetting to hold up my cotton skirt. I was suspended effortlessly. De-light inn-delay—delight inn-delay! It was just lovely being in Vasco Balboa's Pacific vast sea. Nearby, Greg was tugging off his shoes. "I don't know why you couldn't wait until we put on our bathing suits!"

We walked along the water's edge, Greg on the sand, me in the shallows. More people kept arriving, some with baskets or buckets and fishing poles. The tide was turning, the sun setting. Sitting now on the beach, we watched the sun's descent. No buildings, no mountains, no trees. Not even airplanes marred the Pacific sky. Each sun ray, each meld of light and color, was before us, changing moment by moment, giving color washes to the ocean. Gradually the light darkened into twilight, allowing a full moon to be discovered in the sky behind us. The last of the sun was in a golden dissolve on the water before us.

"Look, Greg! We're East of the Sun and West of the Moon!"

I waded back into the water. "Oh! There are funny little creatures in the water!" I cried. People nearby laughed. "The grunion are running! It's that time of the year!"

In minutes the sand was alive with hundreds, then thousands of small silver fish, thrashing in the moonlight as they came ashore to spawn. With each incoming wave, more and more piled up on the beach. People ran around scooping them up, filling their pails. Serenity turned into a festival.

California kept its promises giving us daily sunshine, luscious fruits, my first nectarine! We found multinational restaurants and elegant shops. Ballet classes. We treated ourselves to staying at the Chapman Park Hotel, luxuriating in having breakfast by the pool. If California was our Garden of Eden, it was also our banishment from the theatre: *Bloomer Girl* was closing. The two-week notice was on the Call Board. It was a shock. Unemployment glowered just fourteen days ahead. Dressing rooms buzzed with ideas, questions, "but if's" and "then there's that's." The Company was obligated to pay our return trip to the city of origin; as this lay across the entire country, there were many options. Catch up with family. Get back to NYC in time for fall auditions. Tackle Hollywood?

Greg was unfazed. He had investigated a position teaching Dance at Colorado College. While we played Colorado Springs, he was given the job. Divorced before joining *Bloomer Girl*, Greg was disenchanted with theatre in New York, He wanted nothing better than to be on his own, teaching and treating Dance however he wished. At the same time, he tried to convince me to stop off there, also, to study with Hanya Holm, who taught Modern Dance there each summer. Holm, one of the Four Modern Dance Pioneers, was a marvelous teacher who freed her students to find their own styles, he said.

"I should save my money for New York," I said.

Each performance was treasured these last two weeks as we traveled to Santa Barbara, then San Diego. Sue had Chase, a new man in her life, to drive us down to San Diego in his standard L.A. white convertible. After the show there, Greg joined us for a quick trip to Tijuana, Mexico.

It was nearly midnight when we got there. We stayed out all night drinking tequila, dancing and singing in one cafe or cantina after the other. This was my first tequila. I was not sure I liked it. Essentially a nondrinker, I was soon affected, heady with the excitement of being in an exotic country late at night, stamping out *Viva Faroan.* Sue and Greg joined in, clapping and stamping, as the bands and patrons obliged by clapping and shouting with us, maybe hoping we would just go home.

But we felt homeless. We were homeless. With no deliberate plan, we separated and then came together again as though some invisible playwright were directing extemporaneously. Lapsing into a dreamy wistfulness over our closing, Greg and I danced a gentle, slow motion duet. Chase and Sue whispered, head to head. Then Sue and I were slouching down a dirt street, looking into closed shops and agreeing that being ambitious about our dance careers did not diminish our hopes of finding the right person to share our lives.

At one point in this silly, poignant night, we were all outside wandering in the balmy air when a couple of horses came trotting easily down the dirt roadway. Runaways. Like us. Greg and Sue tried to catch them and I started after them but Chase caught my arm, saying let them go. He wanted to talk to me about Sue. He took my hand and we walked along as the dark began to pale. A touch of coolness in the air was tender somehow.

I listened as Chase expressed his love for Sue, his concern for her future. At thirty-two, he felt he understood more about her than younger men could. Finding someone who understood caring as well as desire was wonderful, I said and began to weep. Chase thought that a girl who could weep was wonderful for she must not be inhibited. We clung to each other and turned back to meet Greg and Sue returning, each leading a horse by the halter. For a few brief moments, the four of us stood there just gazing at each other. When a Mexican came to take the horses, Greg and I put our arms about each other; Sue and Chase the same.

Some of the enchantment lingered as Chase let the car drive us back to San Diego. Evanescence—evanescence! The thought brought me to. I must decide right away what to do! But the moments floating by were not empty; they were full of passion and fatigue. Nothing else to do but sleeeeeep.

The show went on to play Pasadena, San Jose, and then Oakland, which added San Francisco across the Bay to our California beauties. The last days, cast members took their *Bloomer Girl* programs to each other to be signed, unabashed as school kids, wishing each other well.

We were on the train east, fifteen minutes out of Denver, when I decided to go to Colorado Springs to study with Hanya Holm. If I found the classes disappointing, I could always catch another train, right?

192

CHAPTER TWELVE

Summer 1947
  Colorado Springs, Colorado

Hanya Holm left the American Dance Festival in Bennington, Vermont, to set up her own summer dance program at Colorado College in Colorado Springs in 1941. It was vital for me to get back to daily classes, so often forfeited on tour. I hoped my study here would refresh and expand my modern dance technique. It took a good week to get used to the altitude and college regulations with an eleven o'clock curfew. I also signed on for piano lessons to satisfy a belated dream. I was set back as Hanya placed me in the Beginners Class after reviewing my dance credentials. Then I found this class was not even with Hanya but with her assistant, someone called Nik. Noting my hesitancy, Nik, Alwin Nikolais, assured me Hanya put every new student in her Beginners Class. I was still embarrassed.

The classes were tediously simple. Taking an inventory of body co-ordinations, both gross and fine, they recalled Pilates's classes. Furthermore, Nik explained the moves in detail before we could get moving again. I was impatient to get on to advanced skills, but I dropped my prima donna act when Nik casually made a suggestion that improved my balance. (I unconsciously lifted my left big toe off the floor when balancing). I learned to take the classes as they were meant, a fresh start with intelligent guidance. Nik became a valuable, special friend from then on. In a week, I was moved up to Hanya's class.

Hanya wore a black leotard with a black overskirt on a strong, solid body. She taught barelegged and bare-footed.

She wore her hair in a ballet coronet, but Hanya was definitely Modern Dance. Before coming to America with her son Klaus, Hanya had been a favored student of German modern dancer Mary Wigman. Hanya began teaching in her own studio in New York. She then joined the other modern dance pioneers at Bennington's American Dance Festival. Now here in class, no *barre* or mirror was used, no music. Hanya set rhythms on her drums. Hanya's demeanor was quiet and watchful. Her directions were succinct, but she kept a glint in her eye. This could fix a careless student in place or inspire new energies as, with rapid hand clapping, she hurried us along. When class went particularly well, her eyes shone and she had a merry laugh. She did not demonstrate her exercises fully, relying on Nik, Glen Tetley or Oliver Costock to do so. She could (and would) show off by holding her leg extended in second position minutes at a time as she explained a point of theory.

Hanya's technique was a heightened course on body mechanics we take for granted in everyday life. I could not see a defining personal style. She warmed us up by demanding concentration on the action of the muscles instead of line. If a student could articulate the body properly, the line was naturally there. Hanya taught pure movements, a technique that was both solid and plane geometry in action. Our constant state of having a three-dimensional body, so easy for us all to ignore, must be kept in mind. Next we must be aware of being in *a place in space.* That both anchored the dancer in his/her spot but also made the dancer more aware of the placement and actions of fellow dancers. And there was more. Instead of the word Up Hanya used High; for Side, she used Wide; for Down, she used Deep. It helped to think of Leonardo da Vinci's diagram of Man, centered in a circle;

free to move through all the cardinal directions within it; to radiate beyond it. Even a calm position at rest had *more* to it when aware.

People in the audience can see all this right away, but we dancers cannot see our own selves; that is why knowing this spacial concept makes for better dancing. What people in the audience may not be aware of is that they, too, are in the same situation in motion, just walking along with everyone else on the way to work.

As we moved into larger movements, our sense of being geometry-in-motion was continued; thus a skip was basically an undercurved motion while a leap was an overcurve. Then there were *The Circles* in which we moved on the perimeter of circles of all sizes, forward and backward, in scallops. Few people actually make right-angle turns at corners; most of us walk in constant curving paths. Turning the lead foot out a bit and the following foot turned in a bit, makes for elegant efficiency. Dancing the circles could be exhilarating or could be serene. It could also go into a self-perpetuating delirium, as any five year-old pretending to be an airplane can show you. Planing all over campus became habit.

We had very little free time and were grateful for the college swimming pool in the summer heat. The Fourth of July was our only holiday. Greg and I took the Manitou Incline Railway up to Manitou Springs, loitering so long we were going to miss the last tram ride back. The combination of wine and the altitude inspired us to skip the winding path to the station and crash straight down the mountain. Laughing and loopy, we just threw ourselves aboard as the tram took off. One other diversion was a group trail ride through the Garden of the Gods. That became an adventure when we were suddenly in a furious thunderstorm. Lightning ricocheted off the huge rocks and spooked the horses. The smell of ozone was in the air. Fortunately, there was no room for the horses to run, but frightened, they snorted and reared dangerously. It was all thrilling, even though we were drenched. When the storm passed, our leader managed a night fire and a barbecue that tasted marvelous. As night fell, a ghost moon rose, lighting our way back to the stable.

My piano practice was foundering and then died as word came about a Lecture-Demonstration of Holm Technique plus a production of Karel and Josef Capek's *And So Ad Infinitum* or *The Insect Comedy.*. Hanya was to choreograph this show, collaborating with the resident drama instructor, Reginald Lawrence. Nik would assist. In the prologue, a lepidopterist compares insect and human societies as he converses with a tramp. Act One is devoted to the Butterflies.. Act Two, to Creepers and Crawlers. Act Three, The Ants. The Epilogue, *Life and Death.* I was chosen to dance and act the role of the Chrysalis appearing in the last three sections. I was also invited to perform on the *Holm Dance Lecture-Demonstration,* indicating that I must be mastering Hanya's techniques.

As the work went along, two student works were added to the program. In theory class, choreographic assignments were made regularly. Once Nik asked us to choreograph *Pity.* Glen could apparently compose with the same considered direction of energy with which he executed dance technique. Glen was true: his geometric precision appeared to be natural mechanics, but Glen was not without warmth. Quietly going about his work, he was a model for us all. Glen chose to choreograph a character sketch, *Richard Cory,* from Edwin Arlington Robinson's *Spoon River.* Jack

Moore read the poem for Glen's performance. The other student work was by William Murphy, a dance sextet, *America,* set to music by Percy Grainger.

Rehearsals did not take the place of class, of course, but took afternoons and evenings. Being there as Hanya choreographed was enlightening. She came with a clear sense of what she wanted, but without any specific steps. She would tell Glen to "start over there and improvise something light as the Butterfly Felix." She supplied him with butterfly characteristics such as hovering or quick changes of direction, and Glen would then dance his response. The play's concepts, that insects and humans have a commonality, led the Butterflies (Glen and Joan Kruger) to reflect the flirtatious Twenties. This was to be the dancyest, most amusing section.

Hanya continued her presentation of insect characteristics and then depended on the dancers to create the dance movements. Most of us also had lines to speak, but pantomime was to be avoided like the plague. The Beetles had a prop dungball to push around, symbolizing obsessive possession. All insect moves reflected human motivation. As a chrysalis is first a kind of worm in a cocoon, She was to enter with the *Creepers and Crawlers.* Ignoring the others, she was to proclaim heer momentous birth, but every insect ignores her. When the Tramp asks what she will do when she is born, she replies that she doed not know, but something great. Unlike the other insects, the Chrysalis is stuck in place with only axial movements to convey her struggle to be born.

Twisting in various tempos, isolating upper-body moves from the trunk, and body successions were the motions I used to prevent being predictable. My part was one long, slow build to the climax, pushed along by increasingly dramatic moments, until I suddenly die.

Chrysalis:
Harken o heaven, earth give ear!
I will proclaim a mystery
I will solve all things... I will tell
The whole world's hidden mystery!
Harken!... (*falls dead*)

I loved the part. It felt like Greek drama to me. And there was just the right costume in my trunk: a long, gray, silk jersey dinner gown with a cowl neckline. Tubular, the dress was sleek and responsive to the slightest wiggle. The narrow sheath sustained the sense of confinement within the cocoon. Hanya approved. My final moves were simple and sustained, but that did not make them easy. Hanya asked for a s-l-o-w kneel for my ecstatic finish. While my body descended, I must give the illusion my spirit rises into the ether. Hah! Practice kneels again.

Before long, Hanya and I got into a *contretemps* over this. For very good reason, I considered myself an expert on knees-to-floor dance action; certainly an expert on my own knee abilities. Therefore, once I knew exactly what to do and proved I could do it satisfactorily, I knew enough *not* to do it every single time the scene was repeated. Any dancer knows deep *pliés* can be overdone and they are centered. Here, my kneel keeping an unbroken line from opposite shoulder to knee, must be off-center to control the slow descent in character. Overworking the quadriceps and getting stiff for the performance could be avoided with discretion. So, at times I marked the kneel, more times than Hanya wished. All others saw was my not completing the kneel consistently. It bothered Director Reggie Lawrence and embarrassed Hanya, perhaps, but I knew what I was doing. If Hanya sensed a stubbornness in me, she was right. They would have to trust me. This would be the least of my worries.

One Saturday afternoon, about a week before our performance, I found a telegram from home in my mailbox that sent my priorities haywire. Nana, my dear dear Nana, had passed away. Died. Was gone. Never to be with her again.

I called home, crying, full of sorrow and guilt. I heard my mother's voice, very tired and far away. As I sobbed, her voice strengthened and she spoke clearly. "You must not think of coming home for the funeral, Polly."

At the sound of my childhood name, I broke out afresh. "Of course I'll come. I have to come. I want to."

"No. No. There is nothing to do for Nana now. She was very sick. You must think of this as a blessing for her. Stay and finish your work."

"But this is the time I must help you, Mother!"

"Your father is here with me. Jane, Phyllis and Luke are coming. We are all right. You stay. Goodbye, dear."

Nana had been the one to raise me as a child, and now I am being forbidden to come home for her funeral. Every instinct told me to go! But my mother's tone of voice slammed the door shut. My work! The Chrysalis. What a monumental conceit! A flare of brightness against the dark! Even a match could do that. I sent flowers. Tried to write. Couldn't. Went running. Tried rehearsal, but after ten minutes, Hanya sent me gently away. Greg took it upon himself to walk with me until I dropped from fatigue. I had given up praying a long time ago as some form of begging for something I should be able to manage. There seemed no solace anywhere.

Walking me again, Greg led me into a dorm where a friend was playing the piano. The music slowly invaded me. Subconsciously, I began to move slightly to it. Like two Svengalis, the men kept me moving, first with classical music and, gradually, to show melodies. The next morning I felt guilty. Nana would not have approved of this way of dancing out my sorrow. It had given me the oblivion of sleep. Then I discovered there is a gift of life in each death. All senses are re-sharpened, in a manner, reborn. Perhaps the Chrysalis could be a metaphor proclaiming these mysteries of life and death.

In the performance, I thought about the loss of body in death, down in a spiral through me into the earth, A letting go as a spiritual energy rose up through and out of me as I cried out "Harken!" I held my breath until the curtain and then let go a great sigh. In minutes, Reggie came on stage, exclaiming happily about my kneel. Hanya was satisfied.

After the performance, the summer session ended. I took the long train ride home by myself. There I found my mother still dry-eyed, still standing, although spiritually and physically exhausted. She seemed so fragile, my mother, I did not know what I should do. Starchy at my distress, she said, "The time to weep for Nana was when she was in her dreadful, relentless pain. That is when I cried for her, for the little I could do to help her. I can only be glad she is free of it now. You must be, too."

I could not hold my mother for fear she would shatter. I was still the Child. She was still the Mother.

CHAPTER THIRTEEN

Fall 1947
New York, NY

Returning to New York, I found a room in a residential hotel on West 79th Street; then ran to Equity to size up the coming season. By taking the time to study with Hanya, I had missed auditions for Jerome Robbin's *High Button Shoes* and Agnes de Mille's *Allegro*. I made my faithful treks for replacements in running shows and went back to class. I went to Hanya for body alignment, spacial orientation, and those sophisticated stretches that went beyond a strenuous workout. Show auditions demanded ballet. I went to Aubrey Hitchens to maintain my ballet technique, its line, pirouettes and for the fast footwork neither Hanya nor Charles provided. And I went to Charles because it was always dancing.

I had thought that since I had been dancing straight on in professional dance performances that getting a dance job would be easier now. Second verse same as the first: back to tiny meals, back to Unemployment office. And then a rather dear thing happened, which led to some dismay. John, the youngest of the five Canadian brothers, came all the way from Toronto, proudly showing up at my hotel to surprise me. As he stood wide-eyed in my tiny hotel room (bath down-the-hall—half-shelf in the refrigerator), all my glamour dissolved. I could see his Dreams of Broadway Glory go pfft in the air. Though tempted to make apologies, I gave him a quick hug and pulled him out for a great breakfast. Yes, this was life upon the wicked stage in New York in 1947, but I had the day off, so let's see the Town! The problem came when night fell and there was no physical space for John to sleep in my room too. I sent him to the YMCA,

John did not stay at the Y. He was tempted to explore New York further than was smart. He showed up the next morning, much the wiser. I saw to it he had bath privileges and bought him a breakfast. I talked honestly with him about the on/off glamour of the theatre; tried to explain why I accepted temporary poverty to do what I believed in.

"Well, I've been learning a lot about that myself," John said. "In fact, I'll need to ask to borrow some money just to get back home."

"I can give you twelve dollars." I gave him the bills in my wallet. "Just let me know when you get home, OK?" A week later, the twelve dollars was returned with a note. "Made it. Thank you, John."

Johnny Call, coachman in *Bloomer Girl,* hosted a joyful reunion where I learned Carolyn was back at the School of American Ballet (SAB) and job- hunting, too. Margit had married our male lead, Arthur Maxwell, and they were living in my hotel. I did not catch up with them again because I stupidly got sick. Johnny's party went from hors d'oeuvres, steak and all the rest, plus dessert. I had not had such a full meal since returning to New York, and my digestive system shut down. I swelled up so badly, the ER doctor at Roosevelt Hospital thought I was pregnant. They sent me home with Milk of Magnesia to endure one of the most miserable weeks of my life.

When I ran into dance pal Anita Anders making rounds, she told me she knew of a girl looking for a roommate to share the rent on 48th Street, right across from beautiful Rockefeller Plaza. Robin Rull was a new experience for me in female companionship. Short, small-boned, unkempt peroxide-blonde hair, Robin was well named. She moved in quick, quirky movements, but her voice was no song. Her rasping voice told me explicitly what were "hers" and "mine." A one bedroom, I had a cot in the living room against the bedroom wall, where I found myself sharing too much of Robin's huff-and-puff sex life. Robin hung her diaphragm beside her toothbrush.

"You may as well get used to it," she snapped. "I am undergoing psychoanalysis to achieve orgasm. I have to work all day and still have energy for intercourse, so I don't want to waste any ergs on you. Tension is my main problem, so for God's sake don't use all the hot water. I need hydrotherapy at least."

I hated having to tiptoe past sleeping nude bodies to get my clothes from the bedroom and asked why we could not move that closet into the living room.

"That is not a closet. And it is private."

Fortunately for me, a folk singing friend I had met in Colorado looked me up and kept my evenings busy. Terry carried his guitar everywhere we went. On impulse, he would sit down to play it and sing to me. In his white ski-troop parka and Western boots, his beard and twangy voice, he got cheerful attention. As my unemployment ran out, he persuaded his Aunt Calla— who worked at Macy's—to help me get a job.

My first day, I had a Kafkaesque experience trying to be on time. I got totally lost in Macy's Women's Locker Rooms. It had towers of army green metal lockers, room after room, with sounds of metal locker doors being clicked open or banged shut. No one was ever in the room I was in as I rushed here and there to find my locker. I was already late! Pausing and panting, I decided to try to backtrack to the entry, where I was to put my card in a slot and wait for the "ching" before placing it on the rack. But where was back? In quiet terror, I heard faint footsteps and rushed in that direction. They stopped. But began again. And there, as I tore into the next locker room, a girl slammed her locker door and ran out, me desperately following to-Huzzah! the entrance! Then all day I typed up mail orders or answered disenchanting Santa Claus letters.

I took Charles's Company class at night, pleased to get to know company members and learn more Humphrey-Weidman repertory. As a result, I saw little of Robin. The next time I saw Anita, though, we had a sobering talk. New facts emerged:

One: the apartment actually belonged to Anita's boyfriend, Eddie.

Two: Robin had been Eddie's mistress.

Three: Eddie was back in New York and wanted his apartment back.

Four: for Anita and me.

Five: really for Anita and Eddie.

Six: I was the *deus ex machina*.

Seven: On borrowed time.

When I got back to the apartment, it was obvious that Eddie had been there. As soon as I opened the door, Robin screamed at me, "You bitch! You underhanded bitch! You came here just to help Eddie get his foot back in the door!"

Equally furious, I yelled back for a change, "Oh sure! There's nothing I would rather have than no place to live again! Think for once, for God's sake, Robin!" To my overwhelming surprise, Robin threw her arms around me, sobbing. By bedtime, we managed a let-live tolerance. The worst was yet to come.

When she had to move out the coming weekend, I got out of the way, going to my sister Jane's in Philadelphia after work late Saturday. The next week started twelve-hour days during Bonus Week at Macy's, going nine-to-nine for me. I went straight from the train to work, Monday, so it was 9:30 P.M. before I straggled up the stairs to the apartment that night.

The doorknocker was gone. Was I so tired I was at the wrong apartment? I tried my key and it worked. Taking the doorknocker was pretty small, I thought, as I flicked the light switch. No lights. Not by the door, nor— after wandering in the dark—the bathroom. Window curtains were gone. I could now see enough by street light to detect shapes. Only there weren't any! No bookcases, tables, lamps, chairs. No bed! No pots or plates. Towels, soap, cup, fork, knife. My clothes! My money in my blue sock in the second drawer of the missing bureau!

E-v-e-r-y-t-h-i-n-g-w-a-s-g-o-n-e!

Stunned, I wandered into Robin's room. Not empty. That damned box was still there. "You!" I gave it a mighty kick. Half laughing, half crying, I wandered carelessly and tripped over the telephone. Thank God! A lifeline to sanity! Dialing in the dark was a new skill, but eventually I reached Anita in town with Eddie at Toots Shor's Restaurant. As I waited for them, I curiously went back to look at The Box. From the streetlight, I found it was wood outside but metal-walled inside. I had honorably never opened its door before, but now all bets were off. I stooped to enter this empty box and kicked my typewriter case. I dragged that into the center of the living room and sat on it in despair in the shadows of the room. I had a hard time of it as my anger boiled. I tried to get past it by making my hands stay open.

As the days followed, I felt like Sara Crew, the poor storybook child saved by a nearby Prince. Every day brought both pain and hope. At work, wearing the same clothes for the fourth day, I learned that being single reduced my bonus for twelve-hour days to—trumpets please! five dollars. But Anita brought in a bed from New Jersey. My sock money was still gone but Anita brought a lamp, two towels, a chair. A coffee pot! Then Anita herself, protesting that, No! She was not ready to move in with Eddie; she counted on me to prevent that. She could now live with me here, away from Mother in New Jersey. Then Anita seemed very curious about The Box. And, oh, yes! She—and Eddie too! now were going to the same psychotherapist as Robin, Dr. Wilhelm Reich.

Eddie came over from his hotel for a Sunday dinner, a celebration of many sorts. We all carefully acted as though things were settled, knowing they were not. Eddie proceeded to explain to me The Orgone Box. This was a vital source of energy, a Special Energy. Maybe a new form of electricity Dr. Reich had discovered.

"Come on in here, Sharry. Look at The Orgone Box itself. Now The Box is wood and lined with metal, see? If I have it right, the energy goes from the metal to the wood, BUT if one of us is sitting inside, the energies—aren't they called bions, Anita? These bions give their Special Energy to us through heat. It gets really hot in The Box."

"It gets hot inside a closet," I said, thinking out loud.

"Well this energy is special. The metal is galvanized, which has something to do with it. Why sometimes, it makes a greenish light in there we're told."

"Dr. Reich told me it was wonderful for plants, too," Anita chirped.

"Well, I can vouch for the fact that Robin got plenty hot in there."

"Dr. Reich doesn't say 'Sit in the Box and you're cured.' It's just part of the treatment, the whole treatment, to shed the inhibitions generated upon us by a hypocritical society."

Eddie patiently continued to explain. "Our generation is terribly inhibited, Sharry. You know our Victorian predecessors played havoc with our natural instincts. Sexual instincts, I refer to, of course. We've all grown up with these urges, ashamed and frustrated. The tension in all of us is unbelievable. Why when we have a chance for good sex, we fail."

Anita joined in. "You don't know how lucky we are to have The Orgone Box to help us along. That's why Robin was so mad. She knew she couldn't take it with her without getting into trouble with Dr. Reich. Sharry, he is very aware of tensions all over the body. His wife was a dancer and he knows anytime you are just posing. The other day he asked me why I couldn't do anything without pointing my toes. And I didn't realize it most of the time."

"Right. You have got to be able to relax to be intimate with anyone," Eddie agreed. "If you are neurotic about anything, you can't do your best. A tense body wastes energy. Your habits get to be what Dr. Reich calls your 'character armor.' You—we—all wear it and don't even know it!" Eddie laughed proudly and put his arms around us both.

"I'm more relaxed just being away from Mother. Can you believe she still wants me in by midnight! And, oh! She wants to visit to make sure you really exit, Sharry."

Our tentative *ménage a trios* was barely initiated when Anita's mother impetuously arrived late one Sunday morning as we were luxuriating over the *Times*. Hearing a knock, Anita called out lazily, "Who is it?"

"Oh, Anita. It's Mother. I'm so glad you're in!"

All three of us jumped up, electrified. Desperate glances were exchanged as Anita trilled out a high-voiced greeting. "Oh, Mother! What a surprise! Just a min-ute!" Anita frantically pointed to the bedroom but there was no need; Eddie and I were on our way. Eddie dove into The Orgone Box while I piled enough clothes on it to disguise it. I emerged nonchalantly from the bedroom as Mrs. Anders came in the door. (The only door.)

Introductions, a place for the lamp she brought, a tour of the apartment that inevitably led to the bedroom. Anita excused the mess and tried to guide her Mother away. "Well dear, that's why I came to help, so we may as well have at it." She picked up the coat on the top.

"Please, don't bother now, Mother. I...I have...to get brackets. To hang those on—tomorrow! How would you like to go out for lunch?"

"Out? I just got here, dear."

"Tea, then? Earl Grey or English Breakfast?"

Tea would be lovely. Time to get to know Sharry too. So glad we had such a good spot in town, etc. Two hours later, Anita and I were frantically trying to excavate Eddie from his overdose of bions. He emerged almost purple in the face. Could barely croak "Water!" So stiff, he stood hunched over and waddled like a bear as we led him out into the living room.

"Too much of a good thing?" I asked, thoughtlessly.

Eddie's rage galvanized at that, and he let fly a stream of obscenities that astonished Anita and me and then enraged us. The squabble ended as Eddie wavered and fell back on my squeaky bed. Anita caressed him and murmured sweet somethings while I got the whisky bottle. After one more shot of bourbon, Eddie rallied, yanked open the door and tottered out to walk off his humiliation. It was, after all, *his* apartment.

I turned to Anita "Why did we all panic? Doesn't your mother know Eddie by now?"

"Mother is still trying to protect my long-lost virginity. The pretense is tying me in knots, making me feel guilty, when I have a perfectly natural desire for sex. I can't believe she doesn't know, but we're both hypocrites."

Terry brought me a Christmas tree, so we all decided to have a party. At the last minute, Eddie went out on errands and returned with two big boxes. "Here you go, my lovelies! I couldn't resist!"

Inside each box was a delicious white Christmas nightie with eyelet lace and pink satin ribbons. We put them on at once, dancing about as Terry played carols on his guitar. So beautiful, we kept them on for the party. It was a good party, lasting far into the night. Angelic demeanors fell as I caught Anita blowing smoke rings; my personification of Jo in *Little Women* got lost jitterbugging. As the last guest and Terry left, the sky was dawning. Anita and Eddie turned in. I hesitated, took a shower and, dressed, took the next train to Harrisburg. This would be our first Christmas without Nana. I was the one free to come home.

It was well that I did. Our house that had known such joyous holidays and, lately, the comings and going of nurses bustling about and the need for immediate errands, was now stilled. Mother and Dad did not even have a Christmas tree. The best I could do was to insist *I* needed a family Christmas to pull them out of their inertia. Going to Christmas services was a quiet step back into social life. Making Christmas dinner, telephone calls from Phyllis and Toni, and talking about Nana, her many wise sayings, got us through.

Back in New York, I was grateful to have the apartment to myself over New Year's.

Very soon it began to snow, snowing quickly, thick as cotton. All the night long. The Great Snow Storm of 1948 turned all of Manhattan white. Slowly it silenced the Great City until not a single sound could be heard. Ethereal, it was as a blessing from the Heavens, purifying the city with Beauty. So complete and deep was the snow, Manhattan was white silent all that night.

Next morning, people ventured out of their city burrows, smiling as they stood in the hushed streets. There was not even the faint rumble of a subway. It was as though the power of the city was in its sounds. These gone, it was immobilized. Inanimate. It became exhilarating to skate-walk freely down the center of Fifth Avenue. People unabashed playing in the snow, on skis, pulling children on sleds. Everyone was smiling in wonder. I did not know that many people, including my future husband, barely survived the night, caught on the Pulaski Skyway in the storm. Gradually, the underground groans began, the scraping metallic shrieks of snowplows, the banging doors and tearing gears of heavy trucks. People shouted in counterpoint. Slowly the enchantment dissolved.

Back to business in New York meant me, too, going to Hanya in the day and to Charles's company class each night. Everything in the class was refined and polished by

Charles making specific corrections to individuals. Here, too, there was more emphasis on the subjective qualities of the dancing. Here I learned Charles was getting his company assembled for performances in New York and a National Tour.

Despite the fact that dancing jobs were chronically scarce, Charles had many problems putting the company together. One reason was that this would be Charles's first season without Doris. Some regular company members were pleased to dance in and around Manhattan but had no interest going on tour. Peter and Nadine Gae were dancing in *Angel in the Wings* on Broadway and planned to stay there. Peter, who would keep classes going in Charles's absence, taught his roles to Carl Morris and/or Marc Breaux. Bea Seckler declined to tour, so Charles counted on Saida Gerrard for the lead female roles.

The excitement was catching. I had been hoping to dance with a renowned modern dance company; maybe this was the chance. It would mean leaving New York again, but the tour was to last only three months. Nothing else was coming through, and my domestic situation was becoming intolerable. When now Saida, too, backed out, Charles announced auditions for her roles. I went, watching Saida first dance the part of the slave, chased, raped, and left to die in *House Divided*. Then each of us had a chance to try it. Called on early, I was not emotionally prepared nor technically accurate, after observing the movements just once. The idea of rape was a panic to me; I wasn't sure I wanted the role. I stayed to watch the others.

Betts Lee was next, a pretty girl with soft, dark brown, wavy hair and a softer (not weaker) figure than most dancers. The high-floating chest of Humphrey/Weidman was natural to her now, but her airy style did not give enough earthy substance to her audition. Sherry Parker was next with too ladylike an approach to the part. Felisa Conde tackled the role. Tall, brunette, hair waved and worn long in back, rolled bangs in front, Felisa was the company dancer with the most impeccable technique. She was the most accurate, but her attempt was dispassionate despite its vigor. No one was near Saida's work until Emily Frankel tried. She broke the spell, throwing herself into the movements like an animal at bay, proving herself as an actress, as well. Her apprehension became fear, fear became rage, then terror, pain and shame.

Emily had a particular feature that helped— her long titian red hair. It fell across her face, whipped through the air and when the men lifted her up into a cross, it poured heartbreakingly down her back. It was also simply sexier than anyone else's hair. It had taken me a time or two to realize that this scholarship student I had seen cleaning the Studio was the same girl. Emily had projected little more than iron-grey determination in class, her brown hair in a ballet coronet instead of the modern dancers' free flying hair. However, when she changed her hair color, now long and flowing, she began to bloom like the proverbial Desert Rose. Now she was positively dynamic. She got the slave role and others deserted by Saida. This did not solve Charles's problems; it created more.

Not only were old company members deserting Charles; now regular members were in mutiny. The major rebels were: Felicia Conde, Betts Lee, Carl Morris, Betty Osgood. Nick Vanoff and Marc Breaux joined them. They gave Charles an ultimatum: take the roles back from Emily. They refused to tour with her, saying they objected to her attitude, her dancing, her unasked for suggestions and her morals! I was not there when Charles was so enraged he hurled a stack of records at the studio wall, smashing all to pieces. I knew nothing of the mutiny until the day Charles asked me to join the company. I said "Yes" on the spot.

Then I learned a *caveat* or two. "There's just one thing," Charles sighed ruefully. "Do you think you can get along with Emily? Some in the company have told me they will not dance with her. What do you think of that? They say she is trouble. Immoral!" he nodded to the rebellious dancers standing by.

I was astonished. After a moment, I replied, "I have no reason not to get along with Emily. Or anybody else. Choosing company members is up to you, Charles. I can't think what another dancer's morals have to do with my dancing with her on stage."

Charles nodded, gratified. He turned to the others. "Who do you think you are to stand in judgment of another human being?" He rose from his seat, trembling with rage. "Who gives you the right?"

With a haunted look, Charles left them, going to his rooms downstairs. The rebellious dancers stood immobile. I, too, feeling the air between them and myself solidify. Now I had isolated myself from them without dancing a step.

Charles began making new decisions every day. It now looked as though he was being forced to acquiesce to the demands of the regular company members because performances were already scheduled for this month of January. He took some roles back from Emily, but stood up to them by keeping her in the company, keeping her role of the slave. Charles had to do what was expedient, but he would not forget being blackmailed. He used as many of the old company dancers as he could in our pre-tour New York performances.

Rehearsing *House Divided* with Charles and with Spencer Teakle speaking Lincoln's words, I hoped antagonistic attitudes would melt away. No dice. (Emily's immorality consisted of her sharing a railroad apartment with other men and women. Gulp!)

Next Charles started to work on a new piece as sequel to *And Daddy Was a Fireman. Panamic Suite* was a light, colorful folk work, an opportunity for lavish costuming. Then I found out we dancers had to help with the sewing. This was a Modern Dance company, not a Broadway show, where everything was done for us.

Either at 48th Street or 16th Street, my life was caught in the pull taffy of other people's circumstances. I kept three things in mind to prevent feeling powerless: one, there was always a choice to make; two, it was mine to make. And three really *mine* to make! I had left my name backstage at *Brigadoon* and so had Sue Stuart, who now got the first replacement. I went to see her debut, and also Virginia Bosler in the role of Jean. Proud of them both, I felt very wistful not to be up there on stage with them. However, now in Charles's company, I had more dancing than they had in *Brigadoon*.

I saw Papa Shawn at one of the dance programs up at the YMHA. We had a good talk at intermission The Pillow was always on the edge of financial disaster, but despite that, he was hoping to bring the *Danish Ballet* there this summer. I told him I had joined Charles's company and about the dances. Shawn shrugged and smiled as if to say, "A job's a job." It was refreshing to be with this dear man, to know he was still my friend. At rehearsal, I mentally placed Shawn in one of the old Metropolitan Opera seats Doris had cabbaged for the Studio. Imagining Papa Shawn observing my work was a reminder of the rehearsal discipline he had pounded into me.

In rehearsal, I found the emphasis in Charles's dances was not placed primarily on how the movement looked, but on what it meant. The Humphrey-Weidman style came from their principle of rise and fall, as in breathing; the ebb and flow in life. This could lead to sudden rebounds, sustained off-center turns, or at times, long flows of movement. Arrested positions were the result of a resolution of motion; not set body placement. It had been that momentum and meaningfulness that attracted me.

One more week at Macy's.

CHAPTER FOURTEEN

Winter 1947-48
  Charles Weidman & Company in NY & on Tour

Charles Weidman & Company had two performances around New York before taking off across the country. The first was at the *Brooklyn Academy of Music* (BAM), January 9th, 1948. The Company was sharing a program with singer Paul Robeson, sponsored by the Theatre and Arts Committee of the American Labor Party, Kings County. We were on Program III in a series of five concerts of *Music in a Democratic Key*. Our program was titled *Talkin' Freedom*.

Charles chose *A House Divided* and *Daddy Was a Fireman* from our repertory. He prevailed upon Saida Gerrard to dance the Slave in *House* and Doris Humphrey's role as Vesta in *Daddy*. Then I learned she would dance my role as Mother in the Southern Family, as well. I would only dance my role as Worker. I shrugged off disappointment for this gave me a chance to watch the work evolve in sequence. Dancers rarely had a chance to see the dances in which they danced.

Charles did not use a stovepipe hat, but did wear the black frock coat and soft black tie as Lincoln. While he lacked the craggy profile, Charles sunken cheeks and high cheekbones made it possible for makeup to suggest Lincoln's gaunt aspect. Unlike Graham, he was not loath to use facial expressions in keeping with the emotional value of the movements. The spoken word was very much a part of *House*. Actor/dancer Spencer Teakle took the role of *His Voice,* proclaiming Lincoln's words as Charles danced. At times they were man and shadow; otherwise His Voice stayed on the upper level, while Lincoln danced in the forefront. The set had only a draped cross on the upper level at the start.

HOUSE DIVIDED

One woman enters bearing a wreath, which she places on the cross. All join in grieving attitudes, then withdraw. The cross is removed. The Stunned People—Lincoln speaks of The Laborer—The Negro—A Country Divided—His Departure.

Now Lincoln (Charles) enters, gesturing to left and right. Dancers representing the North and the South enter from opposite sides and take stances facing each other. As His Voice pleads for unity, the two sides scorn each other and defy Lincoln with a convulsive body motion, suggestive of laughing ridicule. They exit. Lincoln comes down from the level to dance a solo using large arm gestures. Reaching out, arms extended and hands clasped, he moves in wrenching half turns, back and forth. As he stops to speak again, the Laborers enter. Dressed in brown cotton shifts, four of us enter one at a time, drop to our knees and agonizingly drag our bodies across the stage as though working the fields. At the end of our row, we struggle to rise and drop back down to work our way back. One woman rises to protest and is seized by the Overseer and male workers. She struggles to be free but is cornered. She runs to escape in tangents and pauses with violent head circles, her long hair whipping the air. She dodges as the men press her more and more upstage where they seize her and lift her up into a cross, then she is thrown down and attacked. The rape is seen from the back, the men using violent suggestive movements. They leave the slave for dead.

Lincoln comes and gathers her in his arms, carries her up to place her in the arms of His Voice, who carries her off stage. Lincoln comes back down to rail at a pretty lady who just embroiders during the violence. Now His Voice gives the title speech: "A house divided against itself cannot stand." North and South battle, again coming from opposite sides of the stage, their movement attacking with a vicious swinging leg kick. A threatening arm with a fist slashes back and forth as they rush to change places, giving the effect of waves of attacks. The Father of the Southern Family is wounded, to convey the loss by the South. His family helps him home. Lincoln again pleads for charity and this time the dancers, in ensemble, join him in the hand-clasping-- reversing attitude turns. Lincoln comes forward, arms rising to clasp overhead with a side leg extension, then drop over to the floor; this is repeated by all before a slow, sustained open arm recovery. Lincoln returns to the level, leaving both sides repentant.

The applause was loud and long. On this night, I could see Charles appealing to Betts, Felisa and Carl (the North) to reconcile with Emily, Peter and Saida . It was ironic the roles were cast this way before the schism.

Paul Robeson took over singing a variety of songs from folk to opera to Hassidic chant. Each song received enthusiastic applause. He concluded singing Negro folk songs, and *Listen to the Lambs*. Then Freda Miller took over the piano, beginning Herbert Haufrecht's music for *And Daddy Was a Fireman*.

On My Mother's Side was Charles's first dance about his family; *Daddy* was second. The new *Panamic Suite* was third and had a different structure. In these first two, Charles used the concept of the Greek Chorus. Here in *Daddy,* five of us recited the exact newspaper clippings that recorded the career of Charles Woodman, fireman, in his contest with Chief Malone and fire itself. Daddy also courted Vesta. With cutouts for scenery, the dance had a vaudeville air. Costumes were *fin de siecle,* made by Nellie Hatfield. Nellie also made our hats part of the fun. Felisa's was a cabbage of ruffles that sat on top of her head. Em's feather curved from back to front, ending center between her eyes. Betts's was a mob cap and mine a lace-trimmed straw pancake, tied on with ribbons. Carl Morris was Fire, in bright red tights, a red-striped shirt and black vest. He swirled a long red scarf about as *Fire.* Betty Osgood was the fire Victim in flimsy nightie and curl papers, dancing a hysterical duet with Fire until rescued by Daddy. For his heroism, Daddy was promoted to the Canal Zone.

Daddy never failed to give an audience a good time and this was no exception. Charles was so full of whimsical mischief and glee without a wasted gesture. His movements were selective within modern dance discipline that called for necessity for each movement.

Gradually, I would learn that the ingenuousness that characterized Charles's choreography came from astute observation of society. Charles did not try to glorify mankind; his characters were "normal," which gave them a natural impulse. Another factor that lent credibility to Charles's choreography was the individuality of his dancers. No physical uniformity existed among us; to the contrary, size, shape and body varied widely. Even moving in unison, we were seen as the individuals we were, not a *corps.*

Our second pre-tour performance was in Manhattan at the *Ziegfeld Theatre,* January 25th. With *The New York Times* Dance Critic John Martin as chairman, the Spanish Refugee Appeal was sponsoring a *Dance Festival* for the benefit of

Spanish Refugees in Exile. The best dancers in New York responded to create a star-studded night. Performers included Martha Graham, Sophie Maslow, Jane Dudley. Bill Bales, Nadine Gae, Peter Hamilton, Mata and Hari, Jose Limón, Miriam Pandor, Betty Jones, Rosario, Antonio and us. I caught a quick minute with Betty, learning she was now working in Modern Dance with Jose dancing *Concerto in D* tonight.

Martha was to dance her *Salem Shore* before us. Thus, I was in a good position to observe her. She stood not two feet from me in that personal pre-performance remove. From a backstage perspective, I saw Martha as dancer and not the dance. A small woman in black, Martha was not pretty, but her vitality made her aspect handsome. On stage, clasping the thick, twisted vine, she seemed to retreat from the world. While Douglas Watson recited the ballad of longing, Martha balanced precariously on one hip. Framing her face with the grapevine, she projected an incorruptible intensity. When she moved, her own weight seemed painful. The dance seemed very slow. Maybe it was just my anticipation to dance.

We had good reason for anxiety; this performance was our premiere of *Panamic Suite*. Raised in Panama until he was seven, Charles devised these dances as impressions of his childhood there to music by our own Ada Reif. Using native dance forms, Charles embroidered enough mime upon each rhythm to give each an occasion: the rumba for *Daily Life,* the tango for *Promenade,* the pollero for *Preparation for Festival,* the tamborito as *National Dance,* and the congo for the religious celebration *Semana Santa.* The costumes by Frank Brody were colorful, lush versions of traditional styles. We all brought fresh exuberance to this performance, mindful of accuracy in execution at the same time. Applause was strong and enthusiastic, but it was for *every* dance that night. There was no way to critically evaluate ours. *Panamic Suite* was fun to dance, but not a favorite of the Company. I, for one, would rather have worked hard and eager on a new dramatic modern dance piece.

Charles had received a Guggenheim Fellowship for Dance to choreograph James Thurber's *Fables of Our Times.* I was eager to see what he would do, after my attempt to dance one of the fables for my Master's thesis was quashed. Charles's caricatures were so far beyond my imagination that I was humbly grateful just to watch him create his choreography and dance it. The grant allowed Charles to have Freda Miller compose music for the *Fables.* Freda composed to support the dances, provide mood and transition, to underscore certain words, and to add musical punctuation. Freda and Charles worked well together with a rapport that often allowed them to anticipate each other. Rehearsals can be as exciting as performances. We all marveled at Freda's skill; how her improvising led to invention; inaccurate repetitions became inadvertent improvements, an embellishment extending a dramatic phrase or a stronger body accent. Both Charles and Freda spoke right up to each other in this creative process. The last word, however, was Charles's.

Charles's movements for *Fables* were graphic, modeled after Thurber's posturing of his cartoon characters. For us to capture this two-dimensional bodyline, we used a sharp angularity of elbow and knee, an inertia with arms dangling, knees sagging, feet flat, the gaze diagonal. The hard part was finding the succinct gestures to convey these birds and animals. *Fables* included a veritable zoo of creatures, actual and mythical. In his inimitable genius, Charles used his Kinetic Mime in movements to suggest chipmunks, moles, secretary birds, chickens, beavers, a French poodle, an owl and a unicorn. Our jaws were dropped, cheeks sucked in, necks arched or drawn in, teeth exposed, concealed or protruded, and eyes and eyebrows synchronized in a wide range of expressions. Positioning and carriage of our "paws" and "wings" were equally distinct. For example, Charles wore acorns between his toes, hands tucked under his armpits, shoulders hunched up, and used an exaggerated overbite for the chipmunks. This silliness became the company greeting, provoking many wary public reactions on tour.

I was one of the Beaver Girls, one of Al's play mates in *The Courtship of Arthur and Al.* Charles was the playboy beaver, Al; Carl the industrious worker, Arthur. Betts Lee was the love object. As Beavers, our upper teeth were exposed with a turned up nose, ready for gnawing. Our paws were held parallel, shoulder height, tight elbow, but slightly away from our bodies. Much of our action was frolicking in the "water" with Al, one time swimming on our backs across stage, another time sliding down a "water fall." For gnawing, the back of the hand was held over an open mouth as our heads bobbed up and down.

Our Beaver costumes added much to the fun for us as Beaver Girls. With brown-striped blue jerseys and Dutch-blue ballooning britches, we had a brown velvet cummerbund that ended in the back with a large brown, velvet beaver tail. We wore brown, velvet beaver headpieces with beaver ears, clasped under the chin, matching our turtleneck. Bett's costume was similar but she also wore an apron. Charles wore a frosh beanie, a windowpane checked jacket, complete with velvet tail and brown bloomers. Al's outfit added overalls to his beaver outfit. Despite lingering resentments, we all laughed hilariously rehearsing this dance. We would tickle each other's ears to start giggling before each performance.

In *The Owl Who Was God,* I was the French Poodle, mincing about on my toes. I wore a black leotard and tights with black ruffles at ankles, hip, shoulder and head, with a big pink taffeta bow at my neck and black gloves. Bob O'Hearn designed the costumes for *Fables,* coming up with inspired combinations of animal and human attire. Headpieces were often hats. Nellie Hatfield again got them all constructed for us.

Bob also designed the sets, devising a metal screen about twelve feet long. The upper line of the screen rose in easy curves to about five feet; the lower line was flat. There was a metal flag at the high end of the screen. Used one way, it was our waterfall; turned upside down, it became part of our mountain in *Owl.* For the rest of the *Fables* sets, the gray wooden boxes were put to use in all manners of ways for settings for each fable. For example, the six-foot mountain for the Owl to climb was a rising stack of boxes. The hallmark of *Fables* was the ingenious economy of design throughout: Thurber's succinct wording, Charles's kinetic mime, Freda's concise music and O'Hearn's abstract scenery. Pulling it all together was the Narrator, Jack Ferris, who blandly wandered about the sets, sitting here, leaning there in his business suit. Urbane, detached, he told the *Fables* as he observed our dancing.

While I had been working on my M.A. thesis n 1946, I had asked for and received a letter from Charles's studio, enclosing a paper he had written on *Humor in the Dance.*

Digging it out to reread it, I noted his six rules to apply to achieve humor:

1. Extreme exaggeration or distortion of the natural; example Charlie Chaplin's legs and feet.
2. Extreme contrast in movement...going very slowly, going fast
3. Sadistic humor, or the things that inflict discomfort to a person...falls, kicks, etc.
4. An afflicted person...with gout, toothache, a lame person
5. Sudden changes of thought, direction, or quick new themes
6. Pantomimic representation of a function...fighting, juggling or eating. When the audience recognizes the act, it amuses them.

Later in the essay, Charles explained his search was:

"...attempting to extract the essence of what I wanted to achieve, attempting to extract the essence of any emotion that was projected through motion. The search led me to and was crystallized in a dance called *Kinetic Pantomime*. In this composition, I so juggled, reversed and distorted cause and effect, impulse and reaction, the kaleidoscopic effect was created without having to resort to literary representation. Vaguely, one might explain the movement as one of being pushed, looking for something and scratching of something. These acts in themselves and the way they were done were funny enough without having to tell a story.

New York, New York
December 29, 1944

With so much on his mind, talking to Charles was usually like having a long-distance conversation with poor connections. He stuttered more than usual. He could be sarcastic at times. We had much more to do than dance; responsible for props and changing scenery as well as costumes; techies as well as performers. Ready or not, January 29th came up and the *Charles Weidman and Dance Company* took off early in the morning by bus to Purdue University at Lafayette, Indiana. When we stopped for lunch along the way, I discovered I left New York with more money than anyone else; I had five dollars. Our bus got in so late the night clerk had not saved our rooms. We were crammed together into too few, but glad for any bed.

Next morning, it was over to Purdue to set up and rehearse. While the men lugged the boxes, we girls did the props and costumes. The costumes were so wrinkled they all had to be ironed. We worked through lunch setting up, then rehearsed. I was particularly excited about this performance because my sister Phyllis was coming from Champagne-Urbana to see it. All in all, our first concert was well received. Word came backstage from our hosts saying, "If you're hungry, we'll take you to the greatest steak house this side of the Mississippi River."

We were all ravenous. There had been no time for supper. Thank goodness there was a place willing to serve at 11:00 p.m. We had a great time chatting with Purdue staff, relieved our first program was prized. Charles was in high form and the place rang with laughter at his wit. Only Emily was not with us; no one seemed to know where she was. I had honestly forgotten about her in my haste to find Phyllis, get family news and make sure she had a good time. Phyllis got more than that as the party broke up and it was time to pay the bill. Naive dancers, we thought our sponsors meant to pay when they said, "We'll take you." We had not been paid. Charles was embarrassed. Phyllis graciously stepped forward and treated the whole company. I was very grateful and impressed she had the money to do it. (Phyllis had married U.S. Army Air Corps Colonel Luther Kissick after the war ended.)

We spent a couple days at Purdue, giving master classes during the day and more concerts at night. Roles were now set for the entire tour. Emily took first honors in local papers for her role as the Slave. The four continued to give her the freeze; I was spoken to when necessary. Emily and I prepared to be buddies across the country. St. Louis was next; the routine the same with master classes and performances. Charles began to shrug off his worries and enjoy doing what he did best: teach and perform for new audiences. He also took me to my first burlesque.

When Charles learned I had never seen burlesque, his eyes danced with delight. He dragged me along with him and other company members. The guys enjoyed the seediest acts, egged on the burlesque dollies and, with Charles, got right into the whole raucous mood. "Don't slump down so far in your seat, Sharry," Charles teased, giving me a tickle in the ribs.

The first minute of each act was an anxiety for me; then I either relaxed a bit when it was simply stupid, or blushed and contracted when I understood a dirty joke. The "girlies" had slouching, pathetic bodies, adding to the sleaze. By the time the star stripper came out, I had almost adjusted to the rancid smell of the trash-strewn theatre. I had not yet died of mortification and curiosity was making me braver. Hmmm. Here was a middle-aged woman with a body worse than the rest. Sagging "rubber tires" about her waist and she had a belly! Red satin triangles were tied about her large, drooping breasts on a black string. A black and red G-string with tattered fringe covered her *os pubis*. Carelessly brazen and with a practiced cheery leer, this female paraded and bumped to a bawdy song. Cheap high heels clattered as she minced top-heavily along, then sagged into a hip-slung pose. To my distress, and Charles's glee, she began to caress herself. Next she turned upstage to strip off her bra. She flashed back, not totally bare. Her pendulous breasts had a gold tassel stuck on each nipple. Leaning forward, hands on her knees; Queenie LaMott (whoever) began to swing her tasseled breasts to and fro, then in circles. Between tipples from brown bagged whiskey bottles, the men hooted and yelled for more. So Queenie went for her sellout trick, proudly spinning each breast in opposite circles! That was a new coordination for me.

Then the whole raunchy, miserable, sad exploitation hit me. I began to identify with this over-the-hill dame who ridiculed herself for these filthy minded, lecherous guys. I hated Men. Predatory bastards! Charles grinned and nudged me asking, "How do you like this tough old bird?" Where was there anything funny! Then I felt prissy, remembering burlesque had been a part of theatre for centuries, whenever there had been theatre.

"I'm glad I went," I stated soberly afterward, then had to join Charles and the others laughing at me.

Leland Sage Teachers College in Cedar Rapids, Iowa, was next. Then we went on to the University of Denver, where a surprise was waiting for me. Terry, my folk singing cowboy, in a tuxedo! The next day was our first free day, so Terry took me to Colorado Springs. It was one of those glorious winter runaway days with a brilliant sun in an essence-of-blue sky. A fresh snowfall made me smile at the easy beauty of it. The mountains beckoned but yet forbade a careless approach by their majesty. Fresh air and space!

We rode past ranches where horses with steaming nostrils stamped and snorted in a corral, past a low, isolated ranch house. A nostalgia for the West came over me. Terry started singing and I joined in until we came upon five horses on the snowy range. Here was animal ecstasy. Frolicking in the dry, fluffy snow, the horses jump-started each other to shy and lope away, only to do it again. One horse began to buck, twisting his body while circling in place. Two others started to jump. Suddenly they all began to race.

"Go, Terry! Go!" We drove to keep pace with the horses dashing heedlessly ahead, expecting to see one flip over something beneath the snow. On they all galloped, swiftly shifting spaces until suddenly they all stopped. We left them, chestnut coats gleaming, nuzzling in the snow or standing, poised.

"So, how long can you let yourself put up with the tumbleweed life you've got?" Terry asked me. "Lord above! Can't you see that plain as day you need caring for? What will you have left to dance about, keepin' on like a lost child, woman?" Our eyes met and we broke into a sorrowful laughter at his words.

"I can't leave Charles," I said. "On tour? No. I'm just not…where you are, Terry."

He waited a moment, then sighed, "Well, music pulls me by the nose. Guess I'll have to understand your dancing."

I sat by myself on the train from Denver to Lewiston, Washington, to think. Life seemed to just pour through me. Was I letting it all just go by without considering what to keep? What was there to keep? Just me. Or what to get? Not having things did not bother me very much. I didn't think I needed anyone to take care of me—as long as I was dancing. Well, I had no health insurance, should go to the dentist. But then, what do I give to others less fortunate? I now knew my dancing was for my soul more than others. For now, I *was* needed here. There was enough demand for excellence in my roles to keep my momentum going.

What was missing was the usual camaraderie in show casts. The schism in the Company was a fact nobody mentioned. Or tried to cure. It was wearing on everyone. I was supposed also to be an understudy, but the surly rebels dodged teaching me, or gave such vague directions I had to insist on accuracy and also motivation. I knew it would cut no ice to tell them what solo roles I had had in previous shows. To solve my loneliness, I dove into books.

Charles just plugged along, keeping company with Jack, Freda and his many dance friends along the way. It was interesting to consider how my being promoted in *Bloomer Girl* was immediately accepted. Not a protest. Not a resentful glance from another dancer. No tensions in the air. Here in a Modern Dance Company, where we all danced together in class over and over—a rebellion. Was concert dance more democratic? Less professional? On stage everyone cooperated in the choreography. Only when the North and South came at each other in *House* were there hateful glances from the North. I felt protective of Emily when I learned that her older sister and I were in the same class in high school. Emily never mentioned company attitudes, so neither did I. Hopefully the attrition of traveling, the necessary cooperation setting up, and shared meals would melt tensions away.

On stage, Charles was the consummate professional; offstage, he was often pensive. As company director, he could be deplorably vague and indecisive up to the moment a dancer tried to clarify a point. His drinking affected rehearsals and he had no consistent plan for our master classes. He selected the work on the moment, expecting us to improvise, which we did. Sometimes Charles would be his cheerful self, walking down the street in his Chipmunk guise for the fun of it. Or at a restaurant, tease one or another of us as Al, the Beaver, until we answered in kind and our racket rattled the rafters. Charles could be lovable, and I held a love for him. Knowing he would be uncomfortable to learn of it, I could show it by always dancing my very best for him. And I did.

The long bus trips were tiring. By the time we got through to Reed College out in Washington, the daily need for each other was slowly winning over resentment. There we learned from our Reed hostess, Jean Stevens, that the workmen had not had time to refinish their new stage floor before our performance. Could we dance on raw wood? Charles allowed ballet slippers but they did not move well at all. Worse, as Beaver Girls, we had to swim backstroke all across the stage. Later, Emily, Felisa and I took turns tweezing out each other's splinters. This was the last torment for Emily, who came down with the flu. The extra efforts demanded by one-nighters caught up with other dancers, too. Marc Breau had the flu. Jack could barely keep his voice audible. Felisa was fighting constant insomnia. Charles was exhausted. We had one wet, cold day in Portland to recover. Then it was back to the train and then another bus to Chico, CA.

Spring had come to California! As our bus followed a dirt road through the citrus orchards along the way, we fell into an Eden of fragrant orange blossoms. It was utter bliss to breathe in that lovely scent. Seeing the abundance of these delicate orange blooms, I wanted to jump out the window and sprawl on the grasses beneath the trees, getting drunk on their perfume. My heart swelled as I remembered William Saroyan's *Summer of the Beautiful White Horse.* I could not wait to dance. When the reviews came out after that night's performance, in Chico, California on April 23rd, I was mentioned:

> "Outstanding in their techniques of dance
> were Carl Morris, Emily Frankel and Sharry
> Traver. Modern Dance Group gives top show
> for Chico audience."

John Ferris, Reviewer

Good for my self respect, it finally brought me to the attention of the Company. How come I was noticed? Watch, baby, just watch! Maybe not a lead in this show, but I expected to make a difference any time I went on stage. And to the point, I was dancing in every number that required women but one.

Santa Barbara kept up California's reputation as Paradise. Everyone was feeling much better, much friendlier in the sunshine. One of Charles's many friends opened her studio to us for rehearsal. When we saw it, we were awed. This dance studio was glassed in on three sides, facing the ocean, with palm trees and greenery all about. It was clean, bright with light and gleaming hardwood floors. A dancer's dream. We were so used to smelly college gyms, we forgot something better was possible.

Los Angeles was the best. This was our most important engagement. With rehearsals and performances, we would stay nearly a week. Joe Maronna, our advance man, had done his best to find us rooms. From the beginning, Emily and I agreed to stay on the cheap side to save money. With memories of my lush stay here with *Bloomer Girls,* I was tempted to live it up a bit. What Joe got for us was totally unacceptable to me. The "beds" were 2x4 slats nailed together; the standing lamp wouldn't. No hangers in the open "closet." Walls patched with tin. The "bath" had been a kitchen. Here was a slab of a mirror far from the filthy sink. Surprise! No hot water. Yuk! Emily agreed to move, but when Joe could find nothing else but the Ambassador Hotel, she refused.

"I don't understand you, Sharry. You put up with sleeping in a chair in Iowa, give up your train sleeper to buy books, why are you making such a fuss?"

"In Iowa there was no other way. There must be more than this creepy ex-bordello in L.A.! I can do what I have to, but not with what I can change."

While Em re-dyed her flaming hair, I tracked down a Syracuse Pi Beta Phi sorority sister who was now a starlet at Columbia Pictures in Hollywood, Tish White. By afternoon, I moved into her guest room in her Tudor cottage in Hollywood. Imagine having your own home and a career in the movies! Here was all the glamour: the fur coat tossed onto the bed, the phone calls from makeup and wardrobe, the stacks of glossies of Tish slipping askew on her desk. Tish had a closet full of delicious dresses and a white convertible in the driveway.

It had been 1943 when Tish and I had been close, the only two Pi Beta Phis majoring in drama at Syracuse. Tish was very photogenic, pretty with a soft cloud of auburn hair, an open face with an easy smile. Our sophomore year, Tish already had headshots and an agent. She left for Hollywood mid-semester. Now, although we both had our calls, we managed to catch up on sorority sisters, past, current love life, and where our careers melded or went off on tangents. I definitely felt the poor city mouse but was pumped up with Tish's respect for being in a renowned dance company. Next to the movies, our *Charles Weidman and Company* seemed a one-lung operation. Now I could see comparisons were out of place; our two arts were just different. California Oranges and New York Apples.

Marc Platt, the original dancer for Curley in *Oklahoma!*, was here making movies. He would take Tish to the studio so I could have her convertible to drive over to our Master Class at the University College of Los Angeles, UCLA. Its huge gym enticed Charles to set large-movement dance sequences, giving one of his best Master Classes to these students. I offered to take a company member back from Berkeley with me but had no takers. It was just as well, for after a time on the Freeway, the car just stopped in the center lane.

The car just would not go. Oh, God! I broke Tish's car!

I looked behind me and had a wild time/space/relationship with hundreds of cars hurtling at me. Drivers were terrified, honked, and yelled nasty things at me as I cringed. Then there was a bump at the rear. Then came a few hits more, as a driver bumped me off the Freeway and took off. First I was angry, then managed to call, "Thank Youuuu!" For the first time, I looked at the gas gauge. Humbly, gratefully, I went looking for a gas station.

Buzzing around Los Angeles, I ran into two of my former directors: Reginald Lawrence (*Insect Comedy*), who took me to lunch at the Brown Derby, and Jose´ Ruben (*Starlight Operettas)*. I was flattered that José remembered me by name after two years. Unexpectedly bumping into past fellow thespians is one of the nicest things about the theatre. Rehearsing in the legitimate Wilshire-Ebell Theatre restored some company pride. With four performances, we could present our full repertory. The program itself was professional, listing the cast for each dance. It even had room for a statement by Charles defining Modern Dance:

> Modern!—what does the word mean? The dictionary defines it as 'pertaining to the present time' but it is not enough to be merely existing in the contemporary world. Active life demands that we be mentally and emotionally aware of the world's continual change and realize the constant progressions and retrogressions. The artist who attempts to

escape the present either by delving into the
past or the future is running away from his
'center of being.' But it is not enough for the
artist alone to assume his responsibilities as
mentor and preceptor. His audience must do
so, also, especially in the case of an artistic
form that concerns the theatre. Concert dance
lives only while it is being presented. It cannot
be referred to later in files and books.
Therefore, both the stage and the auditorium
have equal importance. Those who sit in the
'house' must also be of today. They also must
be conscious of and sensitive to their age, for
only then will the dance-work come alive and
project its full meaning and value as the artist
wished.

Wilshire-Ebell Theatre Program
February 26, 27, 28, 29, 1948

I read this with great interest. So far, Charles had let
his work speak for him; so far he had not ever discussed his
philosophy of dance with us.

Tish and I had both come a long way in theatre since
Syracuse University days. I was anxious to please her and
Marc Platt, who came to the program with her. He had
recently starred with Rita Hayworth in *Down to Earth*. How
would we be rated by Hollywood? They took me out to
dinner at Chasen's before our concert, generously
introducing me to this producer, that actress. Our table was
popular enough that I had little time to enjoy the fine food.
Anxious, I left before dessert for the theatre. The best

nourishment was realizing the respect Hollywood people had for concert dance from New York.

Opening night, we began with *Panamic Suite,* followed by *On My Mother's Side, House Divided, Ringside* and *Fables for Our Time.* On the 28th, when Marc and Tish came, we opened with *Dance for Five.* Choreographed by Peter Hamilton, music by Ada Rief, it was pure dancing by Marc Breaux with Emily, Betts, Felisa and me. It was full of Humphrey-Weidman technique with jumps, leaps, off-center head turns and rebounding suspensions. Our costumes were in bright colored taffeta with double skirts and spaghetti straps; our shoes were simply black elastic wound around our feet. Next *House Divided, Ringside* and then *Lynch Town.*

Lynch Town had its origin in Charles's personal experience, a child witnessing a lynching in his hometown, Lincoln, Nebraska. From this gruesome experience, Charles constructed this modern dance expressing the sexuality and cruelty in the animalistic behavior of a mob. It was pure modern dance. *Lynch Town* was demanding to perform and affecting. Our minds must be preoccupied with evil. We had to immerse ourselves in all the negative emotions of human being, loathing, hatred, derision, the perverted satisfaction watching harm done to another, the obsessions of the herd instinct with its hypnotic stupors and momentums. The overall characteristic of the movements was simian: the feet broad based, arms held away from the body, and dangling. Our movements appeared subconscious particularly in the beginning. The quality of our movement with stealthy surges, distorted head and body articulations followed sensually as our mob is pulled from observation into participation.

The action begins with the sounds of Lehman Engel's possessive music score for fife and percussion. There is a murky green path of light from upstage left. Men enter downstage right with a swaying step as they carry the condemned man toward it. We women, wearing off-white sleeveless leotards, smudged with dirt, exposed under our open ankle length burlap garments, sleaze in with hesitant steps, necks protruding. Felisa holds her right hand up to her bare shoulder, her left across her stomach. Em holds her right hand palm out, at the small of her back, her left arm hanging down. Betts carries both elbows pulled back, hands loose. I hold my right hand against the inside of my right thigh, my left hand held lower, dangling between my legs, my body lurching slightly left. Shoulders are carried up for us all. From profile, our stance changes to face the body down stage. First the left foot reaches out, pulling the body into a low, spread second position; then weight shifts to the left, the right arm dangling between our legs, the left arm held away from the body: the classic monster pose.

Syncopated, in turn we rise on our toes with bent knees, fingers ready to grasp. This extension contracts violently into a crouch, one hand held over a silent screaming mouth, the other hand splayed between the legs. In this position we go into a scudding run forward to a point to view the body, then drop back as another goes forward to look. This interweaving projects an irresistible curiosity and the following fear for personal safety in retreat. All this goes on while, the group moves relentlessly toward the grisly scene.

At times, there are duets; one woman jumps on the back of a man and rides him, pointing ahead as he spins her. By now the men have carried the victim off upstage left and the mob leans forward toward the light, mesmerized. As the drum booms, the mob begins to move as one in a drunken stupor, heads protruding, arms dangling. The foot pattern is the classic box step, modified with a lurch forward and back in a trance. The unanimity gives a palpable power, the motion sympathetic with the (offstage) body swing of a hanged man. As the drum suddenly ceases, there is a silence. Bodies freeze. 'Tis done.

But this is only half the dance. The action is reversed, the men dragging the body back on the same diagonal. The same frenzied woman climbs on a man's back, his head between her knees, lower legs bounding on his chest. She points to the corpse and begins to sway until she drops back, her body jiggling upside-down. She sways until her hands touch the ground, then is flipped over to land near the corpse The mob repeats the extension/contraction, encircling the men who are rolling the body down stage right.. The mob, shifting on tangents, accompanies the corpse off stage.

There is always a dead silence as *Lynch Town* ends. Then, always, there is a loud energetic applause in admiration and relief. I always trembled offstage in a convulsive shudder after dancing it. I felt filthy, loathing my nasty self. Who would want to do evil, if you felt like this! And yet I always looked forward to dancing *Lynch Town* for its dance demands, its message.

Reincarnation came with scrubbing off the dirt, changing makeup and costume, to emerge as the saucy black French Poodle for *The Owl Who Was God.*

Here, an Owl simply minding his own business, uttering his too-wit and too-woos, is thought to be answering questions from two moles, a dormouse, a secretary bird, a Plymouth Rock hen, and a poodle. "Why does a lover call on his love?" asks the Secretary Bird. "To woo," answers the Owl. They all decide he is God and follow everything he does. Again, Charles abstracted the peculiar characteristics of each creature; the Moles wearing glasses hovered together; the Hen jumped up and down, picking up her feet to walk; the Secretary Bird changed focus, moving her head abruptly and had a stiff angular walk; my Poodle had dithering, mincing steps, my paws held high, elbows in. I changed focus often, staring. Our company action then was to follow Charles, as Owl, up the mountain (a six-foot heap of boxes) and jump off to die, making sure not to sprain ankles.

The moral in *The Owl Who Was God* was: You can fool too many people too much of the time.

The moral in *The Shrike and the Chipmunk* was: Early to rise and early to bed make a male healthy and wealthy and dead.

The moral for *The Courtship of Arthur and Al* was: Better to have loafed and lost than never to have loafed at all.

In *The Unicorn in the Garden*, the moral was: Don't count your boobies until they're hatched.

Charles discovered endearing as well as amusing eccentricities for his characters. He was lovable and charming as he happily immersed himself in them. Nothing in my life has been such silly fun as splashing in the "water" with Charles as the carefree beaver, Al.

Tish and Marc were excited about our concert, saying we were "Live art." We had a great bull session about dance and theatre and cinema on into the night. Our early reviews were also positive:

Los Angeles Times, February 27, 1948:

Excellent troupe—credit to young men and women who assist him.

Each is an excellent dancer and mime
in his own right… entertainment unusual and
interesting. Fables outstanding."

As usual, we left town before most notices came out but this was enough to celebrate. Now headed back East by the southern route, we had an overnight in El Paso, Texas. There was time next day to cross the Rio Grande to Juarez, Mexico, to poke in little shops for espadrilles and earrings. I treated myself to a silver belt for fifteen dollars. Our next performance would be at my old alma mater, Texas State College for Women. Hmmm. Just keep everything in the present, I told myself.

When we arrived in Denton, I learned Jeanette Schlottman was still in New York. Mary Campbell was still here and it was so good to see her doing well. Several other TSCW pals were around, but it was Dr. Duggan's reception that threw me for a loop. She greeted me proudly with open arms, babbling about my work here, how wonderful "to have one of my girls in your company, Charles." She was at her charming best; welcoming us with a buffet supper, having rehearsal schedules set and PR from the college paper, *The Lasso,* included a special paragraph about me! There was also an invitation to talk to the Modern Dance Group "telling them how what you learned here helped you in your career, won't you Shirley?"

With the student dancers clustered around me, I praised the beautiful studios, the college dance tour, Mary and Jeanette and the vital fact of there being a Dance Major. I finessed praising Dr. Duggan. I just couldn't. All this sudden smarmy praise was such a lie. I could only see more exploitation.

We had a full house for our concert, which included Charles's solo, *On My Mother's Side,* a series of dance vignettes depicting six members of his maternal family. Music was by Lionel Nowak, the text by the poet William Archibald. This was a fine example of Charles's idiosyncratic, kinetic pantomime, which was quickly comprehensible to the student audience. Charles had no interest in being obscure or pretentious; he wanted his works easily accessible to the general public. At TSCW, we also danced *House, Ringside* and *Fables.* The program went well. It was good to show my friends and Dr. Duggan just how much better a dancer I was.

Back on the train, Charles stopped me with a mock-serious frown. "What did you do when you were back there?" he asked. "Dr. Duggan made a point to tell me what a dreadful girl you were. She told me I should throw you out of the Company." Charles eyes sparkled with delight at my instant indignation. Now how could you just leave that woman to heaven?

There was a wake-up call when we played at Hampton Institute in Virginia. Charles had been drinking on the long trip back East and was half groggy, half cranky, getting one of the morning master classes going. I, too, may have been dreaming at the start. Nick Vanoff and I exchanged baleful looks, knowing we would be scapegoats as newest in the company. Charles would correct the class, using us as examples. He was not often malicious, but could be sarcastic and impatient. Dancers are used to getting yelled at; it is a timesaving tool for the most part. I was resigned when he did use me as an example. Therefore I was surprised to have a rather large group of black students gathered around me after class.

They did not ask the usual questions about technique or program content. Instead it was: How did you take that criticism? Why did you accept that humiliation? Is he like that often? Will this affect your dancing tonight? In turn, I explained Charles's right to correct, tighten or expand his work as he saw fit. Yes, I had been picked on today, but the whole company had been reminded "This tour isn't over yet. Classes are as important as performances!" As to could I now perform? You tell me after the show. To their credit, the students did come back to congratulate my work.

Since our California days, company camaraderie improved to the point where we agreed to have our pictures taken together. Freda Miller shared her company with Charles and Jack, but she too became a personal friend to the rest of us. Our last road concert was at the *Museum Theatre of the Baltimore Museum of Art.* Here Emily opened up to announce that she was engaged to dancer Mark Ryder. Everyone seemed genuinely happy for her.

It was raining as I came out of the subway by Rockefeller Plaza, carrying my suitcase and tackle-box makeup kit, wondering whether I still had a home to go to. Neither Anita nor Eddie was home at the apartment. It had been completely redecorated. Wistfully I thought of Nana's embroidered sampler: *Home is where the heart is.* With me, it was *The heart is where the home is.* After Robin returned my clothes, Anita had stashed them downstairs in the back room of *Biff's Barber Shoppe.* Three trips carrying my dainties past eye-rolling, sniggering patrons were enough for me and Biff. Anita and Eddie had names of people wanting to share apartments. I was not ready to live with a stranger.

I went to check out a newspaper rooming ad on Lexington. I followed the owner to the second floor bedroom.

As I was appraising it, I turned to see the landlord coming toward me with that hooded look in his eyes.

"Oh! I just remembered I have a dentist appointment!" I cried as I dashed past him and ran as fast as I could down the stairs and out of the house and down the street for two blocks.

It was back to the relative safety of residence hotels. I found a room, shared bath, first floor but no windows, at the *Pickwick Arms Hotel* over on East 61st Street. This was meant as an available sleepover for the manager; now they were renting it at twenty-five dollars a week in advance. Clean, decent. Good locale. Messages taken at the desk. Now all I needed was a radio to tell me the weather.

Rehearsals were constant at The Studio. We had an engagement at Cedarhurst, one at the Needle Trades High School, and were preparing for our all -important week of performances on Broadway! *Charles Weidman and His Dance Theatre Company* was to be presented by Eunice Healey and Ernest D. Gluckman at the Mansfield Theatre, Sunday, April 18, through Saturday, April 24.

Charles had not forgotten the rebellion. He returned the leads to Nadine Gae, Saida Gerrard and Peter. Beatrice Seckler also returned to dance *Lynch Town.* Betts, Felisa, Carl and Emily lost out until the end of the run. My dances stayed the same. A week on Broadway was sure to be exciting! Performances would end April 24th, with me still in the Company but with no more salary.

Checking with Equity revealed that ANTA (the American National Theatre Association) was sponsoring a one-week show, *Ballet Ballads,* with music, dance and three choreographers: Katherine Litz, Paul Godkin and Hanya Holm. I auditioned and was chosen by Litz, a former H/W dancer, and Holm. Balancing rehearsals between downtown and uptown took elegant timing, but I loved every minute of it.

Charles Weidman & Dance Company received plenty of publicity in the *New York Times* and the *Herald Tribune.* Both Walter Terry in the *Tribune* and John Martin in the *Times* gave generous advance articles on Charles, his works and the company. The newspaper *P.M.* and *Life Magazine* had big pictorial features. Most of the papers were good about mentioning company members' names. Felisa, Emily and I got our pictures in the *New York Times* in our Beaver costumes holding Charles aloft. We danced everything in our repertoire plus a few additions; Peter's *Silent Snow, Secret Snow; Jesse James;* and *None Seeth Me* as well as Bea Seckler's *The Unconquered.* The Mansfield run worked well in every way. It was marvelous for Charles, proving he could survive without Doris.

I was as happy dancing as I had ever been, delighting in every minute of our run. This was the way a dancer's life should be: employed, dancing to full houses in a theatre with a good stage, decent dressing rooms and with another job with artistic challenges in the offing.

John Martin's review after our opening declared our show:

> "an excellent and unusual entertainment"…
> "delightful"… eloquent," and "wonderfully touching"

The New York Times, April 19, 1948

Walter Terry welcomed Charles back on Broadway:

Nine years is much too long for
Broadway to get along without his inspired
clowning, his showmanship, his dance artistry,
qualities which have made him one of
America's leading dancers. These attributes
were very much in evidence; an evening when
Mr. Weidman and his company opened their
engagements at the Mansfield Theatre, for the
program selected for the occasion was
thematically and stylistically varied and the
dancing was of the first order throughout.

The New York Herald Tribune, April 19, 1948

And again, days later, Terry wrote for
The New York Herald Tribune:

Charles Weidman's current repertory
is, in many respects, the most important yet
produced by a modern dancer. It is not the
greatest, for other leaders of modern dance
have produced repertories of inestimable value
to the world of dance, but it is of first
importance because it provides Mr. Weidman
with a way of dance, eminently suited to his
skills, because it is highly theatrical, because it
is diverting as well as emotionally and
intellectually stimulating and because it leads
the general public to modern dance by a route
which is smooth and comfortably familiar.

Later *Dance Magazine* and *Dance Observer* would carry positive reviews. In the June, 1948, issue of *Dance Magazine,* Doris Hering wrote of her interview with Charles following this season. She spoke of his ingenuousness, his gentle humility and asked Charles to state his credo of dance. In his reply, Charles stated that he wanted to:

> "speak in a language all can understand. And that would be my credo, I have no desire to mystify my audience—to send them home with a glazed look in their eyes. I try to be completely clear and choose themes that are from the fabric of America. I like to use pantomime and the spoken word because they are easy to understand."

CHAPTER FIFTEEN

1948
  New York, NY
  Ballet Ballads

"A tree? You want me to be a tree?"

That was what Katie Litz told me at our first rehearsal for *Susanna and the Elders*. Well, why not? I had just been a beaver or a poodle. Now I was to be The Cedar of Lebanon and Ellen Albertini was to be The Little Juniper Tree. It was our duty to shade and protect Susanna as she bathed in a pond by the trees.

Susanna and the Elders would be first in our performances of *Ballet Ballads*. The occasion is set at a revival meeting at which The Parson takes his sermon from the story of Susanna and The Elders as found in the Apocrypha. *Willie, the Weeper,* a sordid tale of drugs and sex, was the second, and *The Eccentricities of Davey Crockett,* a tale of an American frontiersman, the third. *Ballet Ballads* was considered experimental theatre, because the three primary arts of song, dance and music were simultaneous throughout. John Latouche and Jerome Moross created them around the same time that modern dancers and other artists were absorbed in themes about America. It took a decade to bring *Ballet Ballads* to life.

Ballet Ballads program notes:

> During the thirties, John Latouche and
> Jerome Moross were working toward their
> eventual collaboration... Latouche and

Moross collaborated in the Federal Theatre
production of *Frankie and Johnny in 1938,*
one of Moross's first attempts at combining
voice, music and dance. Latouche wrote two
sketches for the long-run ILGWU show *Pins
and Needles* and *Sing for Your Supper* for the
WPA Federal Theatre in 1939.The finale
written with Earl Robinson, now called *Ballad
for Americans* was sung on CBS by Paul
Robeson. It was such a success the studio
audience gave a twenty-minute ovation.
Latouche became famous overnight, stating
his message about human rights "comes out of
my home state…out of a younger generation
that does not accept a defeatist philosophy."

Playbill for *Ballet Ballads,* 1948

Moross was from Brooklyn, Latouche from Virginia;
each in his own way sang of America. While in California
writing music for film, Moross began his association with
Latouche and completed four musical plays: *Susanna and the
Elders*, *Willie the Weeper, The Eccentricities of Davy
Crockett* and *Little Red Ridinghood Revisited.* Both men
were respected; Latouche for his warmth, vigor and wit;
Moross for his fresh diatonic invention, lyricism and
assimilated rhythms.

Jerome Moross:
I do feel that a composer should write not only
to put down on paper what he feels, but in
such a way that his audience experiences his

251

emotions anew. In addition, the composer must reflect his landscape, and mine is the landscape of America.

Playbill for *Ballet Ballads,* May 1948

LaTouche:
    The Ballet Ballads were produced in New York as dance-opera; they were intended to fuse the arts of text, music and dance into a new dynamic unity. When performed in sequence, the fusion takes place gradually proceeding from *Susanna,* which suggests the typical choral-ballet until the chorus is drawn into the action, to *The Eccentricities of Davy Crockett* where the action and character move independently of logical time and space.

Playbill for *Ballet Ballads,* May 1948

    American National Theatre and Academy (ANTA), which sponsored The Experimental Theatre, was in poor financial shape. Blevin Davis, a television producer, lent ANTA sufficient money to do the show. It was budgeted at approximately $25,000 for a six-performance run at Maxine Elliot's Theatre. Assistance also came from Actors Equity and Chorus Equity and from the Dramatists Guild, which allowed leeway in compensation. Later T. Edward Hambleton, director of the Experimental Theatre's executive committee, and Alfred Stern became our financial angels. Our Experimental Theatre, Inc. contracts rolled off an old mimeograph machine: six performances only, $8 each performance, $50 for rehearsal, first performance May 9, 1948. A final statement broke new ground, offering us a share in the profits:

If ET received proceeds from said production as specified in Paragraph Ten of the Basic Agreement between the Dramatist's Guild, in which event the Actor shall receive 1/43 of one half of any and all moneys.

It was a nice gesture.

At our first full cast call, we discovered that we had a large cast, including twenty-four dancers. Seven of us had danced for Agnes, three for Charles, three for Hanya; the others had ballet ensemble or movie and supper club experience. Our dancing star power came from Katie Litz and Paul Godkin (who were also dancing in their own choreography), and notably, Sono Osato. She was our glamorous attraction, having proved herself in *The Ballet Russe, Ballet Theatre, On the Town* and *One Touch of Venus*. There were twenty-five in the singing ensemble and five soloists.

The production staff came from drama and concert stages with little or no experience with Broadway musicals. For Nat Karson, a designer for the stage, *Ballet Ballads* would be his first venture into the financial and technical responsibilities of a producer. He had problems covering overall production chores. As a result, director Mary Hunter had to solve many of these problems. Hugh Ross, the choral and music director, emigrated from England to Canada, where he conducted the Winnipeg Male Voice Chorus and the Winnipeg Symphony Orchestra. Here he had to prepare the choral ensemble and soloists in three differing styles and conduct the performances.

There was to be no orchestra; the score arranged for two pianos. John Lesko, Jr., and Mordachai Scheinkman were both rehearsal and performance pianists. The choreographers/directors of the show also came from the concert stage. Katie Litz and Hanya Holm from modern dance; Paul from ballet. Choreography was not new to Hanya, although she had yet to choreograph a Broadway musical. Katie and Paul had both danced in musicals, but neither had choreographed one nor set dances for an ensemble. They each had assistants: for Katie, Margaret Cuddy; for Hanya, Ray Harrison and Annabelle Lyon; for Paul, James R. Nygren and Olga Lunick.

What *Ballet Ballads* needed to pull these talents together was an exceptional director, knowledgeable in music, dance and theatre. Fortunately, Mary Hunter was all of this. Her experience included founding the *American Actors Company* with Agnes de Mille, Jerome Robbins and Horton Foote. In fact, Robbins originally was to do the choreography for *Willie,* but overbooked, sent Paul, promising to help him along the way.

The sets were correspondingly simple. Karson had designed four black movable step units about five feet high, which could serve as bleachers or steps or mountains. For *Susanna,* these were bleachers arranged in a semicircle for the congregation. In *Willy* and *Davey*, as double steps, arranged to allow Willie, Davey, *et al,* to ascend from behind and descend in front. Simple, but as the Weidman's boxes, this was a perfect answer to the need. And this allowed plenty of space for the dances!

At Katie's rehearsal for *Susanna,* we learned that this was a biblical story of innocence and evil, which we would dance out like a charade. *Willie,* which told of the self-deluded anti-hero, was the sexy part of the program. *Davy,* which celebrated the life of an American folk hero, was third. There were ballads aplenty in this show, but not one classical or romantic-ballet dance combination to be found.

Katherine Litz (1918-1978) came from Denver to New York, where she became a principal dancer in the Humphrey-Weidman Company in the 1930s and early 40s. She danced for Agnes de Mille in *Oklahoma!* and *Carousel.* In 1948, Katie made her debut as choreographer at the 92nd Street Y, initiating her career as a dance satirist and humorist. Katie worked with Paul Taylor, Ray Harrison, the American Ballet Theatre Workshops, Connecticut College American Dance Festival and summer dance festivals at Jacob's Pillow. When the Judson Church opened its doors to dance, Katie was there. Her solos reflected her originality and intelligence. Human frailty was exposed and exaggerated in her work, but always with truth and wit.

A reward for being in an original cast was having the original costume made specifically for you. True in principle, but in practice here, our costumes were bought off the rack in a 7th Ave loft. Ted Cohen took us down to (not Brooks or Eaves) the Puritan Dress Company. There he chose a dress with a fitted bodice, a square neck, short sleeves and dirndl skirt that came just below the knee. This was to do for both *Susanna,* in yellow and fine black stripes, and *Davy,* in large, gray and white checks to project as gingham from the stage. They were new, but regular dresses, they needed gussets so we could raise our arms, and fuller skirts for extensions and high kicks. Our black ballet slippers were supplied. We danced barelegged. In both ballets, we four girl dancers wore our long hair swept up from the side to hang long down our backs. We also wore a white-ribbon bow with streamers.

Katie had a white dress that she soon removed to reveal a white petticoat with ruffles. She also had a white-ribbon bow. So we all had the look my mother called SS&G—sweet, simple and girlish. The men in *Susanna* wore black jackets and pants. The Elders wore "Amish" hats as well. The Angel wore a white suit.

The dramatic structure of *Susanna* is a classic one: one story within a story. The congregation rises in responsive singing to the Parson but is seated most of the time.

Susanna (Katie) comes forward as the Parson tells the story, describing the garden with a high wall outside the house of Joachim, and a pond where "Susanna just doted to swim wearing not a stitch at all." Susanna takes off her dress revealing a white petticoat and goes into the pond. As The Wall is mentioned, Handmaidens (Maggie & Barbara) come forward, one removing a gray shawl that unfolds to become the wall. As The Parson sings of a Little Juniper and a Cedar from Lebanon (Ellen and I), we rise and take our places before the wall on either side of Susanna.

Katie evolved her work from what I would call "conscious improvisation": thinking as she experimented, rather than letting physicality lead her through her music. When it came to us, Ellen and I were to *be* the trees. With only two "branches," we were to respond to the dynamics of the scene. Katie gave us leafy branches at the start, then discarded them to use H-W suspensions to suggest Trees. A fervent tree climber, I soon added tree rhythms to the rising/falling basic motions. Depending of the story's action as the Elders spied on Susanna, I imitated the effects of rifling breezes with that quarter-second after beat just stirring the leaves; heady winds that stirred the trunk itself to the roots and began a counter-swaying. Wild winds sent my "branches" careening, lifting, then clashing in disarray. I used them all, usually in succession, to keep from looking drunk. My head as treetop might move as follow-through. Might, because my Cedar Tree motions were never exactly on the beat. Katie left the phrasing to me to keep it spontaneous. Either I once was a tree or shall be a tree, for I felt marvelously at home as that Cedar from Lebanon.

Katie "swam" with her weight primarily on one hip or the other, her feet upstage or to the side, with flashes of innocent flesh as her petticoat slid up. With her blonde hair, white ribbons adrift, she was the symbol of purity.

The Two Elders grab Susanna by the wrists, telling her they will tell her husband they caught her with another man if she does not oblige them. As she resists, they drag her before The Parson accusing her of adultery. The Congregation becomes the jury as the Singing Susanna sings:

In God I made my testament. He knows all my sin in me.

This starry truth is lent, the truth will set me free.

Now The Angel accosts The Elders, asking each separately: "Was it under the Little Juniper Tree or the Cedar from Lebanon?" One Elder chooses the Juniper; the other chooses the Cedar, proving they lied. The Angel rolls The Elders offstage as the Congregation rejoices with Susanna.

Paul Godkin, like Katie, was both choreographer and dancer in his own work. Originally from Beaumont, Texas, Paul studied with de Mille. He made his debut at the Hollywood Bowl. In 1939, Paul joined Jerome Robbins, Nora Kaye, Marie Karnilova, Frederico and Alicia Alonso, plus others in Carl Randall's ballet trained chorus for *Stars in Your Eyes* on Broadway. After a hitch in the Navy, Paul returned to Broadway for Valerie Bettis's *Beggar's Holiday*

in 1946, then danced in Robbins's *High Button Shoes.*
Robbins suggested Paul for *Ballet Ballads,* promising to
assist when necessary. Inexperienced as a choreographer,
Paul needed constant reassurance to keep from changing or
throwing out whole sections. Ensemble work was hard for
him; setting his own dances came easier. Robbins coached
Paul very little; the final choreography was Paul's.

Willie the Weeper was a total change of pace in lyrics,
music and dance. The show's center of gravity changes
before your eyes from uptight upright to lowdown and out.
Where *Susanna* was concerned with public opinion, *Willie* is
concerned with one man's self-esteem. Where action
between Susanna and The Elders was overt, it is the
imaginings of Willie's "untidy mind" that are visualized here.
The set is black on black. Steps up left lead to a platform and
steps down from the platform, in back. A wide rope ladder
hangs left center that Cocaine Lil will cling to. As in
Susanna, there is a Singing Willie and a Dancing Willie. A
small group of women from the chorus sing for Cocaine Lil.

There are seven Episodes in *Willie,* but they flow
from one to the next. Transitions are made through Singing
Willie, seated at a table stage right. He expresses Willie's
intimate thoughts. Robert Lenn's deep, rich voice had a range
to match Willie's various states of being. The singing chorus
helps describe the scenes and also comments on Willie's life
choices. Example: After Willie runs out of dope for the
crowd, they chase him and beat him up. Willie sings:

It ain't what they tell you; it's what you tell yourself,
It ain't what they sell you; it's what you sell yourself,
You can kill every devil, but when the last one has
died

You'll find the same kind of evil, like a devil in your own inside.

Almost the full stage is available for dance as Willie struts his stuff while on cocaine, then slinks around lost coming off it. The dancing ensemble sways from ignoring him to embracing him to deserting him to threatening him in *Rich Willie, Lonely Willie, Famous Willie, Baffled Willie, Big Willie, Self-sufficient Willie* and *Lover Willie*. While Bob sings, Paul dances to what proves to be a hit song, *I've Got Me!* Paul comes up from the back and dances on the platform, then down the steps, going into a soft-shoe with straw hat and cane. Paul loved dancing it and often stopped the show.

It was the dancers in *Willie* that were sexy, with black net stockings and sleazy outfits. The men wore dark turtleneck shirts, dark trousers and caps. Paul, as Willie, wore long pants and shirts, as did Singing Willie. Ballet dancer Sono Osato, as Cocaine Lil, proved she could go from the classic to the vulgar. Sono had strong disagreements with Nat Karson about her costume, resolving them by taking the responsibility herself. She chose a high cut, shimmery, long sleeved leotard, with flesh colored net stockings and black ballet slippers, cross-tied with ribbons around her ankles. She added a fluff of white feather boa on her right shoulder and wore a large red rose at her left hip. She had a rhinestone beauty mark as well. In green lighting, Sono epitomized SEX. Sono appears in *Lover Willie* slinking down from the platform, posing and clinging on the rope ladder, just out of reach for Willie, aching for her.

Singers: Intraducin' ya to Cocaine Lil
She lives in Cocaine Town on Cocaine Hill.
She has a cocaine dog and a cocaine cat

And they fight all night with a cocaine rat.

Singers introduce Cocaine Lil in their own character: Sniffin Sam, Tessie the Twitch, Hopheaded Maggie, Jerky Slim and Alice the Dip in various states of intoxication. The music turns bluesy as Cocaine Lil oozes off the ladder over to Willie. They meld together in possessive rhythms as Lil sensuously lures him on. When tormented Willie tries to touch her, her pals keep him out of reach. The music turns to boogie-woogie and the place rocks. Then Cocaine Lil takes some snow and offers some to Willie on the back of her hand. Willie sniffs it. When the dope runs out, Cocaine Lil drifts back up the steps and disappears. Singing Willie and Dancing Willie are left facing each other as the singing chorus ends it all:

> *Poor dreamy Willie dreamed himself silly.*
> *So undecided—always divided.*
> *Sunlight, starlight, rain, shine or chilly—*
> *No one, no one knew dreamy Willie.*
> FADE TO BLACK

As in all the *Ballet Ballads,* Latouche's lyrics describe the characters and their action with a mix of amusement and affection. In *The Eccentricities of Davy Crockett,* the third opera/ballet, character and style change again as the psychological weight rises and, at times, soars. *Davy* is a series of episodes in the life of the famous American woodsman. Here, however, Davy has no alter-ego; he sings and dances himself. The main job of our Davy, Ted Lawrie, was singing, but he also had to dance well enough to keep up with our trained dancers. Somewhat to the chagrin of the male dancers, he did. Davy's good-humored braggadocio is celebrated equally with his sanguine courage facing the unknown of the American West. Corny but never camp, this telling is not ridicule. His sweetheart, Sally Ann (Barbara Ashley), also had to dance as well as sing.

Now the cyclorama changes from black to an open blue, daylight sky. The units are set upstage. A platform is centered between two step units, set to allow an opening center beneath the platform. This opening serves as a cave and is used for entrances and exits. This connecting platform becomes a "mountain," a "river" and "the heavens." Down stage space is available for group action.

Both John Costello and I had worked with Hanya on *The Insect Comedy* in Colorado, so we were used to her way of working, except that I never got used to that "nothingness" that was part of Hanya's first rehearsals. Usually choreographers came with dance phrases germinating, but Hanya seemed only to bring an open mind. Hanya's work was exploratory and time-consuming as she told us of the scene and suggested we experiment with one dynamic (not a specific idea) that might take us "across stage left." Her choreography depended on the dancer's ability to evolve the substance of the dance movements. It was trial and error getting the quality and range into movement, but when Hanya decided the sequence was what she wanted, it organically fit the dancer who had devised it. It also avoided any superficial flourishes or affectation.

In *Davy*, Hanya had three aides: Ray Harrison and Olga Lunick were veteran Holm students and both had danced previously on Broadway. To our surprise, ballet dancer Annabelle Lyon was a third aid, recently intrigued with Modern Dance. Olga was to be our Comet, and so worked on her dance separately. Ray assisted with the woodsmen and so Annabelle was referee of the spacing for the four girls. We must faithfully repeat our running circles exactly on the line, forward and backward exactly on the same space on stage each time. No slurring of design allowed. Fine with me, for I understood how perfect spacing projected elegant line.

Davy's first scene, *Out of the Cradle,* is a tableau in front of the cave. As the singers tell of his being fed bobcat stew and grizzly bear milk, Davy springs forth full grown. He takes a rifle from his father, dancing with it. Young *Davy in the Backwoods* has Davy wandering through the forest, singing about his rifle, Betsy. *Courtship of Davy* finds Davy sitting on the steps watching us girls dance games for his benefit as he sings. Each verse he compares us to different creatures: like horses on the mountain, like fish in the water, like birds in the bushes. This song has many dance sequences that sweep us on and off the stage swiftly as the chorus sings a refrain after Davy. When the song ends, Sally Ann drops out and the four of us dance on, running in curves, forward and backward, holding suspensions before changing direction, spinning with a spiral arm-swing into a swift spiral fall that spills onto the stage. Then quick reverse out and up into another curving run, a suspended attitude turn, and a whoosh offstage through the cave space.

This dance was my favorite, some of the phrases lasting seventy-two measures.

Davy and Sally Ann exchange vows and go to live in the Wilderness. In *Indian Wars,* the Indian Chief enters, squats and commands the scene from the platform as the Colonials practice a military drill, frontier style. This was a clever dance, exploiting the use of unpredictable changes of direction in rhythmic patterns. Moross' music had just the right touch for a loose-ordered drill to be amusing, yet brisk enough to demand accuracy from the male dancers.

A fight takes place between the Indians and the pioneers. The Indians take their wounded and leave Davy. On the banks of the Tennessee River, Sally Ann sings her ballad to Davy: *You're My Yellow Flower of the Forest.* A mermaid beguiles Davy, but Sally Ann snatches the Mermaid's parasol and whacks her back in the water. For the *Comet,* everyone else rushes in, crying out in fear for Davy to save them for *"There's a comet comin' with fire and brimstone in its tail!"*

Olga Lunick as the Comet wore a tight buckskin tunic. Her hair was braided with brightly colored ribbons that flowed into a tail. As she whizzes and jumps back and forth on the platform, Davy tries to catch her. Olga dances on the narrow space, fast and fearlessly, jumping high. Davy catches her tail at last and wears it on his hat. For *Bear Hunt*, the male chorus joins Davy in a hunting song.

William Myers danced Brown Bear wearing a vest over a tan shirt and corduroy pants. His posture, with his arms hanging long and heavily from his shoulders and his ambling gait, made him amusing. The clever interchange of bear and hunters made this section a delight.

Ghost Bear brought forth the dimension of American independent character and its price in *Ballet Ballads.*

> Two tenors sing:
> *There is a ghost Bear in this place*
> *No lucky chick-a-saw shakes*
> *Biggest bear you ever did chase—chick-a-saw*
> *But if you want to fight him, Dave,*
> *You'll find his lair in a haunted cave.*

The stage darkens; the cave is lit, revealing dim shapes in the shadows.

Ghost Bear: Brave hunter who kills what does not live. What have you in your heart today?
Davy: Lust and laughter and hunter's skill. And a curious feeling that won't stand still.
Ghost Bear: Turn your gun the other way
Davy: Turn my gun on what and where?
Ghost Bear: On forest and prairie, farm and town, More than animals are hunted down.

Five dancers, each personifying an early American who fought for either personal freedom, public or religious freedom, come in succession from the Ghost Bear Cave. We dance out a portrait of the person as a singer sings why each rebelled:

1. John Oldham: William Ambler/John Costello
"John Oldham was killed for defending
Indians against white aggression by residents
of New York State."
2. Ann Hutchinson: Gertrude Lockway/Sharry Traver
"I, Ann Hutchinson, was driven from Boston
because I believed that man should worship
God according to his conscience."
3. Nathaniel Bacon: Eddie Varato/Frank Seabolt
"Nathaniel Bacon was killed for rebelling
against political injustice."

4. Grace Sherwood: Arlouine
Goodjohn/Barbara Downey
"Grace Sherwood was condemned for
witchcraft in Virginia in 1705."
5. Nathaniel Turner: Arthur Friedman/ Beau
Cunningham
"Nathaniel Turner was hunted for organizing
Negroes and Whites against slavery."

"One thing is essential: to find movement, you have to keep yourself in an emotional state of motion," said Hanya. So typically, Hanya had us improvising movement before she told us we were to represent a particular person. Into the dark of improvisation we went again, searching for movements expressive of defiance, loneliness, strength of character and faith. I was annoyed not to be told I was Ann Hutchinson, for it would have saved a lot of effort had I known. But once informed, I too soon learned that my new moves were dramatic clichés. Hanya was right and I returned to my earlier work, trying to have in my body Hutchinson's strength and desperation.

The stage is darkened, as we come from the cave, one by one, and remain on stage until all five have come forth. Some had four measures; I had eight. John Costello was first. Then as my singer began, I came forward with a propelled walk into my spotlight, stopping with a body twist, my head moving down left—a reasserting stepping forward in independence—a strengthening that came from inside to expand into a high side extension/suspension—that resolved with another step forward—into a quasi-forward posture, the upper body bent, my head and long hair hanging down. As I had to hold this position through the remaining three dancers, I could not see /remember their movements. After the Ghost

Bear's warning, we faded back into the cave, leaving Davy alone.

Davy Goes to Congress believing in doing public works. Members of Congress have a frenetic dance with many gestures. Davy meets President Andrew Jackson and they sing a duet about politics. Davy decides to go back West. He sings a goodbye to Sally Ann. We join her in a farewell dance, a legato variation on earlier choreography. Davy sets off with his rifle, Betsy.

In the final scene, the Chorus sings:

> *Davy journeyed to the Alamo,*
> *It was there he perished as the stormy*
> *sky did glow,*
> *"T'was the sixth day of March 1836*
> *A fatal silver bullet said "Let's go!"*
> *In the earth of Texas they laid him to*
> *rest,*
> *With his old rifle Betsy cuddled close*
> *to him chest.*
> *And the people will tell you that he*
> *never really died,*
> *When a dream calls them onward, he's*
> *riding by their sides.*
> *Colonel Davey Crockett was his name!*

As the chorus sings this, we dancers perform an American square dance before the cave. The final dance figure is the basket-weaving figure: a fast circling of the eight dancers, all with their arms about their neighbors' shoulders, that increases speed until the women are swept off their feet to sail around parallel to the stage as the curtain falls.

The ANTA Experimental Theatre premiered *Ballet Ballads* on Sunday, May 9, 1948, at Maxine Elliot's Theatre. All along, Hugh Ross's joyful enthusiasm had kept rehearsals moving. By opening night we brought a bright, daring confidence to the performance. I wore my Doris Humphrey trunks for luck. They made me feel that I must meet her standards of performance, that in a sense Doris would be on stage, also. We all had that supercharged concentration demanded for a first performance. It seemed to pay off as well wishers came backstage afterwards, excited about us.

I had my friend, Ken Abbott, to wait up for the reviews with me after the show. Lindy's was the traditional Broadway spot opening nights, and the place was thronged with the cast and theatre people. The hubbub went on until nearly 4:00 A.M. when someone shouted, "The *Times* is on the street!"

"Stay here!" Ken ordered. In minutes he was back, leafing through the paper for the theatre section.

"What does John Martin say in the *Times*?" I was beside myself with anxiety.

> "The Experimental Theatre showed
> that its heart was in the right place by giving
> dance its share in its final production of the
> season, Ballet Ballads, which opened at
> Maxine Elliot's Theatre last night. It was a
> gesture, perhaps more kindly than wise, for
> there proved to be very little dance could do
> under the circumstances. The material itself is
> so essentially unchoreographic, however that
> there was not much anyone could do with it.
> Indeed, only Davey Crockett would seem to

be a theatre piece at all with considerable stretching of that category."

*The New York Tim*es, May 10, 1948

My heart sank, although Martin went on to praise Katie as "charming," Hanya as "witty," and Sono, "a radiant flash of life."

"That's not all bad," Ken said. "What do you expect from a dance critic. He wants more dance. Oh, here is the *Trib…*"

"What did Walter Terry say in the *Tribune*?"

"Ballet Ballads has been a long time coming. Ever since Agnes de Mille created the now historical dances for Oklahoma! Our theatre has been reaching toward a form which might be described as a choreographed folk opera… The Experimental Theatre's new production has come closest to arriving at the desired integration of drama, song and dance. Not every moment in Ballet Ballads is a model of perfect integration, but much of it is and here one senses the force of a single concept which may find its expression in acting, in music and in dance, which ever serves it best'."

New York Herald Tribune, May 10, 1948

"Hey! Here you go, Sharry! Terry likes Davy best. Holm superb… choreography…lively…humorous. 'She has

excellent young dancers such as Sharry Traver and William
Myers to bring her dances to life!' "

"Oh! Ken! Let me see it! I love Walter Terry!" I
cried. And there it was in print. And more:

> Katherine Litz devised a pleasant, graceful
> and amusing visualization of the Biblical
> story. Particularly appealing were the dance
> sections of the Cedar Tree from Lebanon and
> the Little Juniper and the judgment scene
> which was a pleasant admixture of pageant,
> parable and barn dance. Miss Litz was
> charming as Susanna.

Robert Sylvester's headline in *The Daily News* April
1948

> Ballet Ballads Belongs on B'way Which
> Hasn't Many Better Shows:
>
> The Experimental Theatre's Ballet Ballads is
> not only the best song and dance show
> attempted by a little theatre group but also—in
> this opinion at least—the best song and dance
> show to reach Broadway this season.
> Watching what producer Nat Karson did with
> last night's premiere—using buttons for
> money—makes you bleed for those
> commercial managers who "can't find a
> script."

Sylvester went on to praise Katie, saying "Broadway could use a dozen more like her," choosing Willie with Paul Godkin as his favorite.

Papers under our arms, Ken and I slowly made our way back toward the Pickwick Arms as the sky began to lighten. I wanted to go by Rockefeller Plaza. It was lovely. The growing light gradually touched the cups of the red tulips and golden daffodils, the yellow tongues of the violet blue iris, the beds of swaying white lilies. Giving all my papers to Ken, I drifted off, slowing waltzing through the aisles of flowers toward Fifth Avenue. Thinking of the wistful times spent here, my eyes flooded in gratitude and relief. But say! Wasn't it great to originate a role and do okay! I floated all the way home.

As Ken brought the papers into my room, I turned to thank him for his faith in me through the years. "Ken, I am so grateful for your help along the way. You are a dear man, the wonderful brother I never had. I…"

"Brother! Hell, I'm a damn sight more than that!" And he crushed me to him, kissing me passionately. Every time I tried to pull away, Ken pulled my hips to him.

I gave a mighty wrench and spun away, crying out, "Stop it, Ken! Stop it!"

"You can't tease a man forever and get away with it! I've wanted you all these years. Now…"

There was a pounding on my door. "You all right in there, Miss Traver?"

I glared furiously at Ken, holding him off with my eyes before I answered, "Oh…I'm okay. Bad dream. Thank you." When the steps died away, I growled, "Now get out!"

A glazed look came into Ken's eyes. He shoved me onto my bed, flung himself on top of me crying, "I'm coming! Oh, God!" Reserves of adrenaline shot through me as I shoved his heavy body off me. He lay on the floor throbbing, then inert. I backed away, shaking with revulsion and dismay.

Slowly, Ken crawled to his feet. He came towards me as I raised my hand to strike him. For an awful moment we glared at each other, paralyzed. Ken broke and slammed out the door. I fell to the floor sobbing convulsively with great exhaling gasps, lost in shock, then bursting out wailing, rocking on my knees, bereft. Oh God! I covered my eyes and ran into the shower.

The water was hot. I let it run over me, clothes and all, eyes closed in a stupor swaying under the spray. My mascara began to run into my eyes. I washed off my makeup...peeled off my soaking dress, my silk slip, everything. Naked I burst out crying again and sat down in the shower, letting the downpour fall over me, cleansing me as I hugged my knees.

My tears had always ended before, and they did now at last. Wearily, I rose, washed my hair and body, dried it off. I decided to put on my new yellow silk pajamas, a birthday present from Mother I was saving for Opening Night. Cautiously, I looked in the mirror. Sighed. Twenty-six and I still did not know MEN!

Ken was my friend.

Ken is not my friend!

How could I ever sleep on that bed again! I methodically stripped the bed, flipped the bare mattress over onto the floor and curled up under a blanket. Last night's reviews lay scattered about the floor, forgotten.

I must have slept as one drugged for I woke too late to go to class. I could not stand to stay in my room. I went out and walked and walked; walked until it was time to sign in. Thank God for the theatre for giving me something to do! Still feeling damaged and vulnerable, I shyly approached the Call Board. A hubbub of excitement there alarmed me. What was happening?

"Oh, Sharry! Isn't it wonderful!" Maggie Cuddy came up to me, eyes shining.

"You mean our good reviews?"

"You don't know?" Maggie threw her head back laughing. "We're moving to Broadway! Yes! It's true!"

"Oh-oh! Wonderful! Really true? I thought I might die the end of this week. No, no! It's great news. You saved my life! When do we go?"

"Next week, I think Mary Hunter said. If we can get a theatre…"

The Call Board was covered with more good notices:

Richard Watts, Jr. of the *New York Post* May 19, 1948:

Nothing I have seen all season in the vital field of American musical theatre has had the imaginative, creative freshness and theatrical intelligence revealed in the program of *Ballet Ballads*.

Hobe in *Variety* May 12, 1948:

Imaginative, entertaining and stimulating, though they may lack sufficient mass appeal for successful commercial presentation on Broadway. The choreography and the dancing of Katherine Litz are captivating and Richard Harvey, Sharry Traver, Ellen Albertini, Frank Seabolt and Robert Trout are notable in the cast.

Wow. *I* was mentioned in *Variety!*

And it came to pass that *Ballet Ballad*s was moving into Irving Berlin's Music Box on 45th Street for a run on Broadway, right along with *Allegro, High Button Shoes, Look Ma! I'm Dancin'!, Inside USA, Annie Get Your Gun, Make Mine Manhattan* and *Oklahoma!*

Next came new contracts: sixty dollars a week and, if the gross went above $18,000, we would get seventy-five dollars a week. I was offered a pink Chorus Equity contract for "dancing ensemble, Cedar Tree and Ann Hutchinson." Until I saw the printed program, I did not know I was featured. And because I had no agent, no one told me otherwise. Everyone had multiple roles, so I was unsure about it. Our financial status was fragile. Were it not for the faith and generosity of T. Edward Hambleton and Alfred Stern, there might not have been a Broadway opening. Now where we had been promised 1/43 of one half of any and all money from ANTA, we were now offered 1.08 per cent of half of the excess of gross box receipts.

The charms of The Pickwick Arms had faded totally for me, so I was thrilled when Maggie asked me to share a basement studio apartment with her on 16th Street, not far from The Studio Theatre. First we agreed on one rule: no men staying overnight. That settled, we would split the $100 monthly rent with our new salaries. There was a kitchen alcove, a large rectangular room with windows on 16th Street, and a basic bath, which we learned we must share with the back apartment. I owned no furniture at all, but Maggie had the essentials: a small table and two chairs, bed and bureau, kitchen stuff. She also had a copy of Andrew Wyeth's *Christina* to place over the fake fireplace. We went to Macy's and bought me a single cot and matching bedspreads.

For food, we each put five dollars in the pot and Saturday morning, we went to market. We set up a nice routine, rising at eight: breakfast with toasted Thomas's Protein Bread, black coffee and orange juice. Class at ten: Maggie to Martha, me to Charles. Back for yoghurt (which we made ourselves every night before going to bed) and more coffee. Afternoon: Maggie went to acting class at the Neighborhood Playhouse; I to Hanya. Soup or scrambled eggs for supper. Sometimes spaghetti. Seventh Avenue subway uptown to sign in at *The Music Box* at 7:00 p.m. Makeup—warm up—8:00 p.m. Dance!

After we opened on Broadway, who should come backstage to see me but Betts, Felisa, Nick and Sherry. They seemed to respect me after all. Emily and Mark did not come; they were working on their own company. Nice things kept happening; A big cover feature in *Life Magazine* with pictures from each ballet. Next a feature in *Dance Magazine*. Then *Theatre World* asked me for my picture. I thought it was some commercial scam and refused until they convinced me it was an important yearly record of New York Theatre. I gave them a head shot from my time at *Starlight Operettas*. When the 1948 volume came out, I was startled to find myself included with many seasoned stars in *Biographies of Popular Broadway Players*, in between Franchot Tone and Sophie Tucker. How could that be! But there I was with a little bio under my picture. With this recognition, *Theatre*

World 1947-48 was saying I was part of legitimate theatre on Broadway in New York, so I finally believed it.

Maggie, blond, blue eyed and beautiful in a Carole Lombard way, was devoted to Martha Graham, exercising at home as well as at class and the show. Maggie and I proved *simpatico* with many facts in common. She had begun modern dance at Bennington College in 1940. Then went on into the summer session where she first saw Martha Graham. She decided to become a dancer, leaving Bennington and going to New York. Her family also disapproved, also would not finance her in any way and also considered dance a shameful life for their daughter. Maggie stayed with her brother in New York, studying at the 92nd Street Y. Doris Humphrey asked her to work with her at one point. Maggie taught ballroom and gave dance exhibitions at the *Arthur Murray Dance Studios.* She auditioned for *Mexican Hayride* and made it as a showgirl, not as a dancer.

"It was awful. I did not know what I was doing and no one would show me. The other showgirls would take my things and I would have to try to make a costume from what they left. I hated it and almost quit but the dresser, Mabel, came to my aid. Charles and Doris hired her as a dancer when they choreographed *Sing Out, Sweet land.* When that closed, she worked with Helen Tamiris at a summer resort in the Catskills. Then there were seven months out of work.

"I gave up five times in my career," Maggie told me. She took a last chance to audition for *Carousel.* When choreographer Agnes de Mille saw her, she said, "Oh, good! You're a Graham dancer!" Maggie was in the original company of *Carousel,* a big success that ran on Broadway for years. Katie Litz also had been in *Carousel* at the same time.

As our show settled in, there was an opportunity to understudy the dances in *Willie*. Fast, sexy, chances to improvise in the crowds, it was fun to dance. I only had a chance to perform it once, but once was enough to shock the cast used to seeing me dancing joy or sorrow. A couple men friends did not "like to see you dancing that stuff," as though it smudged my innocence in *Susanna* and *Davey*. Can't a dancer be versatile? I was a woman as well as a girl!

But "girl" is what both Maggie and I seemed to project. Respecting our bodies, our instrument of our art, we led healthy lives. We did not smoke. I tried but did not like it and my cigarette always went out. We did not have beer or liquor in the house because we did not like it. I could only manage one daiquiri on a date. Drugs? With Willie's preoccupation with weed and cocaine, the subject of "taking something" was *sotto voce* makeup-table talk, but I never knew who or what. Drugs were bad for you. Why ever do that to yourself?

We did have boyfriends. Maggie had Tommy Amato a budding opera singer from Brooklyn who came faithfully to our apartment (later of the *Amato Opera Company* in the Village). I began dating a singer in the show, which enhanced my life. Douglas Martin took me around a New York I had not known before as he continued his Sunday morning jobs as soloist, singing in the choir lofts of various church services. He was Catholic, and although we did not often stay for the whole service, I got a good taste of Catholicism, the theatricality, the subdued light and omnipresent incense, the arrogance of using only Latin. Most of all, the obsequious obedience, the *mea culpa* humility, bothered me. Here God was fearful; not Love, as I had been taught. The spirituality I knew best lifted my soul dancing. Dancing with other dancers, sharing the interchange of space to music was quicksilver-bliss. Doug felt that way about singing.

It was a happy time. And time to catch up with Dottie Spence, who was now dating a writer from the *Times,* Murray Illson. Dottie's epicurean forté was *meatloaf.* When we had a Dark Night (no show), she often would have Doug and me over for dinner. It was great! Wine and intense chatter with the four of us as Dottie set to work with herbs for a lust-right-spiced meatloaf. Big baked potatoes with gobs of butter. Crisp French-cut green beans plus a tangy salad. By the time we sat down it was after nine and we were starving. What can be better than to wine and dine with people you love!

Although we dancers warmed up before *Susanna,* we took the time during *Willie* to do a more thorough warm up before *Davy.* Sono did her warm up then, too, as her scene was last. For her sensuality, she needed a long torso workout. Friendly, Sono soon was giving us a barre warm up. Then she wanted to learn our modern dance techniques. Sono was also a master at makeup, giving Cocaine Lil a pallor and dark, ravaged eyes. She was so skillful that "Lil's" aspect looked the product of years of decadence, not a mask. Sono encouraged us to experiment with our own makeup, showing us how peach could be much better than red for rouge, light, white baby powder instead of the heavier regular theatrical tan. She demonstrated on me, and I found the lighter touch made me feel lighter.

Katie Litz was not content with just doing the show; she was busy on choreography for a solo concert. Maggie sometimes joined in at Katie's studio apartment in Brooklyn, and urged me to come, too. It is the tradition of Modern Dance that after study and performance with others, you are not really a full blown modern dancer until you do your own choreography. Maggie was working on modern versions of folk music. I had my *Woman's Suite* of dances I wanted to do. There were three sections: *Woman Working, Woman Waiting,* and *Woman Wanting.* I remembered a line from Edward Arlington Robinson's *Tristan and Isolde:*

> When a woman is left too much alone, she begins to think…
> And no man knows what then she may discover.

I had things to state in dance about being a woman in my time. I convinced Mordechai Scheinkman, one of BB's two accompanists, to compose the music for me, but it was slow arriving.

In our own ways, as dancers, we were always "on." Obviously, physicality is constantly conscious in dancers but there is more to it than that. Think of Shawn and Delsarte identifying meaning and emotions in body postures. Then consider that dancers are constantly aware of all this in themselves in constantly flowing motions. Not only so in the fundamental principles, intimately aware of any variations in size, strength, emotion, cause and effect, *et cetera*, but also in *meaningfulness.* Dancers must develop and coordinate skills on both right and left and so become ambidextrous in mind and body. As we are always dancing "about something," our minds and emotions are involved simultaneously, perhaps to greater extent than non-dancers. (Doris Humphrey said: "A non-dancer is to a bull what a dancer is to an elk.") We are our own medium, not a Thing, and so must constantly study and be aware of ourselves lest we move untruly.

Yes, dancers are always "on" wherever they are. More than just my older sister have called me "unconscious," but actually my state of mind is quite the opposite. It is true thinking, a concentration with mind, body and spirit that is a constant process in daily living as well as in dance. Our parents were not alone in failing to grasp the concept that dancing was not just what we did but who we were. Good dancers have a strong center, a strong sense of person that starts from the inside out. Isadora Duncan knew it, tried to preach it, but it has taken half a century for her principles to be recognized worldwide. (Now psychiatrists and brain neurologists are talking about use of "The Whole Brain," as if it were something new. Lefties living n a righty world have had to use the whole brain, combining sensory awareness with intellect.

All this is to say that Maggie would forget to keep walking sometimes. I was apt to make little hand gestures while mentally going through dances on the subway or street corner. I understood how she could be suffused with dance thoughts: the phrasing, the experimenting with subtle body mechanics, the sense of each move and transition that makes dancers send out an arm or take a half-turn whenever. We were not always sensitive to others about us.

Maggie, a fellow Graham dancer Muriel Brenner, and I were invited to dance for the New York Association for the Blind. We agreed but had questions: How blind were most of those in the audience? Would they feel better or worse? "Oh, this was an experiment. Just experiment!"

It was a chance for Maggie to try her folk suite with a live guitarist. I chose a fast, jazzy, upbeat dance, to be followed by a lyric dance. Muriel (as I remember) chose an Israeli folk dance. She came by our apartment after our show one night to teach Maggie and me how to tie-dye material for our costumes.

Muriel was a beautiful, dark-haired Jewish girl with deep, dark eyes. She exuded an exotic air, a private passion unexpressed, gazing off in tangents. Muriel thought before she spoke, then looked you in the eye. This night, after our show, she ordered us about, setting pans of bright dyes simmering on the stove, showing us how to tie the knots and where. "Here! Hold this up to you, Maggie. You don't want sunbursts in the wrong place." Maggie laughed and threw the material over her head in embarrassment. After a couple of hours, the apartment was draped like an Indian bazaar and we were starving.

As it was near 4:00 a.m., we insisted on walking Muriel to the 14th Street subway, stopping off at Bickford's Coffee Shop for English muffins and tea. We chattered away, revitalized, but were dragged out again by the time the late-night subway showed up. Muriel promised to call when she got back to her 3rd Avenue apartment. Back home, Maggie was in her pajamas and I was in my slip when there was a heavy pounding on our basement apartment door.

"Open up in there! This is the F.B.I.!"

Maggie and I exchanged startled glances, then frowns. As the irate demand was repeated, a shadowy figure moved back and forth just outside our Venetian blinds, opened this hot summer night. Maggie opened the door a wee crack only to have a black shoe slammed into it. We both pounced on the door, but a leg followed the shoe, body followed leg, and in a moment, a burly young man in a business suit was inside, flashing a badge.

"We've come to question you about your friend Muriel, the one you just put on the subway."

"Muriel!" I cried out. "Is she all right?"

"Yes, Muriel," the man smirked. "All right for now, but we need information from you."

"What has she done?" Maggie demanded bravely, reaching for her bathrobe on the chair.

"Whatever it is, I'm sure you are wrong. We're her friends!" I stated imperiously though in my slip and barefoot.

"We expect you women to cooperate. This, heh-heh, is just a friendly little investigation." As I opened my mouth again, he grew irritated. "Ya saw the badge, lady, and if you give us any trouble, my pal out there will come in and fix you up!"

"Why does this have to be done at this hour of the night, I ask you?" Anxiety sustained my stream of outrage. "Really, you are very rude to force your way in here like this. I doubt if the real F.B.I. would want its agents to question me in my slip. Why can't you wait until morning at the proper time and place? No, no, you don't convince me you are F.B.I." I ran on until he interrupted.

"Hey, Mack! Get in here!" The man fumbled for the doorknob without turning around. I kept scolding.

"You are no gentleman and I intend to report you as soon as possible, so there's no point getting your buddy in here for whatever you think you are going to do. There are two of us, too, and…"

Maggie's eyes grew big at that. "Go! Just go!" she urged.

With no luck getting his buddy's attention, the man turned, grabbed the doorknob and opened the door to yell, "Hey! Mack! Get in here now!"

Instantly Maggie and I hurled ourselves at him, shoved him the rest of the way out, slammed the door and piled chairs against it. There were angry shouts as the two men disentangled themselves in the hallway while we yanked a bed next to the chairs. Next there was a double pounding on the door and trashy, four-letter name calling.

"That just proves you are not F.B.I.," I roared back.

"Hush!" Maggie begged. "Don't answer."

Silence on both sides of the door. Minutes passed. Then feet shuffled outside the door, on up the outside steps to the street to stand by our open-slatted blinds.

"If it's anythin' I can't stand, it's a mouthy broad! Who wants ya!" With backslapping and forced laughter, the two guys took off.

Maggie and I collapsed on the bed. I rebounded to close the Judas blinds. "I'm going to call the police!" Then I remembered the phone was outside the apartment in the hall.

"Why didn't anyone upstairs come and help?" Maggie pondered. "Where was Mr. Messner? Isn't that a landlord's job?"

"Out of the frying pan, into the fire. He's already tried 'to help' me. No thanks. I just don't understand about Muriel." Then of course the phone rang as Muriel had promised. We did not dare go out to answer it.

As we finally fell into our beds, the room — furniture askew, mauve, red, orchid-splotched draperies thrown here and there—was finally quiet.

Maggie: "We forgot to make the yoghurt."

Sharry: "Why wasn't David home? Oh, that's right. Cincinnati."

Muriel forgave us for not answering the phone. The police were dutiful but could only promise to circle the block at night now and then. And no, the guys were not F.B.I.

Our program for the blind was Sunday at their center on upper Broadway. Stage, small but adequate. Full house with an edge of excitement. An M.C. introduced us and described our costumes and the kind of dances we would be doing. My jazz costume was now my red leotard with a short skirt of ribbons plus a red ribbon on my ponytail. (My tie-dye came out a murky, greyish-purple, blotchy thing instead of the cloudy, pink-to-blue, "because you didn't wait long enough for the first color to set," Muriel explained.)

I was determined to use such energy it would blow their hats off, but I knew it didn't. I really felt invisible, and it was odd to receive applause cued by the end of the music. Dancing by myself was not as isolating as this. Maggie and Muriel also got applause, but the whole experiment seemed a variation of *The Emperor's New Clothes.* The M.C. thanked us heartily, saying that at the very least, we had stimulated the imaginations of these visually impaired people.

Muriel had promised us a celebration dinner at her apartment. It was darker and smaller than ours but she had gone to some lengths to decorate it. Lots of pillows with Persian designs; one tall window draped from ceiling to floor allowed a soft shade of twilight to enter the room. A low, round, carved table was centered in the room. There were only two large pillows set facing each other across it.

"No, no, I'm not going to eat anything. I'm on a diet," Muriel announced. "No-no-no. It won't do you any good to protest. This is the way I want it." She went off to her kitchen behind the Indian bedspread. In moments she was back with two glasses of red wine. Next she sat herself near the table, tucking her knees in and watched us drink it. On empty stomachs, we soon felt the wine tracing our entire circulatory systems and began to giggle.

"Come on, Muriel, join us," I urged. She smiled, shook her head and jumped up to return to her kitchen. Maggie shook her head at me slowly, warning me. In moments Muriel set before us a dream dinner worthy of a fine New York restaurant. Fat, juicy lamb chops, roasted potatoes, spiced apples and French green beans with tiny, bright green circles sprinkled over them.

"Chives! Haven't you ever had chives?" Muriel was delighted to educate me. The more food she could stuff into us, the more delighted she became. She could hardly wait for dessert! Ice cream parfait with a wicked pot of black espresso. Oh, the sweet! Oh, the bitter! Maggie and I fell back on our pillows like rolyolys while Muriel clapped her hands for joy. We got caught up in a laughing jag, promising Muriel a giant glass of water at our house and we all collapsed hysterically over that.

Later, getting ready for bed, I asked Maggie about Muriel and her diet. "She's always been sensitive about her weight. She can put it on easily even if she eats little. She has two sets of clothing in that big wardrobe. One size for fat. One size for thin. When the fat clothes get tight, she stops eating for…well, how long it takes to get into her thin ones."

"Then she eats again?"

"Sometimes little, then again everything in sight. It's unhealthy, but I've learned that just say something and she won't eat for ages longer."

"Is she poor?"

Maggie laughed. "No, not really. She's got enough. Can have more help just asking her parents."

"Imagine that!"

There was a knock on the bathroom door. "Don't come in, David," Maggie called. "We're in our pajamas."

"O.K. Just checking on those F.B.I. guys. Good night."

David Stein had the garden apartment beyond ours. There was but one bathroom between us that had to be shared. It was narrow, no tub, but a shower. Door hooks to lock your self in. Recently David had knocked and then came in to complain that we were ruining his love life. "My girl goes into the bathroom and sees all those dainties hanging up in there and she walks out. Happened twice now."

We made a deal, promising to be sure our lingerie was not left in the bathroom by dinner time if he would be so good as to check on us before going to bed himself. David was around thirty, a nice looking man and a huckster by trade. If he was not in department stores selling Slice'n'Dice, he was off at some convention with new shampoos or cleaners. He had just returned from Cincinnati, where he had great success selling balloon animals. Clever, David quickly made a menagerie for us—giraffes, bears, kittens, monkeys. Maggie and I tried and failed totally.

"You artist types think us common types don't have any smarts, doncha? Listen in this bizzness is more to it than you think, am I right?"

Problems in the show arose as attendance at *Ballet Ballads* dropped in the heat of summer. Mary Hunter, John Latouche, Nat Karson and Jerome Moross magnanimously waived royalties to keep the show going. Ethel Madson, our Mermaid, organized the cast to design and print posters, flyers and table cards. We scattered throughout Manhattan leaving a paper trail touting the show. Then we staged a parade in borrowed convertibles, going down Broadway singing our songs and tossing handbills. We girls wore shorts to catch attention—a flagrant misrepresentation—but we were desperate.

There had also been some political agitation over the Ghost Bear scene. Was it slyly Communist? All those early Americans were troublemakers, were they not? You could not trust the theatre; always getting things riled. What were the names of the people in that scene? From the little I could gather, the writers and producers played this calmly. There was a rumor of names going on C.I.A. lists but there was never a company statement about any of this. I was likely on a C.I.A. list already for dancing down Broadway in a Russian May Day celebration and striking against Serge Lifar's performance at City Center because he had danced for Hitler.

Then Sono announced she was going to Europe with her husband, leaving the show. That hurt but we kept stealing publicity any way we could. Douglas Watts gave us a big feature in the *Daily News* (June 14,1948). One week we boosted the box office by $3,500. Olga Lunick took over as Cocaine Lil, but her long, lithe body that suited her as The Comet just made her a long, drink-of- water compared to the deep-belly sexuality of Sono. All this plus summer heat defeated us and we closed July 11, after sixty-two performances. John Latouche held a smashing closing-night party at his Village apartment. Seeing everyone in the cast together out of the theatre and out of costume brought the sad reality home.

Despite our short run, *Ballet Ballads* was by no means a failure for its producers and creators. It was the biggest and most successful venture of The Experimental Theatre. It also sparked Hanya's career as choreographer for commercial theatre. Katie got a boost in publicity for her concert work and Paul was immediately hired to choreograph

That's the Ticket. For Latouche and Moross, *Ballet Ballads* was preparation for their next collaboration, *The Golden Apple,* with Hanya as choreographer.

Everyone from the show ran to audition for *That's the Ticket,* Maggie and I included. As I auditioned for this jazzy show, I hoped Paul remembered my dancing in *Willie.* After finishing a combination, Paul called me forward and said, "Take five everybody."

Giving me a hug, Paul took the time to tell me I was "a beautiful dancer ...too good, in fact, for me to feel right casting you in this sexy show." He kissed me on the forehead and let me go. While others may have thought I was chosen, I left the stage head high, but confused over this new reason for rejection.

CHAPTER SIXTEEN

Summer/Fall 1948
New York, NY
Finian's Rainbow

Maggie decided to turn her back on New York and go up to her island in the midst of the Thousand Islands. She had saved enough to buy a small island while dancing in the long run of *Carousel.* I was pretty impressed. If I had money, buying an island would not have been a first thought.

"My family always vacationed in the Islands. I wanted one of my own. I hardly ever get a chance to go. It is peaceful there."

That left me with a few days of total privacy to play records and work on my choreography.

I read that William Saroyan's play, *Jim Dandy,* was going into production! The producer? None other than Bob Joseph fellow drama student at Syracuse University. Not only was he glad to see me, Bob gave me the chance to join the other actors auditioning the show for backers. At last I was going to be Molly, who dances her responses but does not speak. I wore my romantic, long beige skirt with the handkerchief hem, my Juarez white blouse with lace trim and a long powder-blue grosgrain ribbon sash. A limousine picked me up at the apartment a sunny Sunday, and we were all driven up to the Westport Theatre in Connecticut, for the tryout.

Everyone was cordial, but there was the usual audition subtext. Bob had beguiled the versatile actor Zero Mostel to come on board. He was affable, funny, according to his reputation. He filled in the long silences as we waited outside the theatre while Bob pitched the show inside. Then we were invited within to meet our potential angels. At my turn, I told my theatre experiences and dropped a curtsey. Then we actors were all led outside again to wait to be called back to read parts of this extraordinary play.

"They do not need to see you dance now," Bob explained, so I just kept everyone outside company. Zero emerged with a jovial attitude, encouraging us to be hopeful on our way back to the city. Then it was wait two weeks, heart floating. Get the word, heart broken. Equity required Bob to pay me fifteen dollars for coming to Westport.

Next I tried TV, the new venue for dancers. I passed auditions for a daily exercise show, touting my M.A. in Fizz-Ed. I finally got my postcard telling me I was wanted in the pilot. When I checked in, they told me they used someone else because I did not show up in time. Baffled, I showed them my card, dated *after* the date of the pilot. One more variation on rejection.

Angry and frustrated, I stormed off to the supermarket. Stopped to count my money and found I had seventeen cents. I shook my purse upside down, inside out. Seventeen cents. Standing still, I could feel the July heat from the city pavement burn through my sandals. The noisy power station nearby exhaled waves of increased heat. The trash collector was breaking a thousand bottles at once. I walked in a small circle, coins in my hand, a poor girl on 16th Street in July. Standing still, I was in a vacuum of time—in one of Edward Hopper's sterile cityscapes. The merciless sun was burning freckles on my arms, my nose, frying my hair, turning my lungs into ovens. A voice in my mind said, You will be desiccated like a coconut if you can't move. Soon, flake by flake, you will be nothing but a pile of sweepings to be thrown away.

I pulled my feet out of the cement and ran back to my shady room and played Prokofieff's *Third Piano Concerto.*

It needed walking the city for three days before my twenty-five dollar Unemployment Check came through.

I was invited to be a guest artist on a new TV series at CBS, *Make Mine Manhattan.* Johnny Downs from *Hold It!* was M.C. He interviewed current Broadway performers about their work, and then the performer provided a sample. I danced my lyric dance in my *Jim Dandy* outfit and got paid thirty dollars. The CBS-TV director apparently had had some connection with *Jim Dandy,* for he volunteered that he thought I would make the perfect Molly. Sigh.

Somehow I missed the first Equity call to audition for a new musical, *Love Life,* starring Nanette Fabray and Ray Middleton. Michael Kidd was the choreographer and I was determined to get into callbacks somehow.

I practiced my speech. "Mr. Kidd, you almost chose me…" No, no. "Mr. Kidd, I was in the finals *for Finian's Rainbow.* May I please audition for your new show now?" It had to be short and to the point.

I wore my full, light blue denim skirt, again my Mexican blouse, and a wide-brimmed straw hat with a blue ribbon. As I walked along 46th Street, practicing my speech aloud, I suddenly realized Michael Kidd was walking along in front of me. So I just said, "Good afternoon, Mr. Kidd. I was in the finals for Finian's. May I please audition for your new show now?"

He stopped to look at me. "I don't remember you," he said, "but go along and try." He smiled. "If the doorman gives you any trouble, just wait for me by the stage door." I wanted to kiss him.

Again, Michael made the auditioning process as friendly as possible, but the tension was there underneath. He was always the one on stage showing the steps, ready to repeat instructions. For me, the audition went well until he took us two at a time for pirouettes. Knowing mine were stronger on the left, I did my doubles neatly on that side. And got caught.

"Ah! Did I see a lefty? Once again, this time on the right." Nervous now, mine did not finish as clean. So I was out.

(Most dancers are right-handed and turn better to the right, so choreography is usually designed with that in mind.)

Michael had an announcement for those of us who did not make it. "Right now, they are having replacement auditions over at *Finian's*. If you want to go, tell them I sent you."

What a guy! Usually replacement auditions are not as formal as Equity calls. Frank Neal, the dance captain, showed considerable interest in me when he learned I had danced in *Bloomer Girl*. Yip Harburg and Fred Saidie had worked the book for both shows. And both shows had mixed casts; *Finian's* much more than *Bloomer Girl*. Then I noticed Edythe Udane helping with the audition. She was the dancer with whom I shared my Tally Beatty experience and was now leaving this show…"heading for California" (Hollywood). Everything came together. I danced well and got the job, watched Edythe in the show that night, and began rehearsals next day. Hallelujah! I was in *Finian's Rainbow* at last.

As usual, I studied all the information about *Finian*'s in the *Playbill,* learning it had taken two years to get ready for its out-of -town opening in Philadelphia, December 16, 1946. *Bloomer Girl* had been running just a scant six weeks when Yip (E.Y.) Harburg came back to Fred Saidie with his idea for a new show. The messages again were civil rights and freedom, but time and place would be contemporary America, with an element of fantasy thrown in. Stating his philosophy in *Finian's playbill,* Harburg wrote:

"I don't believe the theatre is a place for photograph reproduction. That's why I am attracted to fantasy. I feel a musical can say things with greater effectiveness about life. It's great for pricking balloons, or exploding shibboleths. Of course, I want to send people out of the theatre with the glow of having a good time, but I also think the purpose of a musical is to make people think."

Jo Milliner, the prolific and versatile set and lighting designer (*Carousel, Annie Get Your Gun*) joined the creative team. Then I discovered another Syracuse theatre alumna, Eleanor Goldsmith, had designed our costumes. Burton Lane, veteran composer of musicals, composed the music. Lyn Murray, of *Firestone Theatre,* set the vocal arrangements. Robert Russell Bennett and Don Walker set the orchestrations. Bretaigne Windust, recognized as one of the five great directors in theatre now, directed. Lee Sabinson was producer, soon taking William Katzell on as co-producer. The problem was finding a native Irishman for the role of Finian. At last Albert Sharpe was spotted in an English film and finally managed passage to the U.S.A.

The story line for *Finian*'s was convoluted, depending on many misunderstandings and illogical conclusions from the very   beginning. Act One, Scene I:

The backdrop for Rainbow Valley, Missitucky, displays a broad expanse of patchwork farmland. There is a full-sized tree upstage left, sturdy enough to hold people, which it does throughout. Act I, Scene 1 opens with the sound of Sonny Terry playing his bluesy harmonica offstage. Soon you hear a chant—"Woodie's comin'. Woodie's comin'"—and citizens, blacks and whites, come singing onto the stage together.

Finian steals the Pot of Gold from the Leprechauns in Ireland, brings it to America and wants to plant it in Fort Knox so it will grow. He has brought his daughter, Sharon, with him. She sings *How Are Things in Glocca Morra?* To calm her, Finian sings *Look to the Rainbow,* which leads into a classic Irish jig that expands across stage and whips up into an exciting finish.

Woodie, our hero, arrives back in Rainbow Valley just as the sheriff is about to foreclose on his mortgage. The next dance to *This Time of the Year,* is simple exuberance in dance and mime. When Woodie comes up short, Sharon gives him enough money to hold off the sheriff, and Woodie and Finian become partners. Woodie and Sharon fall in love. He sings *Old Devil Moon.*

Woodie's sister, Susan, cannot talk but dances out what she wants to say, leading into a hit song, *If this Isn't Love.*

The song went into dance first with Sharon. Then Michael Kidd devised joyous, humorous, inventive duets about lovers. His choreography was a mix of ballet and modern dance that looked like spontaneous dancing. The dances erupted right out of the action:

Two couples: dash fast cross stage, running, leaping, flirting

The Uninitiated: innocent, tomboy stirrings

The Tentative Two: a shy couple with starts and stops
The Intense Pair: vigorous, passionate
The Exuberant Ones: big moves
Triangle: jealously afoot
Another couple: pals
I danced in the first Two Couples and also The Intense Pair. We all danced as ensemble in the last section with cartwheels over the boys' backs, lifts and spins, until finally the girls pose triumphant, the boys kneeling on one knee, each gazing up at his girl. As soon as the curtain closed, we all made a dash to get our Pumpkin Parade props to lead across stage in front of the curtain. Michael filled this coda with lots of big moves: high kicks, hitch kicks, double pirouettes, all up-tempo.

Og, the Leprechaun, has followed Finian. He sings *Something Sort of Grandish* to Sharon. When two surveyors for Senator Billboard Rawkins discover gold in Rainbow Valley, the people imagine what they can buy, and there is a gospel song-and-dance, *Come and Get It Day*.

Edythe Udane had had that solo, so now it became mine. It was the only solo in the show, besides Susan's. All the dancers are seated, the singers in a semicircle around us. As Woodie begins to sing, I rise as the first person to see this dream coming true. The solo starts slowly, dreaming; then switches to quick fast steps and rhythms. The other dancers join in with the big extensions and, on the words "Gabriel's horn", we have an off-center balance on the right foot, arms held as though blowing a horn. We go down to the floor only to rise again, to rollovers, fast lifts, and then stamp it out as the singers belt out *Come and get it and keep it and get it Day*!

It was exhilarating every time. And again on Broadway, no one complained or gave me snide looks for getting all of Edyth's dances.

When the Idle Poor Become the Idle Rich (you never know just who is who or who is which) opened the second act, with all the Rainbow Valley folk in exaggerated versions of classy clothes. Most of the caricatured dancers were on before us. I adored my costume: pink chiffon, Arabian Nights see-through pants, bare midriff, pink chiffon top, and pink turban with a feather, plus gold slippers and a cigarette in a holder. Bob Josias was my partner dressed in a pinstriped suit with extra large lapels and top hat. We were the snooty couple that had a rug rolled out on stage for us before we entered. As we step on it, the rug is pulled out from under us and we fall, rolling back and then forward and up to a standing position to the next steps that lead into a huge, overhead lift that sails up over Bob's head and back down into the next step. I loved that huge lift and always took a strong, deep preparation to help.

Susan's solo was the envy of us all. Sonny Terry's harmonica pierces the night quiet. Susan dances out her loneliness, then is drawn by its glow to the spot where the Crock of Gold is buried. She digs it up, dances with it joyously, but then hides it a new place. Og finds her and wishes she could talk, not knowing he is standing over the Crock. So Susan speaks. Og sings *When I'm Not Near the One I Love (I love the one I'm near)*. Susan and Og dance the refrain together. Og hesitantly decides he might like to become mortal.

The racial theme is threaded throughout the script. Sharon, angry with Billboard Rawkins, wishes he were black. And because she is unknowingly standing over the Crock of

Gold, she turns him black. Ashamed, Rawkins runs off. Og finds him and tells him, "A rose is still a rose despite the color of your nose." Rawkins runs into a group of gospel singers and joins in *The Begat*. All ends well, but there is a caveat as Finian takes off again, with a moonstone in his hand, to Cape Canaveral, as a rainbow arches across the sky. His prophesy is in the hope that the domesticated use of nuclear energy will help mankind.

Harburg and Saidie wrote the book in 1944-45, just as the first atomic bombs brought WWII to an end. The hopes of all were that these bombs would no longer be used for destruction but for peace. For all practical purposes, few people in cast or audience ever paid much attention to this part; perhaps because it came at the finale of the show, with singing more than dialogue. I never heard anyone discuss or talk about this nuclear pie-in-the-sky philosophy or even acknowledge it.

Finian's Rainbow was such a jubilant success, it won thirty-six awards for the show and its performers: The *Ebony Magazine Award* for Improving Interracial Understanding. The *Veterans of America Freedom Award* went to Lee Sabinson and William Katzell. David Wayne won the *Antoinette Perry Award.* and a bronze medallion from *Comaedie Matinee Club* for Og. *Finian's* gave many benefits for *The Actor's Fund, Stage Relief Fund* and the *Union's Welfare Fund.* (Source: *Finian's Playbill*, 1948)

I had been dancing in the show a couple weeks when an assistant stage manager stopped me between scenes. "You are beautiful out there. Do you know that?"

I thanked him and went on to my next cue. The remark was unexpected, but showed I was projecting out there with everyone else. The one consistent trait I have as a performer is in believing who I am and where I am. In *Finian's,* I believe I am a girl in Missitucky, and when Finian sings *Look to the Rainbow,* I see one. I have a feeling of continuity and a sense of growing in character as the action proceeds. Although not a principal, I think myself through the show for the integrity of the role I do have and for the satisfaction it gives me artistically. I consider performing a freedom; that on stage the dance is mine alone to perform as I see best.

Then disaster struck.

Some horseplay backstage (the stage manager trying to tickle me), just before Bob and I were to enter in *Idle Rich,* made us a bit late for our cue. The rug was pulled out from under us before time. We caught up with the dance but when I came down after the overhead lift, I landed wrong and sprained my ankle. Could not stand on it. Was dance-dragged offstage. Damn! Damn!

As my ankle swelled, my first fear was the possibility of losing my job! The stage manager came to our dressing room to check it out, put me in a cab off to a doctor recommended by a sister dancer, Eleanor Gregory. It was a disastrous afternoon. Rage, as the doctor said I must not dance on it for a week. Embarrassment, when I had no money with me to pay the doctor or for crutches. I was too upset to appreciate how lucky I was. The woman doctor trusted me to pay her and then drove me to a pharmaceutical store and let me charge my crutches to her. Lucky - after a fury of frustration trying to catch a cab on crutches at rush hour—to have a fresh-produce truck driver pick me up and offer to drive me home.

My luck ran out, when I opened my door and the terrier I was keeping for a friend burst out and disappeared up the street. The general populace on 16th Street caught the dog for me, got him into the apartment for me. I gave a mighty sigh—until I saw that the dog had ripped up a loaf of bread and scattered it all over the place. Then I cried.

I stayed home that night and the next, but after that, signed in backstage each show before hobbling out front to watch it. No way would I let them forget I was in this show! Before the week was out, I was working my way back into it. Our union rep, Bob Penn, saw to it that the company paid my medical bills. I also received a partial salary (I think!).

(This would be the only time in my lifelong dancing career that I was injured on stage. This and split calluses on my feet were my only dance injuries. Knees? No bad after-effect from *Bloomer Girl!* Lucky!)

I simply adored dancing in *Finian'sRainbow*. I loved the 46th Street Theatre. Loved running up and running down the spiral staircase from our dressing room to dance to full houses, show after show. Even when I broke my engagement and was full of heartache, the joyous dancing pulled me through. .

Maggie was back after a lovely time, but now found it hard to watch me go off to work night after night. I would be joining her sooner than I thought as the notice went up on the Call Board: *Finian's Rainbow* was closing on Broadway to begin a National Tour. We had one more month to prepare, with new costumes, new PR, and photo sessions. New cast! Mimi Kelly took over Sharon. Jay Martin, Woodie. Carmen Guiterez, Susan. Charles Davis, Og. Joe Yule began playing Finian.

Mimi Kelly's father, actor Paul Kelly, was also on Broadway in *Command Decision* at the Fulton Theatre next door. The night Mimi took over, Paul found moments in his show to scoot through a backstage pass to see her. There was a big party on stage afterward that lasted until 2:00 a.m. Bob Penn offered to see me home. "Oh, thanks, Bob. I'm not afraid. I live downtown and you live in the Bronx. Take me home, you'll not get back until four or five a.m.!"

Bob insisted, but I was firm. I was not afraid...until I was on the subway with only a couple scruffy guys and an older woman. I dashed out of the car at 14th Street to make a beeline outside. Took the West Side stairs by mistake. Reversed and suddenly was face to face with A Man.

I inhaled in a scream so loud we both froze. Then The Man sagged, "You scared the hell out of me, lady." And we both dived out opposite sides.

I did not really want to leave Manhattan, but loved the show and needed the money for my concert work. I agreed to go to Philadelphia, where I could stay with sister Toni for two weeks, and then to Boston for two weeks, when I would decide what to do. In the meantime, Joe Yule and I made friends, having coffees and theatre talk at the Edison Hotel Coffee Shop across from the theatre. Sometimes others joined us, and one night Mickey Rooney showed up backstage to see his father. I had also made friends with Coyal MacMahan, a black singer who tried to talk patience to me.

Right after our opening in Philadelphia at the *Forrest Theatre*, word went out that Michael was coming to check out the dances. Fine. Then I learned Hanya was auditioning for a new show the same day as our rehearsal. I danced my very best for Michael the night before. Then told him I could not come to rehearsal for personal reasons. As fast as possible, I zipped back to New York to Hanya's audition. She told me I did not have to audition, for she knew what I could do and would let me know. Hopeful about this *Kiss Me Kate,* I fled back to Philadelphia, arriving too late for rehearsal and was punished.

Michael had taken back my solo in *Come and Get It Day,* giving it to our new dance captain, Eleanor Gregory. I also lost dancing the leading couple in *If This Isn't Love.* This markedly reduced my dancing in the show. I had taken a chance and lost. When Eleanor demanded my costume as well, I began to get mad. No costumes were alike; mine fit me, hers fit her. Why exchange?

Michael stayed to see the show again that evening to check the changes. I asked to talk to him and we sat on the edge of the stage after the show. I asked him the obvious: Why? Answer: You missed rehearsal. It was likely Michael knew where and why I had gone, even understood, for he was his usual friendly self. What I needed to know was why he changed roles. Was anything wrong with my dancing? Performing? "No," he assured me. "Your dancing was fine." We agreed in theory that Eleanor, who had been with the show from the start, deserved a chance at the *Come and Get It* solo; we disagreed in practice. I felt if my dancing was fine, I should not have to give it up.

"But you missed rehearsal. You are not fired, you know," Michael explained.

"That leaves me with so little dancing, it might not be worth going on tour," I thought aloud.

"That's up to you," Michael said shortly and left me sitting there.

I felt especially bad to have lost these parts now, because Toni, her husband Allen and niece Gretchen were coming to see the show. *And* (trumpets please!) Mother and Dad were driving down from Harrisburg to come, too. Seeing me in the arms of black dancers made my parents uncomfortable, but Allen, my minister brother-in-law, wanted a copy of all Og's insightful remarks about racism.

Mother wanted to take me shopping. I explained that none of us dancers had dressy clothes and wore slacks after the show. "Just because your friends are in tatters is no reason you should be," she replied. So we went shopping. It made her so happy. I wished I could be a better daughter for her. Then Dad's car was stolen in downtown Philadelphia. They had to take a train back to Harrisburg. When it was recovered in a couple of days, I said I would drive it back for them. I could take the train back in time for the night show. Bob Penn volunteered to go with me. I changed into jeans and we took off that night after the show.

It was one hundred miles from Philly to Harrisburg. I had not driven it, or even a car, for a long time, so it was exciting at the start. Along the way, Bob, as our Equity Union rep, told me I could appeal Michael's changes, as his decisions were based on political not artistic reasons. I told him I thought not; that I might leave the show in Boston. And secretly I was hoping to hear from Hanya.

Along the way, driving through the night, I got off onto a side route and found we were wandering over in a zigzag way to Harrisburg. The moon was riding high and clear, the sky diamonded with stars when we left Philadelphia. Now it grew misty in the hollows, even though the sky above remained vast and open. As the dawn approached and we found ourselves in between low hills, the mist rose around us, tinted by the rising sun in a fantasy of pastels, ever-changing in hue and chromo: rose, peach, now pale yellow, bluish white. A rainbow had come to Earth.

It was enchanting. As we drove along, we felt this was just a delightful bit of luck and it would quickly pass. To our joy, it went on. We turned here and there, through hills and forest, lustrous with the mists and the reflected glow of the rising sun, still but a yellow ball of haze to the east. Lilac and amethyst, lemon, pink, gray, aqua— now wafted through the air suspending us now, then evaporating to reveal glimpses of the black, macadam road. We had to go slowly to stay on the road. The sun brightened and it was officially morning. Only in the hollows did we find traces of pale vapor to recall the loveliness. Taking deep breaths of the purified air, I felt wondrously alive.

We drove on, gradually realizing even with this errant way, we were still too early to arrive at my parents' door. We stopped at a turnpike gas station for coffee. Even then, the spell of the morning's twilight beauty stayed with us. Not the clatter of heavy dishes or the truck drivers' loud joking broke the spell.

Back in Philadelphia, it was Halloween. My sister's husband, Allen, was chaplain for the University of Pennsylvania and was having a party at their home.. To help, I offered to take my six-year-old niece, Gretchen, Trick-or-Treating before going to the theatre. All went well until we reached a double house. While Gretchen was on the left porch, a black boy rang the bell on the right porch. Both doors were opened, one after the other, the ladies of the houses offering sweets. As Gretchen was accepting hers, I saw the lady next door, take back her proffered bowl of goodies and say "Not for you!" She watched as the little boy ran off her porch. Then as Gretchen came around, she offered her bowl. "No, Gretchen," I said to my baffled niece. "She doesn't have enough for everybody." The woman slammed the door.

The first day we reported to the *Shubert Theatre* in Boston, I handed in my notice, despite friends in the show telling me to fight back (white) or sweat it out (black). One of my black friends, Coyal, told me "You've had a sunshine life. You're lucky. You don't know trouble. Be patient. Stay and wait."

I went to the rehearsal Eleanor called to check on spacing for this theatre and odd things began happening. First Eleanor asked me to teach her my solo, after she had been dancing it in Philly. I shrugged and showed it to her again. During rehearsal, she hurt her ankle. It was opening night, but instead of asking a dancer staying on tour to fill in, she asked me. Bob said I certainly did not have to do it, but I loved the dancing and was happy to do it. Not only did I get my dances back, I got my costume back, too. Maybe the company, or Michael, was tempting me to stay on.

It occurred to me that this endorsement by my new dance captain (Eleanor) might answer later Chorus Equity questions about my work in *Finian's*. I had never given notice before and, belatedly, wondered about the consequences. I was beginning to be embarrassed that I had written my notice in rhymed verse. Waiting to hear from Hanya, I enjoyed dancing the show in Boston for two weeks. One evening at the Vendome Restaurant, my dinner was too late. I danced *Finian's* on nothing but two daiquiris, absolutely loopy the whole show. Didn't miss a cue! Flew higher on elevations! But, oh, what schloppy transitions. Hilarious, I danced laughing out loud. Conditioned reflex and alert dancers saved me from disaster. I was ashamed later, of course. It never happened again.

After my last show, the dancers presented me with their parting gift, a bottle of Emeraude Parfum.

I took the night train back to New York to avoid one more hotel bill.

304

CHAPTER SEVENTEEN

1948 – 49
New York, NY
TV & Concert Dance

Artistically, I was right to come back to Manhattan. There was nothing more to be gained from *Finian's*. The show was not on the road long before there was trouble over the mixed cast of whites and blacks. Racial troubles became worse in Detroit. Soon after, the tour was canceled. That was a very sorry business for everyone.

Hanya did not call me. When I called her, of course, the show was cast. Maggie had not made it either, but we went to see *Kiss Me Kate* together. Loved it! Groaned not to be in it. And we were really offended artistically by Hanya's choosing ballet dancers instead of modern dancers. It was a betrayal of her strong Modern Dance principles. She put them aside and got the ballet dancers to improvise in their medium for the choreography. Pragmatically, I continued to take class with her.

Now my intent was to work in Concert Dance as long as I could afford it. Mordicai had finished my *Woman's Suite* music, but I must wait until he recorded it. In the meantime, I worked with other choreographers. I also taught dance classes for Nik now branching out on his own at the *Henry Street Settlement House*. It was way downtown on the East side, a scruffy area with gutters filled with garbage. The House itself was brick, big and barren, when I started my Children' Classes. Alwin Nikolais (Nik) finally was starting up his own company, eager to try out his strong theories on motion. Many of Hanya's students went to join him.

In his own quiet, cheerful way, Nik soon had rehearsals going for a work based upon *Alice in Wonderland*. He took the Lobster Quadrille into an imaginative dance with great detail in lobsters costumes. Nik continued to fool around with fabrics and props to explore what motions were inherent in anything and everything. He got dancers to animate his constructions, to produce desired motions, or to discover and demonstrate the range and qualities of motion possible. Nik was just getting his ideas into action while I was teaching there. In an early program, I performed in his *Modern Dance Technique Demonstration* but never had the chance to be one of his object animating dancers.

Nik believed human emotions limited the possibilities of dance. He told me how he had personally awakened to the immense power of Motion Itself during an onslaught on a beach during WWII. He seemed to see it all again as he told me that he became aware of the overall factor of *motion*: big in the planes in the sky, endless in the agitation in the waters, on the progress of the landing craft, the actions of the soldiers, the weather itself. All fell within the purview of Motion. Human exploration into ecstatic dance was pitiful movement beside the magnificence of *Motion*. The world soon saw the results of Nik's quest as he carried his motion explorations into music, sound, color and lighting in the world of electronics. His abstractions startled us all into new consciousness. We had been oblivious to the obvious again.

One day Hanya did phone me to answer a job call from WPIX-TV. Reporting, I learned this was for the Gloria Swanson Hour. I found Miss Swanson, in a red dress and heavy makeup, in the center of the TV studio. She pulled a lollipop from her mouth to say "Ohhellotheredarling!" as she shook my hand and smiled. "My guest is Alexander Calder.

Oh! Over here, Sandy! This young lady is going to dance your mobiles!"

I smiled and greeted the tall, raffish-looking man who surveyed me with a bemused expression that soon widened into a smile. After introductions, we both hung around to be ready for whatever. I watched Gloria's style of movement, which went from one modeling pose to another at high speed as she ordered everyone around. What were mobiles?

"Oh, the mobiles! Lord, yes! Helen, show her. We air live tomorrow."

There were three sculptures that moved: two stabiles standing in one studio, and one mobile hanging in another studio. The first, *Gong Song,* had flat, organic-shaped metal pieces, colorfully painted in bright orange or blue, attached with wires to a metal "tree." In motion, these metals glanced off each other, capriciously, creating high, thin sounds in varying rhythms. I jotted down: festive, elegant sound; glancing, sailing motions. The second mobile, *Leaves,* was the most introspective and mysterious of the three. Its black, free-form leaves revolved and dipped, creating contrapuntal after-beats. There was also a sense of mass, which the other two lacked. Its blackness made it abstract to me. Looking at *Leaves* intently, I also caught a quiver. *Snow Flurry* was the most extroverted, the most playful. Here the wires were almost invisible. Here the white metal plates in graduated sizes hung in a falling pattern. Hanging, it easily rotated, the spontaneous motion creating a white flurry.

I was impressed with these sculptures; worried Mr. Calder would not like the idea of a dancer interpreting his art form. So I asked. Apparently, Sandy was taking being a guest artist with Gloria Swanson as a lark, for I was told his only requirement was that "the dancer be pretty."

Choreographing a two minute dance for each mobile slot was up to me. So was finding appropriate music in the WPIX music library. And a costume. No one made suggestions; no one interfered or helped as I found my way around WPIX-TV and got to work. Basically, I took the overall quality of each mobile through body moves, the action of the platelets, through my extremities. I danced under, around them and in opposition to them as I improvised to music by Bela Bartok. At times I was in harmony with the mobiles' motion, at times in counterpoint. Working away, I was glad to be trusted; then, as time went by, feared to be forgotten.

The next day, performance day, I cornered the director. "OK. Gloria and Sandy interview. Then we pick you up with Camera One in Studio B while Camera Two pans the mobile in Studio A. More chitchat. Then we catch you again in Studio B and the other mobiles in Studio C."

"Won't that make it look as though I were dancing through the mobiles?" I asked, trying to envision what he said.

"Exactly!"

On cue, keeping the image of each mobile sharp in my mind, I danced in my black leotard and black longish skirt in empty Studio B, with only the red light bulb to cue me. The music helped. After the three dances, I checked back to see how it had all gone.

"Fine. Fascinating!" exclaimed the director. "Thanks." Fifty bucks.

This increased my faith in my choreography.

The Choreographers Workshop was still going strong up at the 92nd Street Y. Trudy Goth enlisted dancers and musicians for her Executive and Advisory Boards. Louis

Horst was Advisory Board Chairman, with Valerie Bettis, Jean Erdman, Gertrude Lippincott, Muriel Stuart, Norman Lloyd and Winthrop Palmer as aides. The Dance Teachers Advisory Committee also had Louis as Chairman, with Agnes de Mille, Martha Hill, Hanya Holm, Doris Humphrey, Bessie Schoenberg, Muriel Stuart, Anita Zahn and others as aides. The best and the brightest dance minds worked to make the Y the top spot for concert dance in New York City. Experimentation in dance was encouraged; modern dance, ballet or a mix of folk and modern were the most popular styles. (Source: YMHA/YWHA Program note)

Modern dancer Kay Raphael won a slot on a program at the Walton Community Center, also sponsored by the Choreographers Workshop, and cast me in her dance. Kay devised her dance, *Prelude,* for five dancers, based upon Pre classic dance forms with music by Johann Sebastian Bach. This was a typical first effort from new modern dance choreographers, who most likely had taken Louis Horst's course in Pre classic Dance. On this same program was Emily Frankel's solo, *Ballad of the False Lady,* based on an Old English folk song, and Maggie's folk dance with Patricia Newman, *Lolly-koo-cum.* Dancers I knew from various shows were also on the program, a nice way to keep in touch.

Last year (1948) the Workshop had commissioned a major work: Valerie Bettis' *As I Lay Dying.* It was very successful. Now, Maggie reported to me, her friend Virginia Johnson had been commissioned to create a major dance work based upon a poem written by Winthrop Palmer. Maggie was already cast; there might be a role for me. Virginia Johnson taught Modern Dance in Beverly Hills, California, and gave dance programs across the country. Many of her dances were psychological in nature. Her credits included choreographer for summer stock operetta in Memphis, Tennessee, and she had contributed to the choreography in *Mexican Hayride,* which was where Maggie met her.

I auditioned and got the double role of Mother/Wife, Abigail, in the dance-drama, *The Invisible Wife.* The name Winthrop Palmer rang a bell. I had a feeble laugh, remembering it was Palmer's book, *Theatrical Dancing in America,* which had caused me to change my M.A. thesis.

Robert Paget, famous dancer from *Carousel,* was cast as Jonas, first born son; James Nygren, from *Ballet Ballads,* would be Aaron, the second son. Maggie was cast as Rachel, the girl both sons love. Doris Ebener, Billie Kirpich, Raymonda Orselli, Noel Schwartz and David Gold had lesser roles. Miriam Brenner composed the original score for piano, which was played by Florence Weber and enriched with violin, flute and cello. William Cecil designed diminutive furniture for the set. Costumes were by Charlotte Trowbridge and executed by dear Nellie Hatfield.

We rehearsed in Emily's and Mark's Studio, upstairs in Em's brownstone. Ginny knew how she wanted to handle this psychological poem without resorting to mime. She had dance phrases ready first rehearsal. Her movements were inspired by the story's dramatic impulses and expressed through the body in modern dance. The silver cord theme was represented tangibly in the lacy, ten-foot scarf I wore: as Mother to coddle and protect, as Wife, to entice. One significant move common to both roles was a seesawing arabesque (making sure the long scarf did not become a trap). When violence breaks out between the brothers or with Rachel, Ginnie incorporated hands-on contact that was phrased rhythmically without losing dramatic energy.

311

The Invisible Wife

Prologue at the Mother's Grave outside a New England Town

Scene I. Brothers home after the funeral: Aaron sorrows and evokes the spirit of his dead Mother. (A possessive Mother, almost swaddling Aaron in the scarf)

Scene II: Courtship of Rachel by each brother and their fighting each other to win her. Rachel chooses Jonas. Alone, Aaron calls forth his Invisible Wife to have someone to love.

Scene III. After Jonas and Rachel are married, Aaron, frustrated by both his visionary love and the forbidden Rachel, engages Jonas in another fight, killing him. Then he seizes Rachel, who finally frees herself from him.

Epilogue: Aaron hangs himself, anguished at what he has done.

Maggie's and my costumes were long; hers less severe with puff sleeves and stripes of color on her bodice and hem. Both mine were identical in style; long fitted torso that flared to the ankle, square neck, long sleeves in wine for the Mother and gray for the Wife. I wore my hair in a bun for the Mother and long for the Wife. The two men wore light-colored shirts and dark trousers.

Janet Collins, Myra Kinch and Kay's *Prelude* were on the program before our premiere in the *Teresa L. Kaufman Auditorium* at the 92nd Street Y.

The April issue of *Dance News* proclaimed our *Prelude* "a very good opener; a rather simple work in a free style." More space was given to *The Invisible Wife:*

Choreographer Victorious

In the Invisible Wife, the scenario presented
the difficult task for the choreographer but she
came out the winner. She made excellent use
of her material and succeeded in imbuing her
work with an overtone of impending
tragedy...the love duet between Jonas and
Rachel is a touching pas de deux. Aaron's
loneliness, dejection and division between
spiritual and carnal love is brought out
logically and lucidly. James Nygren's Aaron
is the most active role and he performs it with
a full understanding of the character he
portrays. Robert Paget presents a clear picture
of the older brother. Margaret Cuddy is very
well cast as Rachel. The characters of Mother
and Abigail (Wife) both danced by Sharry
Traver, are not as lucidly delineated as the
others, which is probably more the fault of the
choreographer than the dancer. The actual
dancing was excellent throughout... All told
The Invisible Wife is a distinct credit to the
Choreographers Workshop, it's second
production this season.

Anatole Chujoy, *Dance Magazine*, April 1949

From a choreographic viewpoint, *The
Invisible Wife*, a large group work by Virginia
Johnson on a scenarios by Winthrop Palmer,
was a complete success. (It) proved she is in

complete command of her craft, that she is dance-wise is apparent through her use of movement and abstractions of gesture to carry through the complicated story of two brothers in love with the same girl. She is fortunate in her collaborators and performers.

Nik Kevitsky, *Dance Observer*, April 1949

I was embarrassed to be singled out as not bringing strong characterizations to my roles. Ginny and I had both been "accused" and put our heads together over it. We could not identify anything specific. As we were to dance *Wife* again, Ginny suggested a week off to rethink it. Did I have any personal problems, by the way?

A variety of events had taken the bounce out of my usual indecent resilience. Work was my standard bromide. I was now dancing for three choreographers and keeping up with class as well as my *Woman's Suite*. Nik had a performance of his new work, *Extrados,* coming up down at Henry Street. He asked Kay to add *Prelude* to this program. I wondered why, as their choreographies seemed alien to each other. Kay called a rehearsal at her home, a penthouse in The Village. Her husband was an attorney. They had a young daughter with a maid to care for her. They had rooms full of furniture. Two bathrooms. I knew dance was a serious part of Kay's life, but obviously not all. Her lifestyle was a shock to me, a sharp reminder of wider possibilities, less hardship. Consider the comfort of a husband, day in, day out. A child. Having some possessions. Financial security!

I would soon be twenty-seven. It did seem that by now I should have found the right man to share my life. True, there were several notches in my hairbrush, but I regretted none of my refusals. Men seemed to propose to me suddenly while I was unsuspecting. An actor from *Starlight Operetta* came all the way to New York to propose to me. Sometimes, out of a misplaced sense of courtesy, I tried to respond. Other times, I seemed to be wiser than my boyfriend. That scared the hell out of me

I knew I needed an educated, mature man with a strong sense of humor who respected dance and loved me! And there was one: a writer on the *New York Times* who met me one New Year's Eve and pledged his life to me the next day. Jim pursued me in all manner of creative ways; often saying it was an emergency, or promising that this would be "the last time I ask you, Sharry," but always popping up again. He wanted to take me to his hometown of Pearl River, care tenderly for me while I was dancing. I did not listen. No, I fell for a poet who adored me, wrote paeans to my dancing spirit, until I found him married. O.K., maybe a traditional man in secular society would make sense after all. After all, the doctor was the most selfish. My instincts about love cashiered; it was better to dance, Dance, DANCE!

Maggie's situation with Toni Amato was different. Beautiful, blonde, intelligent, she attracted many men but was more wary than I. Laughing, Maggie said her mother told her, "Sex is just like going to the dentist; just something you have to do." My mother never told me anything regarding sex. We both suffered from the old attitude that dancers were "easy."

Maggie and I both had mentors, elder men whose friendship we enjoyed. Wouldn't it be fun for them to meet each other? Both men were exceedingly large: huge! Not a twit of sex appeal, but with fine, productive minds. Maggie's was Louis Horst, Martha's musical accompanist and teacher of *Pre Classic Dance Forms,* among other talents. Maggie saw him daily in class. Mine was Alfred van Duyme, a Dutch translator, amateur poet and sculptor, met through Dottie Spence (now on staff at *Life Magazine.*) Alfred, cynic, and I, idealist, had many philosophical arguments and monthly dinners that alternated between his studio on Bethune Street and ours. Alfred worked at Scribner's, the fine bookstore on Fifth Avenue. Generously, he saw to it that I had copies of the new dance books, including Merle Armitage's *Dance Memoranda* and John Martin's *The Dance.*

We asked them both for Sunday brunch. We sat them at our little table and waited on them, two handmaidens happy to see their mentors appreciate each other. Orange juice, English muffins with marmalade, scrambled eggs and stiff coffee. Maggie and I soon stayed out of the conversation and listened as the two men got into deep artistic analysis. When either chair gave out a painful squeak, we held our breaths. More coffee? Half, please. Then there were jovial goodbyes. Ah!

The phone rang soon after the two men left. Maggie answered it. She came back into the room with an irritated expression, but then laughed. "You'll get a kick out of this, Sharry."

"So who was it?"

"That was a girl from Bennington College. She said she was given my name to contact because she's in New York for winter term field work in dance. She said, "I have only six weeks and don't want to waste my time on something that isn't any good, so what show should I dance in while I am here? I heard *Kiss Me Kate* was a good. How about *Lend An Ear?*

"Oh! Oh! Oh!" I laughed. "What did you tell her?"

"What could anyone tell her! So I said, 'Sure go dance in *Kiss Me Kate.*' and she said, 'Thanks, I will!'"

We both howled laughing and when the thought came to us that, given the right emergency, this dimwit dancer might hit a desperate dance captain at the right time, we roared again. Neither of us had made the rounds recently, preferring concert dance. Dancers who were serious were expected to grow artistically. With *Wife*, we had a chance.

After our week off, Virginia gave Maggie, Doris Ebener and me a new dance with her: *Quator*. This dance was so rich in giving, I felt whole again. The gorgeous music was Bidu Sayao singing to *Villa-Loboss Bachianas Brazileiras* for eight celli and a bass: music that filled every pore with beauty. Its momentums sent us soaring, pouring motions into every phrase. Loveliness came brimming up out of us in suspensions, overflowed in a glory of off-center turnings, reverses, extensions and near miss rushing running patterns. Dancing it made you beautiful. Again Charlotte Trowbridge designed our costumes and Nellie Hatfield constructed them.

Although *Virginia Johnson Dance Company* was preparing for a full length program of its own later, we had a chance to perform *Quator* at the Y on another Choreographers Workshop, May 1st.

In the June issue of *Dance News,* Winthrop Palmer wrote of *Quator:*

> ...With just the mood of the music as
> its subject matter, Quator is rich in
> choreographic invention and projective in
> emotion. Miss Johnson, Margaret Cuddy,

Doris Ebener and Sharry Traver were the accomplished dancers.

Sunday evening, May 22, *Virginia Johnson Dance Company* gave a full concert at The Kaufman Dance Center of the Y. It was an exciting, fulfilling night of dancing. Virginia danced two solos, opening with *Sarabande Bouree,* a modern treatment of the pre-classic bouree, plus one of the highlights of the program, *Crisis,* a dance of personal angst. Maggie was given space on the program for her choreography of *Traditional Folk Songs: Careless Love, Lolly too dum day* and *Common Bill.* We danced *Quator* again, and *Invisible Wife,* plus one older dance of Virginia's, *Within These Walls.* In this, Virginia danced *Woman Figure:* "A woman being heralded for her celebrated deeds, when suddenly she is overwhelmed by the inexorable realization of the ruin she has caused." (program note)

Memory figures included Child danced by Helen Franklin; Husband/Lover danced by Marc Breaux; First Neighbor danced by Maggie; and Second Neighbor, by me. Lucas Foss composed the music

Crisis, an intense, tightly structured and emotionally stirring solo, was the best of Miss Johnson's offerings. The indecisions, the advancements, retreats, the shuddering reflections of self-torture and doubt were stunningly conveyed. At other times, Miss

Johnson's choreography and her own dancing
suggested unnecessary abruptness. *Within
These Walls* was a burlesque, rather than
satire, superficial and repetitious. Portions of
Quator were quite lovely.

...*The Invisible Wife*...disclosed Miss
Johnson's ability in establishing mood and
communicating dramatic intensity through her
choreography was absorbing. James Nygren
as Aaron and Sharry Traver as the dead
mother and invisible wife were particularly
fine.

Walter Terry, *The New York Herald Tribune*,
May 29, 1949

Virginia Johnson and her Company gave a
distinguished recital in Kaufman Auditorium (rest of
paragraph listing cast & program)

This recital had all the components
necessary for a stimulating evening of modern
dance, intelligent and dramatically gripping
content. formal clarity and inventiveness,
sincerity and control of execution and the
unmistakable feeling for theatre. Miss Johnson
danced her solo, Crisis, with a power and
intensity which won her an immediate ovation
from the audience...(More on Crisis)...

The ability to step outside herself, as a
choreographer was even more forcefully
exemplified inThe Invisible Wife. The

inevitable clash of the two brothers, the strange power of the invisible wife and the final immolation were unerringly conveyed. Not a single false note of sentimentality or confused action obtruded itself.

The young dancers performed the work with a passion and devotion which bespoke their respect for it. And the evocative lighting, set, costuming and music all helped to leave a deep impression. This work marks a great advance over Within These Walls...

Not the least of the evening's pleasures was the lovely Quator, a composition in pure movement, tinged with nostalgia and a the super-romantic music of Villa Lobos but essentially abstract. Very few modern dancers of the younger generation have produced any work as strong as this in its genre. Miss Cuddy's Folk Songs were harmless, but tiresomely repetitious and Doni and Jay Saunders left everything to be desired as folk singers...

Robert Sabin, *Dance Observer* May 22,1949

Other reviews had like sentiments. The May I (1949) issue of *Dance Magazine* had a review by Doris Hering, who also found *The Invisible Wife* the strongest dance on the program. In a parallel article about the Choreographers Workshop, a picture of James and me dancing was included. Maggie did not grieve about her work being damned with faint praise, but was very disappointed. I felt that I had vindicated my being cast in this mother/wife role. For all this work, hours of rehearsal and performance, Maggie and I each earned fifty dollars.

Two days after our concert, Peter Hamilton with Felisa Conde´, Betts Lee, Emily Frankel, Jack Ferris and Ada Ref, pianist, also presented a concert at Kaufman Auditorium. *Dance for Five* was the opener, and Peter asked me back to dance this for him.

In his *New York Herald Tribune*, May 29, 1949 review, Walter Terry called Peter "one of our best dancers."

His movements are not only facile by nature but highly expressive by reasons of his application of technical principles to emotional ends. His high easy leaps, his frequent use of suspensions, his awareness of spacial values, his simplicity of his pantomime and his responding to and resisting the pull of gravity, all contribute to his dance effectiveness.

As choreographer, Mr. Hamilton is not as consistently effective...*Dance for Five*...pleasant...gay, imaginative. awkward in spots. *Silent Snow Secret Snow* wonderfully poignant dance story...Joe Kitchener Jesse James...best works. *Prospice,* with score by Romeo Cascarino, represents ambition. It is, however, pretentious and not so very profound expansion into dance terms of the Robert Browning poem. *Prospice* is sometimes pageant, sometimes explicit movement, sometime ritualized mystery, sometimes pure dance.

Terry completed his critique of Peter's work praising "the beautiful dancing of Emily Frankel" and the fine support of others in his company.

Alfred had me over to dinner after my Peter Hamilton concert, spoiling me with shrimp salad and a crisp white wine. We talked overlong, making it after midnight as I waited for the Eighth Avenue bus home. When it finally arrived, there were few people on it, an older woman with bags, a couple of men sprawled in the back seats. As I dropped into the nearest seat, the older woman looked at me and began talking.

"What's a young girl like you doing out this late alone?" she chided. "It's only us old ones that can go it. My work keeps me out down Wall Street offices. You look tired. You work nights too?"

"Often I do." Her tone was friendly, so I answered her.

"I've a daughter, just younger than you and I don't like to think of her goin' home alone late night. Where'd you live?" I told her. "Well I'm gettin' off the bus and takin' you home."

I protested, telling her I had my Purposeful Walk that had yet to be challenged. If anything, I should be taking *her* home. All the way up to 98th? When I got off at my stop, this tired, old, cleaning woman got off with me, despite my concern that it would be over an hour before her next bus uptown. Taking my arm, and keeping to the street side of the sidewalks, she pointed out dangerous doorways where predatory men could hide, just waiting for a young thing like me. Touched by her concern, I tried to limit her efforts by pointing out our apartment, now just a block away. She could watch me run home and go no further out of her way.

She hesitated but a second. "No! I promised I'd takin' you home and I'm keepin' it all the way!"

And she did. I asked her in, for tea perhaps? No, she had to skeedaddle back to 8th Ave. I gave her a hug, then stood waiting to watch her go. She stopped, hands on hips, insisting I go inside before she would leave. I never saw her again, but I'll never forget her kindness.

EYE Magazine was doing a feature on New York dancers, our careers and lives offstage. They asked to interview Maggie and me for a four page spread and came by our apartment to meet us. Journalist Ira Peck and fashion photographer Peter Martin asked us about our job-hunting experiences, performances, and took homey pictures of us making yoghurt, Maggie answering the hall phone, etc. In a shot of me, I'm wearing my dark raincoat, slouching philosophically in my Nana's rocking chair, holding a cigarette as though this crass pose was my style. Throughout the interview and photo shoot, we four became very friendly, so we all went dancing off to The Village for ice cream.

My parents were going by ship to Europe to see Pummie and Herbie. They embarked from New York, so we had a short visit. In a euphoric mood, *My Father Gave Me fifty dollars!* The only money he ever gave me since I had become a dancer. Nik paid me fifteen dollars for teaching. Even so, I was broke, for my *Finian's* unemployment benefits ran out. I could not afford only concert work. I needed a show job. Then two streams of energy flowed into my life in conflicting directions.

Marc Platt had come back to New York in search of live theatre, finally taking the dance lead in the road company of *Kiss Me Kate*. Marc wanted me in the show, and that was manna from heaven for me. There would be good dancing and money. Marc promised to speak to Hanya on my behalf. At the same time, Felisa called, asking me to consider a summer dance-teaching job; one she had first agreed to, but then backed out of. She promised to look for a replacement. Go out of the City? No! Touring was one thing, but teach at a girls' camp? Thanks, but no thanks, Felisa!

Before Marc could speak to Hanya, her secretary called me to come see Hanya.. I delayed a day but could not put it off because of seeing her in class. With a happy smile, Hanya told me she would be pleased to have me run her New York studio for the entire summer while she was out in Colorado Springs. This would involve day and some night classes, as well as managing her studio. The salary would be fifty dollars a week. Hanya looked at me expectantly.

It was an honor to be trusted with this responsibility. I thanked Hanya for her confidence in me. Then I had to respectfully decline. Without offending, I explained how desperate my financial situation was, that all these teaching hours would prevent me from dancing anywhere else and, therefore, fifty dollars a week would not cover my living expenses. I would be available, however, for the road company of *KMK* and would be grateful for that opportunity. Also, I knew Marc. Would that be possible?

No.

Disappointed at my refusal to manage the studio, Hanya refused to let me in *KMK*, despite Marc's speaking up for me.

While I was smoldering over Hanya's spiteful treatment of me, Felisa's camp director pestered me. Tuck Duboff had a spiel that ran on no matter how you tried to cut her off. How many times did I say, "Sorry! Gotta go!" and hang up. She came by the apartment and, though not exactly thrusting her foot in the door, babbled about her "camp that really is a summer school for the arts" before I could even be rude. Finally, I let her have her say to get rid of her. It was a Jewish camp, but she liked to have Christian counselors as well. Students were serious, already studying dance in New York. I would have my own dance studio. There would be choreographic opportunities, putting on the yearly musical. I would have one day off per week when the studio could be mine alone. The pay was $450 for two months work, plus tips.

My *Woman's Suite* was stuck until I could rent a studio for space, but I could not afford the $5 per hr. fee. I was getting so desperate for space that I considered getting a college teaching job nearby just to get a studio. I had even written to the employment office at good old TSCW to see if anything was near me. Of course, I had to reaffirm a love of teaching. To her credit, Dr. Duggan replied she would look for a place by fall. What had I started! Now my top priority was doing my own work, using my own dance voice, as soon as I could afford it. Maybe even taking that camp job to work on my stuff. Come back to New York in September and turn it on its ear!

I gulped and called Tuck Duboff, agreeing to come. Being out of the city in the mountains for eight weeks? How bad could it be?

The very next day didn't I get a card asking me to please come audition for swing girl in the Broadway production of *Kiss me Kate!*

"Oh, Sharry!" Maggie agonized with me. "What are you going to do?"

"I am sick and tired of waiting for someone to say 'Yes, you may dance…Oops! No! You may not dance! It's *my dancing* and I am going to decide when the hell I'll dance. I'll…I'll audition just for the hell it. Then tell them I don't want their lousy job!"

There were only three of us auditioning; Emily, which surprised me as she had no use for Broadway, and another girl, obviously a ballet dancer. Glen Tetley was dance captain. Now he showed us the audition combinations, some including lifts. The audition lasted an hour-and-a-half as Glen took turns with each of us in dances from the show. My sense of independence freed me to have fun with the dances, and I danced well. So did Em. As we three stood in line center stage, I saw one of the producers point to me. I also saw Hanya shake her head "no." Em and I were excused. I stood and stared at Hanya a full slow four counts before turning on my heel and marching offstage. Glen looked at me with chagrin, holding out his hands and shrugging helplessly.

Back in the dressing room, Emily told me she had just learned that the winning girl was *KMK* dancer Shirley Eckl's roommate. We had just been called to legalize her audition. Worldly, Em chalked it up to politics as usual, but I went into a black boiling rage. How devilish Hanya was! She had completely "gone Broadway!" She was totally vindictive to one of her best and most faithful dancers. Me!

But I had a strong solace to get me beyond this. Glen had come to our Virginia Johnson concert. He came backstage afterwards to give me a hug and to talk to me.

Glen praised me, adding, "Sharry, you have come fully into your own as a dancer." Coming from Glen, dancer supreme that he was, that affirmation was higher praise than any dance critic's. One of my own assured me I was ripe to do my own works.

The itch to choreograph my own dances was already strong but confidence in its being concert worthy was a sometime thing. Glen's push was what was needed. And now with studio space available, there was the chance and the challenge to create a major dance work.

It was thrilling to think of it!

CHAPTER EIGHTEEN

Summer 1949
  Camp Birchwood, Vermont

Oh God! What had I done!

When I had entered Grand Central Station with my suitcase I heard this loud, boisterous singing. When I spotted Tuck, Camp Birchwood director, in the middle of the mass of screaming campers, I groaned out loud..

In the confusion, I backed slowly away. Too late. Tuck saw me and seized me, bringing me forth into the crowd with a shrill whistle. "Listen up! Here is your new Dance Counselor from Broadway! Sharry Traver!" Screams filled the air. Tuck made sure I made it on the train. In the midst of basketballs, hockey sticks and teddy bears, I almost got off at 125th Street. At counselor's pre-camp, I wished I had.

Before I could teach dance, I must be prepared to care for a bunk of teenage Jewish girls by proving I could operate a heavy fire extinguisher, inspect the septic tank (and keep weekly records of the girls' BMs), pass a physical by the camp nurse, and pass lifesaving partnered with the Arts and Crafts counselor, Mara. For all this, we two were led around by the Assistant Director, Beverly. Last she demanded a canoe test. Rank beginners, Mara and I floundered, paddling around in the canoe out on the lake and began to giggle.

"Stop that!" cried out Beverly from the dock. "Now dump it!"

"What's dump it!" yelled Mara.

"Turn it over! Dump it! Don't you artists know anything!"

"Why? Do we have to?" called Mara.

"YOU HAVE TO! NOW!"

I was suddenly enraged. Got up on the gunnels of the canoe rocking it violently and tipped us both over into the lake. We emerged far from each other to hear Beverly shout . "You dummies! You lost your paddles! "

Treading water, I yelled, "Go to hell, Beverly!" Mara thumbed her nose.

My first night with my bunk teenagers, the girls had asked question after question: Did I really dance on Broadway? If so, why was I here? Did I know Celeste, the dance counselor last year? Did I have a TV? What kind of dance would I teach? Had I seen the Broadway show *South Pacific?* Is that summer nightie all I brought?

"I'm sure I'll be fine, girls. We better talk more tomorrow. Nitey-nite."

I woke up in the middle of the night shivering. I woke up in the morning, covered with blankets. These Jewish Princesses who had brought everything they had at home along with them, had fun supplying me with anything from a flannel nightie to chocolates. Veteran campers, they showed *me* the ropes.

After our first campfire by the Indian totem pole, a ritual contest between the Gold and Silver Teams ended in wild hysterics and tears. I talked to Tuck about it. "Oh yes, that is why I hire Christian counselors. You are not as emotional."

She admitted the girls were spoiled, but took time to tell me that most of these girls were first generation Americans, born of the early refugees from Europe. In many cases, these children were all the family their parents had left.

Grandparents, aunts and uncles, even cousins, all lost in the Holocaust. Their parents were both doting and demanding.

"Why do you think Jewish kids are so often at the top of their school class? Because they feel guilty. The Indian totem pole? To get them to remember America goes beyond New York City and it is not all cement. To remember they are *Americans*, not Europeans. And just as important, we want them to have fun here as just kids."

So the two teams were allowed to spontaneously upset the days' routine with their own ideas. More than once, giggling at my surprise, the leader of the Gold Team came running through my class, taking my whole class with her.

My dance studio redeemed everything. It was beautiful and big with a sprung hardwood floor. It had a *barre*, a standing mirror on one side and a stage, broad and deep enough for a cast of twenty. My dance classes in Modern Dance and Ballet were established as rigorous; my rehearsals as serious. I moved on into solid choreography, working with the music counselor, Sally. The production was to be Gilbert's and Sullivan's *Patience;* casting was on the Call Board the day after July 4th. My heart lifted as I drifted into dancing about in my dream come true.

Now I could get to my *Woman's Suite: Woman Working, Woman Waiting, Not Knowing, Woman Wanting,* sentient conditions in my life and common to most women, but undervalued, I believed. My attitude to each was not flat "yes" or "no." That was why I wanted to reveal dimensions of each.

I swore off men for the summer, but then, when a counselor from our brother Maple Tree Camp asked me to go to a local July 4th Dawn Square Dance, I got Tuck's permission to go see how Vermonters danced.

Well, this man, Wynn Underwood, turned out to be a local fellow who picked me up in his Army jeep. He rattled us up and down hills into a yard filled with cars and trucks by a shimmering lake. There was the white Dance Pavilion, like a one-layer wedding cake sparkling with lights. Fiddle music sounded into the airs outside. Inside it was a wild, wooly, ya-hoo blast. As soon as we were spotted, we were pulled into a square where the joke was to keep Wynn from getting me back as his partner. I was swung as on a daisy chain from one guy to the next, all laughing up a storm. Rescued, given food and drink, I had enough. Wynn drove me back through the mountain mists, suddenly enclosing us, then ghosting away.

I had to ask, "Have you ever seen the show *Brigadoon?*"

So far away.

So near!

There was worse to come. The whole camp was quarantined. In the summer of 1949 in New England, there was a serious epidemic of poliomyelitis. Working with parents and Vermont Department of Health Officials, it was decided that these young girls were safer in camp here than at home in New York City. The night Tuck announced this at the campfire, the expected uproar was patiently calmed with factual information and specific procedures, finishing with a unifying ritual and Birchwood song. The rule was: nobody in, nobody out. On my way to our bunk, Wing Li, our Chinese cook, brought me a note:

Meet me at the lake tonight. Wynn .

Oh dear.

After lights out, I stumbled down to the shore, trying not to use my flashlight. Well, where was he? A red glow from his pipe led me to turn my flashlight there and a canoe appeared. I quickly turned the light off to avoid discovery, only to have him yell, "Keep it on! Get in the canoe!"

"We're quarantined! You have to go away!" I stage whispered.

"I know that. Why do you think I am here? Get in the canoe!"

He was making so much noise, I finally got in the canoe to talk quietly with him. He quickly back paddled too far off shore for me to jump out, turned the canoe and headed for an island in the lake.

" Hey!" I protested. "You can't..."

He beached the canoe, handed me out, still protesting. Taking his pipe out of his mouth, Wynn asked, "Do you have polio?"

"No! Of course not!"

"Neither do I." Then he kissed me.

"Hey! Wait one minute!"

"Want a beer while I make a fire? I want to apologize for those woodchucks the other night." He kept talking as he built the fire. And it was nice, being there under the stars, away from camp. "I was wondering if you might have met my sister, Judy, a time in New York. She's a dancer. She was in *On the Town*. You know of it?"

The last place I would have ever looked to find a kindred soul was a tiny island in the middle of a lake in Vermont.

Nights that I did not have Quad guard duty I would sneak off after lights out to meet Wynn at the water's edge. He paddled three miles up the lake. Then we would paddle out to the island. I became a good canoe paddler, but he still had to paddle three miles back. I would not break quarantine by going out in public, so we either went to his house or drove up into the mountains. That meant twelve miles paddling in the dark for Wynn—who I learned was a disabled veteran from the Army 10th Mountain Division Ski Troops. It all became ridiculously melodramatic, involving an underground network of local folks to get messages back and forth.

One night we were half way between camp and Wynn's shore when a terrific summer thunderstorm blew up from nowhere and drenched us in seconds. The waters whipped up nearly swamping us while Wynn yelled, "Sing! I've been working on the railroad." We both yelled and stroked in rhythm together, keeping as close to shore as we dared. The cold rains were relentless, filling the canoe, making it heavier. Lightning frightened me so I yelled louder. We were barely able to drag the canoe ashore. Barely able to get the jeep started to get to his house. Hastily we peeled off our outer clothes, wrapped ourselves in blankets, took a shot of brandy and dropped exhausted to the hearth. We slept like the dead—until bright morning sunshine woke me.

Ohmygod!

As we arrived at Camp Birchwood, everyone was gathering for Reveille. My teenage girls spotted us coming down the campus and rushed towards us. Tuck blasted her whistle. Wynn immediately snapped a salute to the flag. Then everyone else had to. We held the salute as two young campers finally got the flag raised. Wynn unsnapped his salute, did an about face and strode off. My campers clustered around me, only to be whistled off to breakfast. Beverly gave me a furious look as she joined them. That left Tuck and me. She looked very stern. I started to apologize.

"Tuck, I guess this looks pretty bad…"

Tuck looked about the empty Quad.

Then she burst out laughing!

"Aren't…aren't you angry?"

"I have every right to be. Oh, you should have seen yourselves! If it weren't for Bev…who wants you fired by the way…I could not have lasted. Look Sharry. I knew I couldn't bring you here from Broadway and not expect a few broken curfews. As long as you didn't go out in public…"

Stunned, I asked, "You knew?"

"You forget you have a bunk of teenagers?"

"Everyone knew? Oh, what we've been through!"

"I was concerned about you in that storm, but I'm not angry. I try to keep the big pictures when it comes to kids. I don't know how we would have lasted through quarantine if it weren't for your 'secret romance.' You look terrible. Get some sleep. Your kids are worrying about you."

I saw my girls in this new light, coming to care for each one for herself, rather than a group of girls. Four of my five were good dancers, one good enough to audition to attend the Fiorello H. LaGuardia High School of Music and Performing Arts. My own work on my *Woman's Suite* was still not finished to my satisfaction. Getting my dancers ready for Parents' Weekend now came first.

Weeks later, with an OK from the Vermont Department of Health, Tuck ended the quarantine in time for a Parents' Weekend. *Patience* was better than I first expected. There were activities all over campus, including a Refugee Bazaar filled with Mara's pottery and other crafts for sale. My best students choreographed a *Refugee Ballet*, roughly based on *The Little Match Girl.* And I danced for everybody too.

The next night, Wynn drove us up into the mountains under the Harvest moon to get us away. He had things to talk to me about. He wanted me to know he had plans. After coming home from the war, he had run for Town Representative and been elected to the Vermont State Legislature. Now he had applied to different law schools. Harvard and Yale rejected him as he had joined the Ski Troops before finishing his degree at Dartmouth. Boston University Law School had just accepted him on the G.I. Bill of Rights.

Starting this September!

"I know I'm rushing you, but Sharry, I want you to come with me. 'Come live with me and be my love'..."

The quote sounded like just one more proposition. "That's what you want?" I asked. "You want me just to come live with you?"

"Yes! You know that I love you!"

"If that is all I wanted, I could have had that long ago." I walked back toward the jeep. Wynn ran after me, taking me by the shoulders.

"If you love me, why won't you marry me!" he cried in distress.

"Marry you? Is that what you truly mean?"

"What else could I mean!"

"To be your mistress."

"MARRY ME," he shouted.

"Can you stand someone dancing around all the time? For I will, you know."

"Yes! Marry me!"

"Oh, I will, Wynn. I will!"

I told my parents, first with a letter and then, as we had only ten days before Wynn had to report to Law School, I sent a wire. This was all pretty fast. I had just met Wynn six weeks ago. I tried to think about him objectively. Why

Wynn? Why now, when I wanted to take my dances back to New York?

I could not stop loving this man.

And why ever was that? For one thing, he could admit he did not know something to a girl! Wynn would simply say, "I don't know enough about that to say."

Wynn's aspect was appealing; tall, lean, brown eyes, and, yes, handsome in a Lincoln-esque way. His stance was one of quiet strength. He said what he thought, but did not chatter. Wynn was true. True the way a ruler is inherently true. He was a man who knew himself.

And he deeply loved me.

We learned to know each other quickly, alone together during our melodramatic courtship. We were both at turning points in our lives. We had both *been around*; both of us needed to redirect our lives. He was straight with me, saying that after Law School, he wanted to return to Vermont "to have a hand in how things in the State were going." Would three years in Boston be enough city life for me? By then, there was no choice: I could not see my life anywhere without Wynn.

My next day off, Wynn picked me up to take me all around Vermont, which proved to be by farms and fields, then over the mountains to a small village called Rochester. It was a pretty village. White clapboard houses with porches stood on three sides of the Green, with a bandstand in the center. Thirsty, we went to the local General Store for drinks, and there I spied the latest issue of *EYE Magazine*. I grabbed it and began looking at our feature article.

"What is that?" Wynn asked. I showed him. "Now don't tell me you want a divorce?" he kidded.

"Not yet!" I smiled. But I worried as we drove through forest after forest, small town after no town but more farms. Who would I ever dance for here?

We drove on up to Montpelier, the capital of Vermont. The capitol itself while smaller than my Pennsylvania capitol, had a handsome greensward approach. Classic in design, the capital had a golden dome with a statue of the Goddess Ceres. Wynn proudly took me within the House of Representatives, now in recess. Showing me his desk, he told me how he dared run on a Democratic ticket in this Republican State.

"I'm sure being a Vet helped me win but at twenty one, I was the youngest Representative in the House. Would you like to meet our governor? I'll see if Ernest is in"

"You call the governor by his first name?"

Wynn led me down the hall to the Governor's office.

Governor Gibson was a man of medium build, graying hair, but with a handsome visage. He was energetic and gracious.

"Hello, there, Wynn! Come on in!" Governor Gibson smiled.

"Glad to find you in, Ernest. Governor, I'd like you to meet my intended, Miss Sharry Traver."

Governor Gibson congratulated us and asked if Wynn would be running for office again. "Law school? Coming back to Vermont? Hate to lose you."

"I plan to, Sharry being willing by then."

Wynn completed this trip around Vermont by going on to Burlington, showing me Lake Champlain, and taking me to a fine restaurant across from City Park. I was relieved to find Vermont indeed did have a city. Thrilled to see Wynn's stature grow with each new experience.

That night I devoured the write-up by Ira Peck in *EYE Magazine.* Stared at the pictures of dance friends, of Maggie and me.

> Today's CHORUS GIRLS can dance
> A revolution in Broadway Musical has shifted
> the accent from shapely legs to dancing
> ability...
> ...*Oklahoma!* threw out the hoofers
> and show girls and substituted ballet and
> modern dancers whose dancing was a
> continuation rather than an interruption of the
> plot. The successful integration of book, songs
> and dances in *Oklahoma!* created a new
> standard for musical comedy and a new
> standard in chorus girls.

This was old news to us but newsworthy to the general public. Peck also had information about a recent Chorus Equity Survey of its over 5,000 members.

> 1. The average chorus girl today spends at
> least ten years and
> $4,000 studying dance, singing and dramatics
> before she even attempts coming to Broadway
> for a career.
> 2. Even after she makes her bid for a career,
> she continues with her studies, devoting two
> or three hours a day to them whether working
> or not.
> 3. Despite her intense professional training,
> she has managed to acquire a year or two of
> college education.

4. Although the minimum pay for chorus work is $75 a week, very few chorus girls average that much pay for any length of time. For competition in their field is terrific and unemployment the rule rather than the exception. Of Chorus Equity's more than 5,000 members, fewer than 1,000 of them are likely to be employed in Broadway shows at any one time. Before the war, the average chorus girl worked only sixteen weeks a year at her chosen profession. In recent years, because of the fabulous success of such musicals as *Oklahoma!* and *Carousel,* she has managed to do better but not nearly well enough to afford anything like security...

Peck closed his article with a quote from Marianne Sanders that spoke for us:

"Dancing is terribly hard work. I prefer to live that way. I want to accomplish things. My favorite field is concert...that's the type of dancing I really want to do. That's serious work. You never make a tremendous living out of it. Even if you are topnotch you still don't do terribly well. But there you really have a chance to develop your own style, or if you have something to say in dance, to say it, to create something."
EYE Magazine, August, 1949

It was unnatural for me and the dancers I knew to think of ourselves as "chorus girls." We were not. Even the title "chorus girls" was no longer used on Broadway Play Bills. The term now was Dancers, and our names were listed. First, I was a dancer, a natural, independent, freelance dancer. So were we all. Then we danced according to our choreography in ensemble or as featured performers in Broadway shows, on concert stage, in movies, on TV, in circuses, in parades, schools, night clubs. churches, festivals, camps, with or without music, together or alone.

It would be scary for me to leave New York now, but it would force me to be independent. It was expected of Modern Dancers to progress to the point of dissatisfaction with the *status quo* and evolve new concepts in dance. I was ready.

I was teaching *Laces and Graces,* a round dance, to the combined girls and boys camps for the Co-Camp Summer Square Dance, when I was called to the office. Busy, I ignored it until the third time. Stamping up there, I was stopped in my tracks.

"Daddy! Mother?"

They had dropped everything to come up to Vermont to save me from myself. No, Wynn was not a farmer and he was not even here. He was in Boston looking for an apartment for us. Yes, to be a lawyer. What would we live on? I would have four hundred dollars soon; Wynn had four hundred and fifty, and the G.I. Bill would pay Wynn one hundred dollars a month. We'd be fine! I took them all to meet Wynn's parents, whose genteel ways calmed the situation.

Wynn's parents showed them a picture of Wynn; then took us all to a classy luncheon at Hyde Manor. A visit to their antique shop rewarded Mother with a pair of brass candlesticks.

Finally I had to say, "Mother and Dad, I would like your blessing, but I must tell you that I am going to marry Wynn with it or without it."

My Dad took me aside. "You are sure you really love this man? He loves you?"

"Yes, Dad."

"There's nothing better than living with the one you love. I'll talk to your Mother."

My mother's parting words were, "Now, Shirley, don't you give yourself to Wynn before any wedding. You know what I mean!" That was the only thing my mother ever said to me about sex in my entire life.

Then I told Tuck. "You're really going to marry this guy? Wait 'til your kids find out," she laughed. She agreed to let me leave two days early.

My kids screamed, going beyond the usual hysterics, swamping me with hugs. Could they be my bridesmaids? Was he a good kisser? Would I kiss him before he brushed his teeth? (The real test of love.) Would I still dance? Do we want children? Boston? Will I come back to Birchwood next year?

The last days at camp were in a whirlwind. Finding time to call Maggie, who said, "Oh. OH!" Then came the telegram from Dr. Duggan offering me "a great job" at some university in Missouri that seemed oblivion for me. A passionate letter from our fashion photographer, Peter Martin, arrived from Paris, frantically asking me to marry him. And then came a letter from my parents, making a brave effort to accept Wynn, sight unseen and offering home for the wedding before law school.

When Wynn came to pick me up to take me off, the whole camp went bananas. The Gold and Silver Teams took turns screaming corny cheers, decorating the jeep, loading my stuff. Wynn tossed my things in the back as fast as he could, yelling, "Come on, Sharry! Let's go!"

As we took off across the campus, the kids ran after us all the way out singing *"Some enchanted evening, you may meet a stranger across a crowded room..."*

342

CHAPTER NINETEEN

September 1949
Boston, MA
Middlebury, VT

Wynn had found an apartment for us on Beacon Hill. It even had a fireplace. Boston University Law School was up the hill behind the State House. Down the hill was Charles Street with its shops and restaurants and just ahead there was the Boston Common. Perfect.

As Wynn settled into law school, I was welcomed into the *Boston Dance League.* While I deplored its name, I quickly respected the Modern Dance talents of its members. These young women were the dance teachers in all the colleges in and around Boston. Saturdays we met at rotating colleges to choreograph and rehearse new dance works. Two of my new dances were included in our first performance.

In no time, I was giving master classes at Wellesley, teaching at Pine Manor, the Cambridge School, and then at Emerson and Tufts Colleges. I also volunteered to teach at the Harriet Tubman Settlement House. I kept up my ballet at the Boston Conservatory, performing there as well. I danced in the *Boston Opera* production of *Iphingenia* and earned cash dancing in Filene's Department Store fashion shows.

Then I got pregnant. It was a surprise, but we were delighted. Boy or girl, we did not care. Due in August, I could continue my teaching through the spring. After the babe was born, I planned to resume teaching and dancing next fall.

People have said "A dancer's life is short." I was finding that flat statement simply was not true. If you *are* a dancer, you continue to be a dancer all through life. I did not see my life as "Home town girl makes good, marries and has kids, joins Hospital Board."

People may be referring to the performance years of a dancer, which can or cannot be short. Modern dance changed the ground rules so that age is not the determinant, but creativity and ability. Now as a wife and mother, I would have ever more things to dance about.

We had a beautiful baby girl whom we named Sky. (What!! said Mother.) We moved back to Vermont for Wynn to set up his law practice "and have a hand in how things were going in the State." We settled in Middlebury, mainly because I felt a college town would be more congenial to live in than a small mountain town. Middlebury College had no dance department at that time and had no wish to start one. There was no dance studio in town. I could find only one ballet dancer, in Springfield, in the whole state of Vermont. There was no arts council. The only space big enough for *a tour jeté* or a circle of spins was the Ballroom at the Middlebury Inn.

Artists try to understand what they are living, responding through forms of art. These forms celebrate the moment of thought or feeling. With most arts, the artist turns intangible concepts into tangible forms, sooner or later shown to the world. Here the artwork has an independent entity that can continue to exist without the artist.

This is not true for performing artists: theirs is a living art form that cannot exist without their persons. Yes, actors have scripts; musicians have scores. Dancers can join in recordings on film or television. But all these are only images at a remove of time and space and size from the original performance; they lack full measure of being.

Where a sculptor, photographer, potter, architect, writer, weaver, painter can live and produce art while living apart from society, if not without it, a performing artist cannot live apart. A dancer must have someone to dance for or the dance flows away, ungiven. At times, I think of the apple bud brought to blossom, to fruit that ripens to a rosy cheek with the sun, to go unpicked, to drop and rot. Does the apple know it is wasted? Dancers can tell. Dancers cannot wait to have their work respected years later. Despite notation, the dancer's aura will not be there.

This evanescence must be remembered to understand why I cannot turn in to self, why turning away from others to dance alone cannot suffice. Why I insist upon dancing in this touchingly beautiful place. So I am swallowing my pride and going tomorrow to audition. Oh, not in one of my beloved New York theaters but at the Middlebury Inn. Not auditioning before choreographers and producers but before a lawyer, a doctor, and the current President of the local Lions Club. What dance gig do I hope to get? A chance to dance for assembled guests at the Annual Lion's Club Spring Dance.

Later: At the Inn for my audition, the three sat on straight chairs in a row while I danced to the zither music waltz from *The Third Man*. They withdrew to confer. I was approved.

At the dance intermission, I was introduced.

"Mrs. Wynn Underwood will now do us a dance!"

Some people wandered off to the bar. No one said anything afterwards and the general dancing resumed. My thought was to dance something pretty on a spring night. Maybe they were disappointed, expecting razzle-dazzle and spangles. After all, was I not "that Broadway babe Wynn Underwood has gone off and married up with?"

At first I thought I was resented for some reason. It was worse than that. Nobody cared whether I danced or not. It had nothing to do with them.

"But they need me!" I complained to Wynn.

"Well, you'll have to find a way to convince them," he said.

When you are a dancer, you gotta dance.

I started a class for children, renting space in the old Town Hall. My first class there were three five-year olds, two sixes, one seven, plus our Sky.

First, we all try to stand very still.

Next, we check all our parts and pieces.

This makes us laugh, so we run all over, and then freeze!

Now what does the music feel like?

Slow-motion tag...

Moving tiny...moving huge...

Running backwards...

Skipping with a partner....

And then the best...Sailing around on one foot — arms wide singing "I feel—I feel—I feel like a Morning Star!"

Is it so hard a thing to see
The Spirit of God whate'er it be
The law that abides and changes not, ages
long,
The Eternal and Nature-born—
These things be strong?
What else is Wisdom? What of man's
endeavour
Or God's high grace so lovely and so great?
To stand from fear set free, to breathe and
wait.
To hold a hand uplifted over hate;
Is it so hard a thing to see
And shall not loveliness be loved forever?

The Bacchae by Euripides

349

CODA

One wistful winter day in Vermont in 1977, I decided to write to Agnes de Mille and thank her for her dances in *Bloomer Girl.* To my delight, Agnes de Mille answered me. A short correspondence developed, bringing me to meet her at her press conference for her *Agnes de Mille Festival Week* with the Boston Ballet the following spring.

Despite her limitations after her stroke, Agnes looked attractive and alert. She wore a black dress with a diamond brooch. Her graying hair was drawn back and held in place with a black ribbon. She could walk with measured grace using a cane and light support. There was also a degree of motion in her right arm. She was seated in a comfortable chair upon a low platform so that she could see and be seen.

After introductions, Agnes de Mille was presented with a Citation from the State of Massachusetts and given the Key to the City of Boston. Agnes de Mille Week was declared. Virginia Williams of the *Boston Ballet* expressed her admiration and gratitude for working with her Company. *Boston Ballet* dancers presented two excerpts from de Mille ballets. Next, her book editor, Edward Weeks, praised her affectionately and notably for "being the one who really changed the attitude of the public to dancers by giving them respect as persons in her choreography." He named Agnes de Mille the Greatest American Choreographer. She shook her head, but looked pleased.

Agnes then rose, leaning on the adjacent piano and expressed her unhappiness with the presentation of her dances. Speaking in robust terms, she explained that the excerpt from her new ballet, *Summer,* should have been partnered and on point. She called Ms. Williams to account for not explaining that the girl in this ballet was dying. Softening, she thanked the Boston Ballet dancers for "all their splendid patience with her now that she was hurt."

She then went on saying that Mr. Weeks had treated her not only as a friend but that he was also one of the very few gentlemen she knew—she did after all work in the theatre—and she was confessing now to a secret love held for him all these years.

Seeing me rise and then retreat, the MC came and asked if I was one of Ms. de Mille's dancers. "Then bust right in," he said.

When I explained who I was, Agnes clapped her hands and said "Talk to me! Talk to me!"

They moved us to a table and we sat there, knee to knee chattering away as though there was nothing exceptional about it. Agnes leaned forward, speaking again about how her new dance should be. I was touched she would confide her worries to me. She asked if I didn't think Ted Weeks had been gracious and wasn't he fine? I agreed and told her I had told him so.

When I gave her one of my Vermont Dance Company T-shirts, she was enthusiastic about it, saying she received them from other dancers. Then Agnes de Mille said, "Tell me about your work? Do you have a studio?"

"My work" seemed so pitiful in light of hers that I demurred.

"We'll talk about it in New York when you come to tea," she smiled.

"I am sorry but Ms. de Mille must go on to the next event," her manager said.

Suddenly overwhelmed with affection, I asked, "May I kiss you?"

Startled, Agnes exclaimed, "What!"

Then she leaned forward a little as I gave her a light kiss on her cheek before saying goodbye.

How did I dare do that!

352

ADDENDA

In 1993, five of us Agnes de Mille dancers got together in New York for the first time in forty years. In no time, Carolyn George, Margaret Cuddy, Virginia (Winkie) Bosler, Jean Kinsella and I were chattering away as though we had just finished a show together. We laughed over show stories, spoke about Agnes herself, how we feared and loved her.

How was she now?

"Frail now," Virginia reported.

We had all left Broadway, joining dance companies for concert work. Comparing our opportunities with those now in '93, we agreed we were the luckiest generation of American dancers, here when new ideas of dance and dancers were changing in exciting ways.

"It is much harder to find a job now." said Carolyn.

"The technique is much harder now, too," Virginia nodded. "It doesn't seem to be as much fun as it was for us."

"Yes, we were like sisters," we all agreed

" Now it is not outrageous to be a dancer," I said. "There is some respect."

Agnes de Mille passed away two weeks later.

Credits:

Virginia Bosler: *Gentlemen Prefer Blondes, A Month of Sundays Out of This World*. Agnes de Mille Dance Theatre Soloist in Valerie Bettis's Dance Theatre. Two films: *Oklahoma!* and *Brigadoon*. Teaching Dance Notation, Secretary of the International Movement Notation. Virginia married Herbert Dorris. They have a son.

354

Carolyn George: *Bloomer Girl, Oklahoma!*. San Francisco Ballet Company three years. New York City Ballet. Carolyn became soloist in 1954. Married NYCB star Jacques d'Amboise. Four children, two dancers: Christopher, Artistic Director of the Philadelphia Ballet, and Charlotte, Broadway musicals. She took up photography, internationally recognized for her excellence. Carolyn passed away in 2009.

Margaret Cuddy: *Mexican Hayride, Carousel, Sing Out Sweet Land, Ballet Ballads, Wonderful Town My Fair Lady*. TV series, *The Triad*s. Toured with Columbia Concerts in *Musical America*. She became interested in Yoga. Maggie married artist Murray Sherman; they have a daughter, Brook.

Betty Jones: major dancer with José Limón as Desdemona in *The Moor's Pavane*. Work with Doris Humphrey in Limón's Company. Betty married Fritz Ludin formed a duo company in Hawaii. For many years, taught Modern Dance at the American Dance Festival at Duke University. Betty received the 1993 Balasaraswati/Joy Ann Dewy Beinecke Award for Lifetime Service.

Jean Kinsella :continued to dance in shows. She worked with Carolyn in her private Ballet Studio. She married dancer/choreographer Peter Genarro. Jean was also interviewed for the *EYE Magazine* feature on Broadway dancers

We also learned Emily Frankel carried on the *Dance Drama Company* in USA and abroad. She became a soloist performer until an accident interrupted her career. Emily returned to dance, performing to Mahler's *Fifth Symphony* at Lincoln Center. Emily married actor John Cullum. They have a son, David.

Jeanette Schlottman Roosevelt became director of the *American Dance Festival* at Connecticut College. Teaching at Barnard College, she created the Dance Department at Barnard. In 1986. Barnard founded the *Jeanette Roosevelt Dance Library*. Recorded historical Conversation on Dance with Louis Horst.

Sharry Underwood: In 1968, founded the Vermont Dance Company with Graham dancer, Gloria Shaw, bringing theatre dance into Vermont. Writing dance criticism since 1976. In 1985, honored by *Flynn Center for the Performing Arts for Fifty Years of Devotion to Dance in Vermont*. In 2000, Reconstructed *Lost Dances of Ted Shawn* for Jacob's Pillow. Husband Wynn became a Justice on the Vermont Supreme Court. We have four daughters and one son.

356

NOTES

The major point of this book is that it is not derivative. It does not depend upon second hand information for its veracity. Where dance reviews are included either to describe the dances or provide an expert opinion, credit is noted on the spot. Program information is credited likewise.

There are other personal dance histories, each distinctively different. This is mine to add firsthand reporting for the evolution in theatrical dance in America.

Note: in 2009, *Finian's Rainbow* was revived for short run at *Encore!* an organization which mounted many revivals, in New York City. Its production of *Finian's* was so successful, the show went back on Broadway.

In December 26, 2011, on cable TV democracynow *A Tribute to E.Y. Harburg, The Man Who Put the Rainbow in the Wizard of Oz*, reported that "*Finian's Rainbow* is still so popular that it is produced thirteen times a month in high schools and colleges across the country every year."

RESOURCES

Because of the nature of dance, it has been important to keep programs, pictures and other ephemera related to dance as resources for names of dancers, cast members, directorial staff, production dates *et al*.

The Dance Library at the New York Public Library at Lincoln Center, New York, provided dance collections of Charles Weidman and Denishawn with additional general information on dance during the 40s decade. The dance films of this period were sparse but ones of Denishawn reinforced my information.

The dance descriptions are my own from the status as performer and/or observer. Pictures, dance notes and my personal dance journal brought the dances back quickly The lack of performance descriptions of these dances elsewhere was another major reason for this book.

BIBLIOGRAPHY

Armitage, Merle. *Dance Memoranda*. New York, NY: Duell, Sloan & Pearce, 1947.

Duncan, Isadora. *My Life*. Liverright, London.

Ellis, Havelock. *The Dance of Life*. Cambridge, MA: Houghton Mifflin Company, 1923.

Lloyd, Margaret, and Alfred Knopf. *Borzoi Book of Modern Dance*. New York,   NY: Princeton Book Company, 1949.

Magriel, Paul. *Isadora Duncan*. New York, NY: Henry Holt and Company, 1947.

Martin, John. *The Dance*. New York, N.Y: Tudor Publishing, 1946.

Shawn, Ted. *Dance We Must*. Pittsfield, MA: Eagle Printing & Binding Company, 1940.

Shawn, Ted. *How Beautiful Upon the Mountain*. Private Publishing, 1942.

Sikelianos, Angelos. *The Dithyramb of the Rose*. Ted Shawn, Privately Published, 1939.

Traver, Shirley. *The Development of Ballet on the Concert Stage of America Between 1940 & 1946*. Master's Thesis. Texas State College for Women

Underwood, Sharry. *Ballet Ballads.* Dance Chronicle, 9.3 (1986). P 279

SUGGESTED READINGS

Bordman, Gerald. *The American Musical.* New York, NY: Oxford Press, 1978.

Chujoy, Anatole. *The Dance Encyclopedia.* New York, NY: A.S. Barnes & Co., 1949

Clarke, Mary, and David Vaughn. *The Encyclopedia of Dance & Ballet.* New York, NY: Putnam's Sons, 1977.

Cohen, Selma J. *Doris Humphrey, An Artist First.* Middletown, CT: Wesleyan University Press, 1972.

Gitelman, Claudia. *Liebe Hanya.* Madison, WI: University of Wisconsin Press, 2003.

McDonagh, Don. *The Complete Guide to Modern Dance.* New York, NY: Doubleday & Co. Inc., 1976.

Osato, Sono. *Distant Dances.* New York, NY: Alfred Knopf, 1976.

Sherman, Jane, and Barton Mumaw. *Barton Mumaw, Dancer.* New York, NY Dance Horizons, 2000.

Sherman, Jane. *The Drama of Denishawn.* Middletown, CT: Wesleyan University Press, 1979.

Stodelle, Ernestine. *Deep Song.* New York, NY: Dance Horizons, 1984.

INDEX

371

Nina, 34

14659592R00232

Made in the USA
Lexington, KY
13 April 2012